AMBITION AND SURVIVAL: BECOMING A POET

BOOKS BY CHRISTIAN WIMAN

POETRY

Hard Night (2005)
The Long Home (1998; reprinted 2007)

PROSE

Ambition and Survival: Becoming a Poet (2007)

Christian Wiman

▾ ▲ ▾

Ambition and Survival

BECOMING A POET

Copper Canyon Press

Port Townsend, Washington

Copyright 2007 by Christian Wiman

All rights reserved

Printed in the United States of America

Cover art: Keith Carter, "Giant" (1997). Toned gelatin silver print, 15″ × 15″.

Copper Canyon Press is in residence at Fort Worden State Park in Port Townsend, Washington, under the auspices of Centrum, a gathering place for artists and creative thinkers from around the world, students of all ages and backgrounds, and audiences seeking extraordinary cultural enrichment.

LIBRARY OF CONGRESS CATALOGING-IN-PUBLICATION DATA

Wiman, Christian, 1966–
Ambition and survival: becoming a poet / Christian Wiman.
    p.   cm.
ISBN 978-1-55659-260-7 (pbk.: alk. paper)
1. Poetry – Authorship.   1. Title.
PS3573.I47843Z46   2007
811′.509 – dc22

2007013417

9 8 7 6 5 4 3 2 FIRST PRINTING

COPPER CANYON PRESS
Post Office Box 271
Port Townsend, Washington 98368

www.coppercanyonpress.org

ACKNOWLEDGMENTS

I am grateful to the editors of the following magazines, where the essays in this book first appeared:

The American Scholar
Harper's
Harvard Divinity Bulletin
The Hudson Review
The New Criterion
Poetry
Poetry Review (England)
The Sewanee Review
Southwest Review
The Threepenny Review

"Poetry in a Visual Culture," "In Praise of Rareness," and "In the Flux That Abolishes Me" are copyrighted by the Poetry Foundation and reprinted with the Foundation's permission.

I am grateful to the editors of the following anthologies, where some of these essays were reprinted:

After New Formalism
Pushcart Prize XXVII
Twentieth-Century American Poetics
What Makes a Man: 22 Writers Imagine the Future

I am also grateful to the MacDowell Colony, where one of these essays was written.

Finally, and mostly, I would like to thank David Caligiuri, Danielle Chapman, Matt Fitzgerald, Anne Halsey, Naeem Murr, Elizabeth Stigler, Laura-Gray Street, and Michael Wiegers for their help with this book.

1/08

Contents

III

▼ ▲ ▼

IV

▼ ▲ ▼

V

▼ ▲ ▼

Preface

When I was twenty years old I set out to be a poet. That sounds like I was a sort of frigate raising anchor, and in a way I guess I was, though susceptible to the lightest of winds. When a visiting poet at the college I attended said offhandedly that he thought young poets should travel rather than go to graduate school, I spent four years dragging my big ambitions and bigger ignorance from one impermeable place to another. When I read Samuel Johnson's comment that any young man could compensate for his poor education by reading five hours a day for five years, that's exactly what I tried to do, practically setting a timer every afternoon to let me know when the little egg of my brain was boiled. It's a small miracle that I didn't take to wearing a cape.

I regret none of it, or at least not the iron aim of it. There are always casualties of mastering passions, casualties deep within oneself if not of others (though all too often of others, too). These one does regret – or, hopefully, grieve – a topic that some of these essays explore. But the ambition and fierce focus, the hunger of it, the sense of a life shaped by some strong inner imperative: all of this – even the moments easy to mock, even the years when I wrote only bad poems, or no poems – I find myself cherishing. I still believe that a life in poetry demands absolutely everything – including, it has turned out for me, the belief that a life in poetry demands absolutely everything.

This book is a record of that belief, and shaped by its evolutions and confusions just as surely as I am. The oldest essay here is "Finishes: On Ambition and Survival," which I wrote twelve years ago when I was just beginning to have some conscious sense of the tension between life and death that can be played out within a single poem. The most recent essay is "Love Bade Me Welcome," in which issues of life and death are considerably more literal and personal. The essays could not be more different, but they are so intimately related that I think of them as parts of a single work. Indeed, I have had this book in mind for so long, have for so many years meant it to *be* a book rather than simply a collection of miscellaneous prose pieces, that I am relieved now not to have published a selection of exclusively critical work or woven the personal pieces into a memoir, both of which I have been on the verge of doing at one time or another.

I don't mean to suggest that there is no difference between critical and personal writing. There certainly is, and I have tried in my critical writings to get at truths that transcend my own creative urges and anxieties. But I do believe that a reader should feel the *pressure* of the personal even in essays from which an author is scrupulously absent. A critic for whom literature is not rooted deeply in life, whose ideas seem to have no relation to lived experience, doesn't hold much interest for me. By the same token, any writing that is merely personal, that does not manage to say something critical about life in general, is equally inert. Our own experiences matter only insofar as they reveal something of experience itself. They are often the clearest lens that we can find, but they *are* a lens.

In 2003 I took over the editorship of *Poetry* magazine. It's taken some getting used to. Not only had I grown accustomed to constant itinerancy and gentle poverty, but I had just begun to accept the fact that the only responses I would get to even the most flagrant things I said about poetry would be either absolute silence or some lone gleeful approval scrawled on bark and ornamented with the hair of the yeti. How things change! I've now lived in Chicago longer than I've lived anywhere in my adult life, and for most of that time I've been at a magazine and foundation that, thanks to Ruth Lilly's gift in 2002, has an endowment of almost two hundred million dollars. That last fact has created a lot of media interest around *Poetry,* and part of my education as an editor has been to watch some of my offhand and ill-considered comments to reporters ricochet around the Internet with alarming speed. There's nothing I can do about that at this point, but I am including three essays that originally ran as editorials in the magazine, which I hope speak in a more considered way to some of the questions about the public life of poetry that get posed to me all the time.

For a few years I reviewed new books of poetry regularly. The bulk of those reviews seem either too superficial or too callow to reproduce, but I've included a handful here ("Eight Takes") whose judgments I can still stand behind, and which are focused on poets whose work has continued to exert some hold on me. For the most part, though, I have not been comfortable as a reviewer, and most of the essays in this book were not written on assignment or were the result of assignments that some very generous editors allowed me to manipulate for my own immediate purposes and interests. "A Piece of Prose," for instance, began as a review of a whole box of books (listed in the Notes) and ended as a general meditation on the prose of poets. It is itself a kind of preface, I guess, in that it offers definitive criteria by which to judge a poet's prose. I hope I haven't simply woven the rope for my own hanging.

Finally, this book begins with an essay on homelessness and unbelief and ends with an essay on rootedness and faith, begins with health being taken for granted, ends with it being taken away. It is at once assuring and eerie to me how utterly the first essay points toward and even foreshadows the later one: assuring because such symmetry suggests that what I have experienced as random and chaotic movement has in fact had a coherent course; eerie because I have no sense of having been in control of that course. So many poets deprecate their prose, relegate it to a sort of adjunct status with regard to their poems. I myself have done this at times. What I have come to realize, though, is that prose is absolutely integral to my life in poetry, and not simply in an intellectual sense of working out ideas or staking positions. It has helped me to stay alive to all the buried impulses and impressions out of which poems are made. Which is to say: it has helped me to stay alive.

2006

AMBITION AND SURVIVAL: BECOMING A POET

I

On Being Nowhere

Last month I moved to Chicago. By "moved" I mean I drove here one day from Philadelphia. Not that I was living in Philadelphia. I'd merely left my car there for a few months while I was in San Francisco. I have lived in Philadelphia, though. By "lived" I mean I remember the streetcar clattering up Germantown Avenue, and the fungal smell of the back rooms of William Allen's bookstore on Walnut, and the three-foot snowfall that buried my car just a few days before I packed it up and "moved" to Austin.

I'm thirty-six. *Nel mezzo del cammin di nostra vita,* as Dante says, in the middle of my life's journey. This assumes my life span conforms more nearly to the country's average than to my family's, the latter being a considerably sharper slope on the downward side. In any event, I'm at an age of appraisal, and sitting down to work this morning, looking out at the sun winking off of Lake Michigan, I find that I've just made my fortieth move in the last fifteen years, that I own nothing that won't fit easily in my car, and that my purchase on a place has become so tenuous that at any moment I might blink and be on my way to Marrakech.

Certainly it's been a choice. I've had good health, good friends to give me some sense of ballast in the world. I've had a somewhat crazed and commercially irrelevant ambition – poetry – as well as a willingness to approach middle age in a state in which all my assets are... well, aren't. And yet I've come to suspect that my itinerancy isn't *merely* a choice, that it might be some combination of my time and temperament, and thereby expressive of something broader than my own admittedly eccentric brain.

I was having a conversation along these lines not too long ago, in fact, with a group of people I got to know in New Hampshire, where

I lived, briefly. They ranged in age from their midtwenties through their midforties. Though I was an extreme example of the type I'm describing, between us we'd lived in every state and dozens of foreign countries. Not a single person now lived anywhere near where they were born and raised. At one point I mentioned Simone Weil, who wrote: "We must be rooted in the absence of a place. We must take the feeling of being at home into exile." The concept, if not the quotation, was immediately familiar to everyone. This may be another characteristic of the sociological segment I'm describing: an ability to swallow paradoxes on which our parents would have choked. I have noticed, though, that many of us tend to have unsettled stomachs.

I've noticed another characteristic, too. We often simply won't ask each other where we're from, skirting the question as if it were either too intimate or, more likely, too involved to broach. When the question is asked, though, it invariably elicits a perceptible pause and narrowing of the eyes while the person who has been asked tries to figure out exactly which version of the question they're meant to answer. Where have they lived longest? Where did they most recently leave? Or is this the earliest version of all, seeking the one place that, though they may never return to it, inevitably returns to them? As for me this morning in the early, attenuating dark the lake was not a lake at all but the long and barren landscape where I was raised, cotton and killdeer and cactus all imminent, and for a moment too brief to measure I teetered at the brink of that bald dawn.

My own reactions to this state of affairs are complicated. I value the breadth of experience, the ability to be at ease in many different places and among many different kinds of people. And I do actually enter the places I'm in, not merely move through them like a tourist. Indeed, I'm a lousy traveler when traveling is the aim, grumpy without my hours of work, easily and all too literally dyspeptic, and mostly impervious to the scripted intensities of sightseeing. But there is a certain intensity, a certain kind of seeing, that seems available to me only when I've cast the old anchor of work into the waters of a brand-new place – Lake Michigan right now, for instance, wind raking light across all that blue. It's habit I hate, the gleam going out of things. I leave before the lake leaves me.

And yet, believe me, I am my own most persistent prosecutor to the obvious charge: all this itinerancy is a "commitment problem," and either symptomatic of, or certain to lead to, despair. I can't altogether absolve myself of this charge. There is something missing from all this motion, some hunger that all this seeing never sates. But insofar as that phrase suggests a shallowness of attachment and immaturity, an inability to put away the things of the child, it's probably unfounded. Discipline and depth of feeling I do not lack. Indeed, it may be precisely this combination, operating at this particular historical moment, that is the problem.

Adam Phillips, a British psychoanalyst, wrote a brief, compelling book called *Darwin's Worms,* in which he talks about a common contemporary phenomenon wherein people who have lost faith in permanent things come to place their faith in loss itself. It amounts to an ascetic, secular sort of religion, he says, and involves not so much an absence of commitment as a fierce commitment to absence. Phillips's emphasis is on a sort of internal traveling and has obvious implications beyond simple attachment to a place. I expect he'd see itinerancy in that light, though – part mission, part malady. Indeed, I expect he'd recognize immediately the ease with which that group in New Hampshire accepted the Simone Weil quote as a prescription for a viable life, as if you could inhabit wholly only what you'd left, no scene so gorgeous as the one that's gone.

I leave my furnished sublet and walk through Lincoln Park, heading south along the lake, thrilled once more as the variegated light and lines of the skyscrapers come into view. Surely Chicago is America's best downtown, with its signature but integrated architectural styles and clear perspectives from which to see them; the El snaking through the buildings, giving sudden glimpses of sky and river, the towers of glass contriving to confuse the two. It's been a while since I've been so struck by an American city – something about the combination of brawn and sharpness, angle and plane; something so, well, *American* about it, from the naive Gothic imitations to the confident Art Deco, from some of the charmingly ugly vestiges of the late sixties and seventies to the pure postmodern assertions of steel and glass. It's telling, no doubt, that my very favorite building – 333 West Wacker Drive – should be from this last group, and that, though it is beautiful, curving sheer and green along the river, I should love it less for itself than for the way adjacent buildings ripple in its sides, as if it were ghosted by the styles it had outgrown.

Where are you from? Where are you from? Where are you from? One gets asked this question in Chicago much less often than one does in, say, San Francisco. I suppose that's because Chicago is a place where people really *are* from, whereas in San Francisco to meet a lifelong resident is, though not unheard of, certainly more unusual. In any event, I don't find my answers coming any easier. To the couple with whom I strike up a conversation at a concert I say, "San Francisco," because that's where I was last. To the bartender at Sterch's on Lincoln Avenue I say, "Virginia," because that's where, in the last few years, I've been longest. But to the woman cutting my hair downtown, who asks me while holding my temples steady in the mirror as if it were myself I have to answer, I tell the truth.

When I go "home," as I do a couple of times a year, I go not to the tiny town in West Texas where I was raised, but to the strip-mall city not too far away, where what's left of my family now lives. There, you can walk five miles in any one direction without anything to tell you you're not in any one of a dozen other midsize cities in Texas, and only the scrub vegetation, aridity, and spectacular sky to distinguish the place from all the anonymous American cities and suburbs our consumption has consumed. No doubt this is one reason Chicago's downtown is striking – even moving – to me, because it seems at once so singular and so American, whereas I'm accustomed to a different, leveling sort of national impulse with regard to place. Indeed, sometimes when I'm home, or traveling through the immense and thriving nowhere of Middle America, it occurs to me that there must be millions of people as addicted to absence as I am, and that our lives, for all their apparent differences, are expressions of a similar loss.

But that city in Texas is the place I return to, not the place that returns to me. No, this latter place, the one I see before the lake has lightened, or in my own eyes in the mirror, is outside of town, outside of all towns. The land is flat as far as you can see, and the white aisles of cotton make a stark contrast with the black ribbon of the road, the sky's blue. Maybe a lone, arthritic mesquite tree breaks the plane of the fields somewhere, or a pumpjack bows over and over to the ground. Mostly, though, it's just space and glittering distance, the sky so wide it seems curved to the horizon on every side, as if, should you walk too far in any one direction, you might fall endlessly into it.

The *feeling* of being at home, Simone Weil says: that's what we're meant to retain, that's what will save us. Amherst and Antigua, Oxford and Ocracoke, Paris and Prague, Seattle and San Miguel – I have had addresses in all of these places, homes in none. But after the woman cutting my hair asks me where I'm from, and I find myself thinking of the stark, annihilating beauty of that sun and sky, I feel truly rooted in the absence of that place. And I take that feeling with me as I walk out into the shadow and dazzle of downtown Chicago, and carry it up Michigan Avenue, buses and cabs blasting by, and hold on to it as I head north along the lake, where the last sailboats of the season are out, and the water glitters, and the air is sharp with the first hint of a cold that, I'm told, will be like none I have ever known.

2002

Milton in Guatemala

And yet, the ways we miss our lives are life.
RANDALL JARRELL

S ome books are so bound up with the circumstances in which you first read them that you can't ever think of them apart from those circumstances. The effect can be perverse. I first read *Paradise Lost* while living on a roof in Guatemala, and to this day I can't open the poem without catching some quick whiff of strong coffee, avocados, and black beans. I had traveled there from Mexico with only a very small bag, which had room for only one book: *The Complete Poems of John Milton.* I'm not quite as odd a person as I was once on the verge of becoming. "Long is the way / And hard, that out of Hell leads up to light."

My room was a tiny box made of corrugated tin and cardboard. It was clearly a desperate and hastily conceived entrepreneurial effort by the young, careworn couple below, who slept in one room with their three children, two of whom were infants. Through a large hole in the middle of the floor I could see the kitchen. Through the vaguely rectangular window slashed in one wall I could see a smoking volcano. It was the hole that caused me some anxiety. When I knew I was going to get drunk (a person who carries Milton into a jungle is a person who plans his benders) I'd set various objects around its edges in the hope that a kicked can or bottle top might clatter down into that underworld before I did.

My first problem was the light. There wasn't one. I wasn't accustomed to going to bed as soon as it got dark, and even if I had been the amount of coffee we drank with every meal would have precluded that. I read by candlelight at first, then later – ingeniously, it seemed to me – by a flashlight hanging from a string. I had to strain to make out the words in my compressed Cambridge student's edition, a minor discomfort that mostly pleased me. This was going to do me some good.

Other hardships, though, tested my sentimental asceticism. It was *cold.* It had been pretty cold in Mexico City, but I figured that a jungle – red-rumped baboons, big squawking birds, that sort of thing – had to be hot. It wasn't a jungle, and it wasn't hot. I read wearing every piece of clothing that I had brought, wrapped up in the sheet and blanket from the bed. Because I had originally meant to make my way through the entire *Complete Poems,* I set myself a goal of fifteen pages a night. It was like eating lightbulbs. I took comfort from the words of Mammon, not yet wise to the fact that Milton had put them in the mouth of a ruined devil:

> Our torments also may, in length of time
> Become our elements, these piercing fires
> As soft as now severe, our temper changed
> Into their temper; which must needs remove
> The sensible of pain.

That's from the second book, when the fallen angels, after having gone to war with God, have gathered in Hell to lick their wounds and plot the best course of future action. It remains my favorite part of the poem. It's full of bizarre but very recognizable characters, rhetorically impeccable sophistries, and just flat-out great writing. It's also where we first get a good sense of Satan, whose individuality, defiance, and raw willfulness constitute a single insidious energy that all of the poem's ponderous dogma never convincingly crushes. Satan is the saving flaw, more human than the humans in the poem.

He is also in some essential sense Milton himself. Just as Satan was once one of the highest of angels, Milton, in the years before *Paradise Lost,* moved at the margins of highest power. He was close to Oliver Cromwell, who had dissolved the monarchy. Everything changed in 1660, when Charles II returned to England. Some of Milton's books were ordered to be "burnt by the hangman." Shortly afterward an order went out for his arrest, which at the time was tantamount to a death warrant. There remains some mystery as to why the arrest was never made (others named on the warrant were killed), though it can probably be attributed to some highly placed, sympathetic figure. For a while, though, Milton must have thought he was done for, by mob violence if not regal edict. Indeed, when Cromwell's disinterred corpse was carted to Tyburn for public gibbeting, the mob salivating alongside passed very near Milton's new lodgings. He must have heard them. He must have still been hearing them shortly afterward, as he backed away from public life and, in a fury of redirected ideals and will, plunged into *Paradise Lost.*

I wasn't aware of any of this then. I wasn't aware of much of anything then, it now seems to me, outside of the narrow focus of my *own* hypertrophied will. I was in Guatemala because I thought a writer needed a store of EXPERIENCE, and I was reading Milton because I thought that the only way to write GREAT POEMS, which is all I wanted to do, was to come to terms with the GREAT POEMS of the past. I haven't altogether outgrown those ideas and impulses, though I am less inclined now to go around in my daily life talking in capital letters.

What interests me – haunts me even – is the almost absolute rift I maintained between these two ambitions, experience and poetry, and the extent to which I mostly missed both. For a long time literature existed not in the context of the life I was living but in a sort of stark, almost oppositional relation to circumstance. I seemed to arrange the two – art and life – with just this sort of incommensurability in mind. It was as if I didn't want my art and my life to have anything to do with each other, or wanted art only insofar as it could set life in relief, in both senses of that word. Some jolt was needed to join the two. At that time of my life – "O innocence / Deserving Paradise"– the jolts were mostly gentle.

I first fell through the surface of *Paradise Lost* early one morning on the dirt roads at the outskirts of Antigua. Fog in the trees, wraithlike dogs in doorways, the tiny tortilla lady barefoot and balancing her day's deliveries on her head, everything creaking awake inside me: I almost ran right into the two Americans. I had met them earlier, a striking couple even in the rather theatrically disheveled state they were in that morning. Each had the kind of varied history that suggests a distinctive individual sensibility, but they also had that abstractedness and enclosed focus that comes with intense love, particularly that kind of love that is sudden, disabling, and, because of circumstance or temperaments, unreplenishable. The tank was almost empty for these two, and they knew it. Or at least that's what I in my wise, twenty-two-year-old detachment knew for them. There was a passionate sadness about them, or a passion that implied sadness, was shadowed by it.

It turned out they had spent the night up on the volcano. Sleepless but wired, they wanted only to keep whatever energy they'd unleashed up there from dying out. We went to breakfast together, where they told me about their night up in the Empyrean. I, to whom it hadn't occurred to climb the volcano much less make love on it, got interested, but I quickly lapsed into almost total silence. They didn't need me. They talked with a fervor that was at once intimate and desperate, finishing each other's sentences, unable to stop touching, recalling even the details of their lovemaking without embarrassment or even much consciousness really. It was almost as if by articulating their experience together they could in some way – and here it was getting a little weird – experience it again.

The obvious connection is not the enduring one here. Of course I couldn't help but begin seeing these two as a sort of handy Adam and Eve, the volcano Eden, their fuck our fall, this manic postcoital passion our long curse of unquenchable desire. All of this occurred to me, sure, but superficially. Some deeper shift, some bedrock rupture from which the rubble is still settling, occurred in me when the woman, right in the middle of some memorable moment she was reconstructing with her lover, leaned over the table and asked me, "Are you in love?"

I was. Some months earlier I'd fallen for a woman in Virginia, for whom I would presently leave Guatemala, and with whom I would live for an intense, itinerant decade. I had spent a lot of time thinking of her olive, angular face, the charged interior world she inhabited that had so unsettled my own. I thought of the last place we'd made love, some hotel somewhere in Dallas, rain on the windows, rainlight gauzing the walls, the air, us.

"No," I said.

▼ ▲ ▼

Blake thought the imagination, because it was infinite and "pure," a higher faculty than memory, which was finite and corruptible. The imagination, he felt, is our residual divinity, through which we feel something of what we once were and may one day be. Memory, on the other hand, is our mere humanity, telling us only what we wretchedly are. *Paradise Lost* was for Blake one of the greatest of poems because it was addressed "to the Imagination which is Spiritual Sensation & but mediately to the Understanding or Reason." The crazy cosmological scheme and the vague Eden, God talking like a pipe organ with a law degree, all of the visual difficulty that T.S. Eliot thought was the downfall of the poem – for Blake, these weren't defects but virtues. The poem wasn't aimed at clarifying or imitating life but transcending it. To attain this higher, more spiritual sort of consciousness, Blake felt, requires an art that is as unlike life as possible.

I wasn't any more aware of Blake's distinction than I was of Milton's biography, but sometime after that woman's question I think I began to read Milton, and many other things, differently. Any major work of art requires a massive effort, in preparation if not in actual execution, but there is something singularly willed about *Paradise Lost.* The poem has a rock-breaking, unromantic rigor about it, which has alienated many twentieth-century readers. The problem is not simply that the poem is often dogmatic and abstract. The real barrier is the poem's style, which is clenched and labored and just generally *unreal,* its thickets of syntax sometimes so dense and thorny that getting through them can be pretty tough.

Now, though, I began to attend much more closely to moments in *Paradise Lost* that seemed qualitatively different to me, moments of surprising, brief, incorrigible human feeling. Satan is the most obvious example. Over and over you find him resisting not only his worst inclinations but the very role that Milton has in mind for him. He won't quite ever become the uncomplicated, unsympathetic agent of evil that the myth requires him to be. There are many examples of this, from his insolent and philosophically acute answers to the angel interrogating him outside of Eden ("let him surer bar / His iron gates, if he intends our stay / In that dark durance") to his first, truest reaction to seeing Adam and Eve, "whom my thoughts pursue / With wonder, and could love." He's a type of character that since the Romantics has become very familiar: interior, reflective, motive and will all raveled up with doubt and guilt. This led Romantics such as Blake to see him as an artist-figure, his godlike brilliance and ravening ambition at once his strength and weakness, gift and curse.

And yet, the comparison is not quite right, neither between Satan and the artist, nor between Satan and Milton. For if the character of Satan is compelling because of Milton's imaginative identification with him, Satan's actions – starting a war with God, wrecking the world God made – have an immediacy of consequence and palpable reality that Milton's (and most artists') lack.

There are people of abstract passion, people whose emotional lives are intense but, for one reason or another, interior, their energies accumulating always at the edge of action, either finding no outlet into reality, or ones too small for the force that warps them. This is my sense of Milton. Even his actions in the public sphere often seem to have a misfocused or balked ferocity to them. He was inclined to expend energies out of all proportion to the importance of the issue, or, when the issue was truly important (the right to divorce, the right to kill a king), to apply his ideals and passions so inflexibly to messy circumstance that the results were more inflammatory than efficacious. By the time he gets around to devoting himself to *Paradise Lost,* it doesn't feel as if he's doing so by default, but that he's finally coming to fully inhabit his proper element, which, really, was the maze of his own mind.

But life goes on. It went on around Milton. Probably the most notorious anecdote about *Paradise Lost* involves Milton's three daughters, two of whom, because he had gone completely blind, he forced into what amounted to bare servitude. They were apparently taught the phonetics but not the meanings of each of the many languages that Milton had mastered, so they could appease his endless appetite for books by reading to him at his pleasure. During the years that the lines of *Paradise Lost* came to him "as if they were dictated in his sleep," his young daughters, whom he would eventually disinherit for being "undutiful," took down that dictation by daylight. By all accounts, they were growing very, very angry. "That is no news," one of them is said to have remarked upon hearing, from the maid, of Milton's third marriage, "but, if I could hear of his death, *that* would be something."

The old crux – how does a bad man make great art – is not really what I'm getting at here. I'm interested in these moments of human feeling I've mentioned, these softened spots in the hard-hearted style. If art exists for the sake of life, and if one recognizes a certain detachment and even numbness in the life of an artist who has produced moving work, then what is the feeling in the work *for?*

One of the most memorable of these moments of complicated human feeling in *Paradise Lost* occurs when Eve is first created out of Adam's rib. She wanders to a pool of water and promptly falls for her own image. The feeling persists even after her first sight of Adam, whom she finds "less fair, / Less winning soft, less amiably mild, / Than that smooth watery image." She's almost immediately wrenched into a right frame of mind by Adam's "superior gifts," but the damage, you might say, is done, a whole history of human fallibility and pain implicit in that gesture. In that moment you get a sense of Eve's volatility, which is the volatility of imagination. She is everything the will can't control, an expression of the appetite and passion for a life more intense and eternal than the one that reality offers – which, incidentally, is the passion any imaginative writer is trying to appease. It is troubling to me that the form this passion first takes in Eve is self-love.

Walking home from breakfast that morning in Antigua, oblivious to Blake, the black volcano, Eve, and everything else but the self-enclosed world that I was, I began to have my first dim sense of a rift between what I imagined and what I remembered. I was still some years away from finding my way into work that would intensify and confuse these elements utterly for me, as well as make me realize how disorienting and disruptive it could be to one's life to inhabit that confusion for any length of time. But sometime after that morning I began to take the first steps toward formulating my own version of Blake's distinction, in which I would come to identify the imagination with art and memory with life. I began to see it as a choice, and to wonder if it were one that I, as my immediate and instinctive answer to that woman's question revealed, had already made.

▼ ▲ ▼

Every year during Holy Week in Antigua there is a series of elaborate processions and rituals to mark Christ's death and resurrection. The night before Good Friday, the people spend all night working on what are called *alfombras* – meaning, literally, rugs – in the streets. These are large, elaborate designs made of colored sawdust and flower petals, many of which depict some religious scene or symbolism. There is frequently an effort to individualize the *alfombra,* some token of a family's or individual person's private life – a photograph or family name, some memento, or even in one instance little cakes that were presumably a source of particular pride – made part of the larger design. The atmosphere is charged and festive, tourists and flashbulbs everywhere, but there is also something portentous in the air, some element of, if not quite gravity, at least readiness.

The father of the family I was staying with woke me at three that morning. With his oldest child, a bright and lively girl of about eight years old, we wandered the streets for three hours. Everything seemed charged and mysterious, and time has not dulled for me the eerie clarity of those hours. I remember not simply the vaguely coffeeish color of those cakes waiting to be arranged on that one *alfombra*, but their vaguely coffeeish taste, too; for when she realized that she'd been seen, the little girl held out to me the half-eaten piece she'd pilfered, so that we shared in that sweet perdition. I remember the moment when the first cock crowed from the open-aired center of some house that could have been our own (vile animal – "Gordo," he was called, Fatso), and I remember the moment just after, when the father, with an infectious seriousness, leaned close to his daughter and whispered, "Now Peter is denying Christ."

As one by one all the roosters in the town began to cry, the procession began. I have forgotten exactly where I was when I first saw it coming toward me, teenagers and children first, then a phalanx of

Roman soldiers pulling a large wooden cart, some blindfolded and impassive local Christ riding high over a crowd of costumed penitents and various historical personages, the air around them clouded with incense and myth. Slowly, seriously, street by street, and *alfombra* by beautiful *alfombra,* the procession passed on its way to Golgotha, leaving in its wake swirls of colored sawdust, crushed keepsakes, indecipherable designs, and silence.

The most apparent connections between Milton and my experience are again the least important ones. Much of what is for Blake metaphysically suggestive in *Paradise Lost* is for me merely physically vague. Having these palpable representations of some of the ritual and characters relevant to the poem helped to ground it for me, just as those two tall, carnal incarnations of Adam and Eve had helped me earlier. It's a silly, reductive way to read literature, I know, but I was really *struggling* with this poem. The procession gave it a connection with my immediate life, a physical focus, if only a superficial one.

But there's something else. When we got home shortly after dawn, we all went to sleep before the more formal services later in the morning. I came down in a couple of hours to find the father waiting for me at the foot of the ladder. He asked if I would mind watching the children for thirty minutes – and here he paused, smiled slightly, and said, "or maybe an hour." I sat down in the living room with the little girl and the two infants, all of whom were awake but reasonably sedate, whereupon he went back into his bedroom and closed the door.

I had wondered how they made love. I don't mean the mechanics of it, but how they managed to have a sex life with their children sharing the room. It seemed apparent that they did *have* a healthy sex life, as there was a conspicuous affection between them. Often, over dinner or watching television afterward (next to my ramshackle room was a ramshackle antenna), their eyes darted the same "contagious fire" that consumed and ruined our first parents. Many nights I had vaguely imagined, from the vaguely literary stupor I was in, what ensued, the whole house under me acquiring some medium denser than mere darkness, the two of them moving through it so slowly and deliberately they seemed underwater, some immense tenderness and silence. Nice, in a sleepy-headed sort of way. And yet I had also imagined the little girl waking occasionally, dimly aware of some beast with two backs in the bed, little radioactive Freudian fragments sealing themselves away in her brain to leak out years later.

The underwater part of the scenario may have been right. So quiet were they that there is an element of conjecture in my memory of that morning. Were it not for the sly look the father had given me when he increased the length of his request, and the sly look his little girl seemed to mimic from the far side of the couch, I might have concluded that they were simply taking a much-needed nap. If there were doubts, though, their appearance later dispelled them. A bit disheveled, a bit embarrassed, they came out just in time for church, their faces flushed with the flush that is not sleep.

I don't want to sentimentalize this. The life this family lived was harsh, and if it's not depressing that they had to go to such lengths to obtain thirty minutes of time together, it is depressing – to me, at any rate, from this distance – to think of them renting out a room they desperately needed to some middle-class American in search of EXPERIENCE, to think of myself up there dreamily feeding my imagination upon their hardships.

But there was an element of genuine good in that moment as well, both in their lives and mine. Their elation and relief, the warmth with which they embraced, and were embraced by, their little girl afterward were apparent. We went off to church in high spirits, came home to a meal of strong coffee, black beans, and avocados – though this time there was a bit of meat and some celebratory rum. The effects of that morning were less immediate for me, I'm sure. But whether or not there was any consciousness of it at the time, that morning has become emblematic to me of the kind of feeling in life that I have come to value most, a tenderness that is both released and defined by necessity, some act whose poignancy and simplicity of feeling depend upon the very harshness and severity of the climate, be it circumstantial or psychological, in which it flowers.

And what is true in life is, for me, true in art. The Milton I still respond to is not Blake's Milton, not the Milton of unmoored ascendancy, "breeding wings / Wherewith to scorn the earth," but the

poet of those unguarded and altogether earthly moments: Eve lean-
ing over the water in love with herself; Adam in the moment before
his fall, in love with Eve ("How art thou lost! how on a sudden
lost"); the two of them as we last see them, "hand in hand, with wan-
dering steps and slow," leaving Eden for good. Blake loved the poem
for its upward aspiration, its otherworldliness and immense ambition
to "justify the ways of God to men." I love the poem in pieces, trust
most its backward glances, those moments when the willful style al-
most relents to the force of some mastering passion.

But they are moments only, and they depend for their effect upon
the fact that the style, finally, does not relent, the will behind the
poem does not relax. Much as the beauty and fragility of those *alfom-
bras* are due to the fact that they are being constructed only to be
crushed by Christ, so those moments of passion and real feeling in
Paradise Lost, those glimpses of, in Wordsworth's phrase, "human
life, or something very near / To human life," are attributable to the
fact that they are in a sense rolled over by this willed, unlifelike style.
Unlike that ceremony, though, in which art is symbolically sacrificed
to life, the imagination to memory and history, in *Paradise Lost* this
gesture is never really made. Indeed, I wonder if this gesture ever re-
ally can be made by an artist, or at any rate by a certain kind of artist,
who finds that life is most life as it is being obliterated by – or, more
accurately, into – art.

Life goes on, though, on and on. And what happens to a passion
that, though it fuels art, remains in some essential human sense ab-
stract, never altogether attaching itself to any one person, any one
time or token of the perishable earth? Does art, at least in some in-
stances, and for some artists, *demand* this, that they always feel most
intensely the life they've failed to feel? Is it worth it? The will, at least
in its higher manifestations, is not a capacity that humans have
learned to exercise with much precision. Always there are secondary
casualties, collateral damages inflicted upon whoever happens to be
in the way. To love is to really be in the way. Faulkner once famously
said that Keats's "Ode on a Grecian Urn" was worth any number of
old ladies, by which he meant that any enduring work of art has a
higher value than any human costs its making may have exacted. I

can't agree. If life is art's price, if imaginative creation is contingent upon, or even just coincident with, the destruction of reality ("They shall have no other benefit of my estate, they have been very undutiful to me") or the exploitation of reality ("if I could hear of his death, *that* would be something"), then art, even the greatest art, just isn't worth it.

Surely this is a fake kind of accounting. I have come to think that the artist is someone for whom this anxiety over the relative value of art and life, imagination and memory, cannot occur, at least during the moment art is being made – someone who, like Eve in her first infatuation, comes to love the objects of his or her imagination *as if they were life*. It's too simplistic, finally, to call this self-love, for the world is what one imagines, and real experience is what any artist needs, though there is inevitably an element of satanic pride and egotism in falling in love more deeply with the world one imagines than with *the* world. It goes without saying that there are big practical and personal problems up ahead for those so consumed or deluded, but the questions come after the fact, are posed and answered by people giving lectures or writing essays, whose Eden is over, and who now, back in the brute fact and formlessness of damaged circumstance, either pound some podium to convince themselves and others that it was worth it, or perhaps just ghost their prose with the notion, but never quite the knowledge, that it was not.

One of the moments of genius in *Paradise Lost* occurs late in the poem, after Satan has seduced Eve and returned to Hell. For a moment it looks as if the original convocation in Book II will be transformed into genuine triumph, but when Satan ascends the dais and prepares to receive his legions' gratitude and adulation, all he hears is a confused sibilance, all he sees is a massive tangle of snakes. And even as he registers his defeat, he himself is transformed back into the shape in which he sinned, his voice a hiss, his body becoming a single sinuous length, "a monstrous serpent on his belly prone." Not simply one tree of knowledge then, but row after row of them rise around the fallen angels, the fruit as boundless as their sudden hunger, which only increases as each piece turns to ashes in their mouths. This is Hell, we are meant to understand, not so much the consequence of sin as its endless reiteration, to inhabit forever that moment when we were first presented with the choice that defines a life – *Are you in love?* – and to make that choice again and again and again and...

▼ ▲ ▼

I had a dream one night in Guatemala that my room was moving – the walls breathing, a little tremor traveling through the hard boards that were my bed – then woke to find it was: the smallest of earthquakes subsiding even as I felt it. I can only guess that no one else in the house noticed, or that it was too tiny or common to be mentioned, because no one ever did. Though I believe in my bones that it actually happened, I can't quite be sure, for after that moment of half-woken awareness I dropped back into sleep and, until long after I'd left Guatemala, forgot all about it.

It was another jolt, less gentle, a decade later, that brought it back – not the memory of it, which I had recovered before, but the sensation, that trembling instant between waking and sleep, reality and dream. I was living in San Francisco then, with the woman from Virginia I mentioned earlier. It was late at night. There was a sharp, single concussion that shook us awake, then a slow, or what seemed slow, series of waves that went through the floor. In that instant, too brief to be afraid, too strange to speak or reach out for each other, I remembered: it had been real. Then the walls and windows, the floor, and everything but my heart, grew still. It was over.

▼ ▲ ▼

When I first began to think about writing something about reading Milton in Guatemala, I mentioned it to a particularly blunt friend of mine. "Oh god," he moaned, "I hope it's not going to be just what you'd expect from a piece with a title like that." I asked him what exactly one would expect from a piece with a title like that. "Lots of phony, forced connections between Milton and Guatemalan history and culture, some *meaning* in the meeting of the two, rapturous crap about how it changed you."

I don't think that's a problem. It would take a moment for me to find Guatemala on an unmarked map; my knowledge of Milton is fragmentary and superficial; and if I am changed, it is, alas, only in awareness and not in inclination, only as Adam and Eve were changed the morning after their fall, waking to find "their eyes how opened, and their minds / How darkened."

Still, I'm uneasy at the aptness of some of the anecdotes I've related, the way in which, from this distance, my reading and my experience seem to speak to each other, if only to illustrate some essential estrangement. If you one day find that you are living outside of your life, that whatever activity you thought *was* life is in fact a defense against it, or a crowding out of it, or just somehow *misses* it, you might work hard to retain some faith in the years that suddenly seem to have happened without you. You might, like Milton, give yourself over to some epic work in which you find a coherence and control that eluded you in life. You might, like me, begin recounting vaguely exotic anecdotes to account for a time when you were so utterly unconscious you may as well have been living in Dubuque – might present them in such a way that your real subject remains largely in the shadows they cast. You might find that the hardest things to let go are those you never really took hold of in the first place.

The night before I left Guatemala, the father of the family I had stayed with rode his bike into town to buy a pizza. He picked bananas for his living, and this gift – for it was that – would have cost him at least a day's wages. It was a gesture of immense kindness and affection, enlarged by the hard necessity out of which it emerged and which it momentarily flouted. We ate the pizza, drank coffee, and talked around my bad Spanish late into my last night there. The little girl crawled sleepily into my lap and asked when I'd return. It was life, I think. So it is both painful and chastening to me now that I, who have in my head all these pieces of *Paradise Lost,* can't even remember their names.

1998

Filthy Lucre

Growing up in West Texas I always thought I'd be rich. It seemed to me as inevitable as my future career as a professional athlete, though the two ambitions were related only insofar as I saw wealth and athletic talent as inherent. *Blood will out,* my father must have muttered at the dinner table at some point, if not quite in those words, all of us nodding solemnly over our Frito pie. That no one in the family was wealthy and some were distressingly poor, that I had to quit basketball in the eighth grade because that uniform was simply *not* flattering – this was nothing. I was going to leave and come back with moneybags and miler's thighs. I'd flutter pulses, glitter when I walked, be the man about whom those tanned and tobacco-spitting men outside the feed store said, "He's shittin' in tall cotton now."

▼ ▲ ▼

All through my twenties I had two terrors: that I was going to have to get some sort of regular job, and that I would never write great poetry. I still live in the shadow of the latter, a huge black bird hovering at various heights above me, though at least it's not perched on my chest when I wake every morning. I'm used to it, have learned to work under its relentless arc and appetite, and would be worried if it suddenly went away. The former, though, dolor of pad and paperweight, domain of those the martyrs call the world, can still cause me to wake in a dead sweat. I think of telemarketing in Seattle, filing in Buffalo, tending the grounds of a nursing home in Abilene, and what comes over me is not despair but absolute blankness. "The only choice," Camus writes at the wizened old age of twenty-four, "is of the most aesthetically satisfying form of suicide: marriage, and a forty-hour work week, or a revolver."

▼ ▲ ▼

I've never experienced real poverty, not the sort of soul-killing privation that you read about in Céline or Orwell or Dostoevsky. The only time I was ever desperately short of money was in Morocco, where the combination of weeks of hard travel, a transportation strike, and my own stupidity left me with four dollars and a very high fever. An American in Tangier took pity on me and gave me enough money to get to Gibraltar, where I convinced British Airways to fly me to London (I had a ticket from Barcelona). It was a miserable few days, but you know you're not in any real danger so long as what's happening to you still seems to be "experience."

The only time I've ever had too much money was in Prague. I was teaching, ironically, at the Prague School of Economics, which, because it was the year after the Velvet Revolution, and because the school had been a bastion of Communism, was quite a confused and confusing place. I was paid by a fat hand that exploded out of a little slot at the end of ten thousand dark hallways, in unstacked cash, as if there were simply a huge barrel of it just beyond the wall. The money was worthless outside of what was then still Czechoslovakia.

A week before I was to leave the hand inexplicably paid me several fistfuls more than my usual salary, which I could never spend all of anyway. But in a city where at the time there was nothing to buy, and for a man who was just developing what's turned into a full-blown phobia of owning things, the money meant only a few days of frenetic shopping misery. Finally, after overpaying for a meal and realizing that not only did it not matter, but that it actually felt pretty good, I gave the whole pile to my weird, sweet landlord, Pane Hnilička, whose only English words, which he would say with uncomprehending enthusiasm at random moments, were for the first time all year apt: "Lucky weekend!"

▼ ▲ ▼

I lived with a woman who was constantly discovering cash in her pockets. Though we were often broke, this didn't "count" for her, and it had to always be used for something impractical, something fun. Gathering the laundry, she'd make a little pile of treasure and declare, always with the same elated surprise, that we were going to a movie, going to the zoo, going out for lunch. The habit reveals something essential about her character, its careful carelessness. And that it's taken me a strong dose of solitude to realize the charm in that habit reveals something essential about mine.

▼ ▲ ▼

After college I spent a couple of summers as a tennis pro – not to be confused with a professional tennis player – at a posh club on Long Island. My sugar daddy was a man I'll call Mr. Plack, whose family owned half of Manhattan. He was probably in his late seventies, but still plenty vigorous to play tennis, of a sort, every morning from 7:30 to 9:00.

It was my job to hit with him, a lucrative but delicate and exhausting transaction, because it was quite clear that I was to hit it perfectly to his forehand every time, run down even his wildest shots, and never, never presume to offer him instruction. *Harder,* he would yell, *harder,* with a frenzied glee that at the time seemed to me a bit odd, and that in retrospect seems *really* odd.

Midway through my second summer, when I was living in a mansion with Louis xiv furniture and vaguely pornographic topiary, I began to lose heart. I hustled a bit, playing some of the club's juniors, who would blithely sign chits for my fee, "double-or-nothing" matches with a racquetball racket or left-handed. And at Mr. Plack, who each day drove to the courts in a different vintage car, who never took off his silly tennis vest while I sweated through three changes of shirts, and who was constantly forgetting my name, I began to take aim.

One morning he came to the net. This in itself wasn't unusual, because typically he'd come in for me to lob some patsies, which he would smash, yelling *Get it, Get it, you* as I scurried around the clay, crashed into windscreens, and generally abased myself.

On this particular morning, though, he wanted it *hard,* so I kept drilling balls right into his raised racket until, Raskolnikov in tennis whites, I hit him cleanly in the throat.

He crumpled like a buck. I ran to the other side of the court where he lay moaning for a few moments, clay all over his shorts and vest. Finally I helped him up, apologizing effusively, feeling the tip I'd figured into my fortune palpably vanish before my eyes.

"That's not good fun," he said.

"Excuse me?" I said, dusting off his shoulder.

"That's not good fun," he repeated. Then he walked off and never played with me again.

▼ ▲ ▼

Money didn't destroy my family but it certainly hastened the blaze. My father, after selling vacuum cleaners, Bibles, driving a bus, working in a library, and teaching junior high, decided to go to medical school when I was a child. I don't remember ever lacking things before that, or even feeling very "poor," though I know that at one time there were five of us living in a forty-foot trailer. I think of us, perhaps only with a nostalgia intensified by all that happened later, as happy.

My father set up a practice in the small town where he'd grown up, and the money poured in. He bought a motor home bigger than that first trailer, which he wrecked, an airplane, which he wrecked, a great big house, which the bank eventually reclaimed. We had nothing again, but it was a different kind of nothing, a scorched field in which it would take years for anything to grow.

▼ ▲ ▼

Back in San Francisco after a year in Virginia and North Carolina, it takes me days to get used to the gleam. Partly that's because I've moved from a house on an island to a basement sublet in the Haight, a gloomy little cave from which I emerge every afternoon like a shocked troglodyte, raw and blinking. But I've never been in a city that glitters like this one, or one I've loved as much. A life here, though, the kind of life I want to lead, seems less and less possible.

Can money obliterate a place, drain it of its life even as it makes it more physically attractive, more productive, more comfortable? It would be disingenuous for me to lament the destruction of a certain kind of San Francisco culture, because I've never really known the city otherwise, but I believe my friends who have. "Living in this city," one of them told me recently over a bowl of West Lake minced beef soup, on a day so bright even my cave couldn't keep me inside, "is like being married to a beautiful stupid woman who can really cook." And who, he might have added, has begun to tell some of her more marginal and improvident lovers that it's time to think about moving on.

▼ ▲ ▼

Having your chief passion divorced from your means of making money is at once liberating and crushing. It separates you from the steamrolling economy, by which our culture is defined and leveled. With some notable exceptions, such separation is necessary for the production of original art. It can also leave you quite vulnerable, though, and you may look up just in time to feel yourself being made part of the pavement. "No man but a blockhead ever wrote, except for money," Samuel Johnson once said, a statement that it sometimes seems even the dullest of steamroller drivers knows, shouting it cheerfully as he chases you down the street. Johnson wasn't a poet, though, especially not in his poems.

Poetry *is* a special case, I think, and not simply because one can't make a living off of it directly. I find I can get prose written in just about any circumstances, but I've never been able to write poetry, which I find infinitely more satisfying, without having vast tracts of dead time. Poetry requires a certain kind of disciplined indolence that the world, including many prose writers (even, at times, this one), doesn't recognize as discipline. It is, though. It's the discipline to endure hours that you refuse to fill with anything but the possibility of poetry, though you may in fact not be able to write a word of it just then, and though it may be playing practical havoc with your life. It's the discipline of preparedness. Camus again: "There is dignity in work only when it is work freely accepted. Only idleness has a moral value because it can serve as a criterion by which to judge men. It is fatal only to the second rate."

▼ ▲ ▼

When my grandmother died, we discovered she'd been living for almost thirty years on sixteen thousand dollars a year, roughly half of which she was giving away, mostly to her confused and thriftless grandchildren. At one point in my midtwenties I lived for several months in her backyard, in the very trailer where I'd lived as an infant.

One afternoon a college girlfriend happened to be in the area and visited me. She'd married into a powerful California banking family and spent a large part of the visit detailing for me and my grandmother her Santa Barbara mansion, the extravagant wedding, the honeymoon in the south of France. At the time, when even sunlight seemed like a reproach to me, I felt acutely the ignominy of my circumstances. After she'd left, though, as I was getting ready to go back out to my trailer with its flood of books and unpublished poems, my grandmother, the one uncomplicated love of my life, put her hands on my shoulders to stop me. "Honey," she said, "you may be smarter than all of us put together, but you're dumb as a blue pig to sit listening to that gab."

▼ ▲ ▼

The Walker Evans exhibit at the SFMOMA was too much for me to absorb in one visit, so I spent most of my time in the room containing portraits from the WPA project he did with James Agee, which resulted in *Let Us Now Praise Famous Men*. It's a book I've never been able to read. The voluptuous, self-pleasuring quality of the prose seems to me altogether inappropriate and misguided. You can practically feel Agee pumping his fists and saying, "Subject matter!"

It *is* the prose that's to blame, though. Evans's photographs are always aestheticized, but they retain a documentary quality, a feeling

for reality, that Agee's language does not. That's not simply the na-
ture of the medium. Evans believed in the necessity and inevitability
of an individual style, that no artist could ever simply hold up a clear
pane in front of reality, but a man who sneaks a camera onto a subway
to eliminate all trace of "pose" is a man who also has a feeling for hard
fact. Detached from Agee's captions, Evans's WPA photographs have
always seemed to me quite moving.

But in that immaculate, sunlit museum, leaning close with all the
other well-dressed and cosmopolitan people, I felt a coldness for the
images similar to that which I've always felt for *Let Us Now Praise Fa-
mous Men.* The woman in the dress made from scraps of sacking, the
young scruffy man whose handsomeness indicts anyone who would
dare notice it: the context turned them into curiosities. What had
seemed depth of character now seemed like a bourgeois notion of
"soulfulness." After a while I felt the same sour look on my face, the
same need for air, as when, at a dinner party with writers in New York
once, when the conversation was about the ways in which one's work
was both rooted in and hampered by one's past, a woman of means
and cheekbones said, wistfully, "Poor people are so *interesting.*"

▼ ▲ ▼

I almost went to work at Citibank in London. That is, I thought about
it for about three minutes. I would have been, I suppose, an invest-
ment banker, though I still can't quite imagine what that means be-
sides having to wear a suit and work a thousand hours a week. I knew
a top executive of Citibank's European operations. It was a tennis
connection. Among a certain social set, tennis opens a lot more doors
than intelligence.

He offered me the job as he was showing me around Hyde Park
Corner, where he and his family lived when they weren't in New York
or Switzerland. I was twenty-one, living in Oxford (though not, as he
thought, actually *attending* Oxford), obsessed with poetry. That's
what I told him, the poetry part, that I had no time for anything else.
He stopped in the middle of the street and stared at me, trying to de-
cide if I was serious. That's one thing I can be: *serious.* He clapped me

on the shoulder and burst out laughing. All the way home, his arm around my shoulder familiarly as if we were on a debauch, he laughed and he laughed.

▼ ▲ ▼

Money is beauty, money is sex, money is a party to which I've inexplicably been invited, wasabi roe and squab liver crostini, stock options like pheromones in the air, a ten million dollar house in Pacific Heights around which I wander with the discontented purity of a palace eunuch. Money is my father – crafty man, Odysseus of the desert – renting a truck at twenty-one and driving all night to New Mexico because, he's heard, the price of wood is so much lower there than in treeless West Texas that if he can just bring back a truckload he'll be, well, not rich maybe, but at least not broke, not fucking broke. Money is the dawn so full of promise, his blank fatigue, the ax that slips and lays his leg open to the bone. It's the hospital bill, the cleaning bill for the blood in the truck, the ticket he gets on the drive home. Power and terror, means and end, fat man in a Philadelphia bank who, after I've explained proudly that I've just paid off my last debt with a poetry prize, denies me a car loan for that reason, his oleaginous jowls jiggling ever so slightly as he says, "How else can we know you exist?": money is shit.

▼ ▲ ▼

Disheveled, disgusted, I leave my apartment in the middle of the morning to make a completely unnecessary trip to the post office, where I run into a former student, who looks glossy and prosperous enough to buy the entire postal service. She asks me if I'm teaching, and I say no. She asks me if I'm writing, and I say no. She says, "I guess you make plenty off of your poetry anyway."

I look at her sharply, but there's no trace of irony.

"Why yes," I say, smiling and nodding my head, suddenly in love with this city, myself, her. "It's good fun."

2000

A Mile from Hell

Elder, Today, a session wiser
And fainter, too, as Wiseness is –
I find myself still softly searching
For my Delinquent Palaces –

EMILY DICKINSON

In the summer of 1993 I found myself traveling around East Africa with Southern Baptist missionaries. Getting at the origins of this trip requires, to some extent, unraveling my own.

My father's wife had died, after a protracted bout with bone cancer. Her daughter and son-in-law, Ellen and Scott, with their four children and fifth on the way, had recently become Baptist missionaries in Tanzania, sponsored by the same small-town church in West Texas my family attended throughout my childhood. After his wife died, my father, wanting to remember his wife in some way, but wanting to forget all the details and circumstances of her death, decided he'd go to Africa. Having never traveled, he decided that I, who never stopped, would go with him.

We met at a hotel in Dallas, my father ashen, trembly, his blood pressure dangerously high. He attributed his condition to the difficulty he was having getting adjusted to his new cocktail of medicines, which he mixes himself and takes for an assortment of physical pains, depression, and who knows what else. Given the precarious pharmacological equilibrium he's maintained for years, this explanation was certainly plausible. His general health has long been bad, though, and the extremes of grief and exertion he'd just gone through had inevitably exacerbated that.

We spent the next twenty-four hours debating whether or not the trip would take place at all. I voted no. My mother, brother, and sister, who had come to Dallas to see us off, voted no. All the old crackling dynamics asserted themselves.

32

"Hey, Pop," my brother said, sitting next to my father on the bed, feeling his brow. "You got your will sorted?"

"Why don't you two just watch this," my sister said, looking up from the lion mauling a gazelle on television. "Bond that way."

My mother pulled me aside in the hallway. "Your father looks terrible," she said. "I really think he'll die if he goes. You've got to *do* something."

My father stewed and swooned, extracted and rejected pity, almost, it seemed, as if he needed some critical mass of dissent and concern to initiate the action he knew he was going to take. When he finally cast the only vote that mattered, bounding out of bed with just enough time to make the drive to the airport exciting, it felt for a minute as if the whole family were going, felt almost as if we *were* a family. Speeding up for yellow lights, careering around corners, he could have been taking us on one of the many abrupt, half-manic trips of my childhood, when we might drift asleep thinking of the green trees and snow-covered mountains we were headed toward, then wake in a desert.

We landed in Nairobi. Despite all my warnings, my father's unlocked luggage arrived intact, even the cornucopia of drugs (much of which he'd brought for the missionaries) untouched. My own bag showed up two days later, locked, empty but for my underwear – a thief with a gift for detail, I guess, or a conjurer. In any event, a pattern was set. While he contrived a patois of signs and smiles to communicate with people, who flocked to him, I followed a few paces behind, watching hawkishly for the first sign of the treachery to which I was certain he was making himself – and me – vulnerable. He ate food off the street with no consequences, eschewed his mosquito netting, and seemed to draw strength from the strangeness. I grew bleary and weak, as if at the edge of an illness my body was fighting off, and steadily shrank into the shadow he cast. When our maid at the hotel, a furtive, big-eyed girl of about fifteen, spoke for the first time since we'd been there, it was inevitable that she should direct her words to my father.

"What did she say?" he asked me.

"I don't speak Swahili, Dad."

Assuming she wanted a tip, he sighed and reached for his wallet, which was so stuffed that he could hardly keep the money from falling out of it. The girl began unbuttoning her blouse.

"Dad," I said.

He looked up just as she peeled it off, sharp-shouldered, her breasts small, her smile vacant.

"Oh, Christ," he said, wincing as he looked away and thrust the wallet toward me. "Give it to her," he said. "Just give her the money."

Scott, who'd had difficulties making the two-day drive from Shinyanga (that's all he said, "difficulties") showed up a couple of days after our arrival in Nairobi. Blunt, boyish, with one of those edgeless and preternaturally pink faces I associate with middle-American Protestantism, he could have been the choir director greeting us on the steps of our church, as indeed he had been and done. He took us to the main assembling place for Baptist missionaries in Nairobi, an impressive complex of hotel rooms, playgrounds, and meeting halls in and out of which missionaries came and went brisk with purpose and efficiency. But for the city seething just beyond the gate, and the occasional snatches of Swahili in which you could hear the twang of Texas, the longer drawl of Alabama or Mississippi, we could have been back in one of the Baptist encampments of my childhood getting ready for revival, that electric, intensifying energy in the air, which, when night came, would be both unleashed and suffered.

Or back even further, because as we left Nairobi and made our way into Tanzania, both the circumstances, and the faith and efficiency with which the missionaries met them, grew harder. I was working then on a long poem set early in the twentieth century in West Texas, when many people from the deep South, like my family, moved west out of pure desperation, and I was steeped in stories in which experience was a battering ram the Lord used to shatter men's hearts. There was my father's father, who had toyed with the idea of being a preacher until the war, then afterward had buried himself—and his family—in work and willed hardship, wanting only whatever god he had encountered in that war to let him be. There was my great-grandmother, whose breast cancer was so advanced that, during a hymn one Sunday, her chest began to bleed. Two days later, both breasts gone, she was out milking the cows.

It was easy to imagine similar feats of courage, possession, or blind compulsion among the missionaries in Tanzania, most of whom had acquired a pioneering kind of competence. Each of the huge, white sport utility vehicles they drove was fitted with what was essentially another SUV inside – everything but an engine block, it seemed – which, should circumstances arise, and they did, a missionary was meant to assemble. Some went months without enough water to bathe. Some, if they were in remote areas, learned to perform minor surgeries like stitching a wound or extracting a tooth. There were stories of snake-infested houses, malaria afflicting whole families at the same time, highway robberies, and worse. Whatever I thought of their aims and methods, there was one thing that had to be said for these people: they were *tough.*

And some, inevitably, were mad. It was in Mwanza, a sprawling, filthy town just south of Lake Victoria, where my father and I met Clyde, a man of such finished features and primordial silence that he seemed less born than hewn, and Mindy, his wraith of a wife, who fluttered and chattered about their thirty years in Africa, the quality of guava, and the devil of which she'd been dispossessed.

"So how'd she get rid of it, Clyde?" my father asked when Mindy went to make dinner, after having told us, right in front of Clyde, that this devil wasn't so much a physical creature as a feeling she had, a vague sense that, well, she didn't love her husband, had never loved her husband.

"God," Clyde said.

The word might have been a discovery, an explanation, or just some raw sound his body had emitted.

"Think it might come back?" my father asked.

"Don't bear thinkin' on."

When Mindy returned to the room, after having clattered in the kitchen for an hour as if a great feast were being prepared, humming one disturbingly accelerated hymn after another, she offered us nothing but a plate of peanut butter and jelly sandwiches with the crusts cut off, deep fingerprints in every piece of bread like the touch of ghosts.

Then there was Chuck, the pilot of the thunderously loud WWII transport plane, with whom, because it seemed I was getting sicker, my father and I hitched a ride back to Nairobi at the end of the trip. The plane was designed for two pilots, I think, but Chuck flew alone, and seemed visibly discomfited when my father sat in the empty seat in the cockpit. Midway through the flight, though, despite the fact that he'd not said a word on the tarmac, and was so gaunt and indrawn a man it seemed he might simply implode into his own reticence, he eased back into the hold and began screaming intimacies at me, telling me everything from his mother's earliest inadequacies to his own disturbing dreams. "Brother in Christ," he called me, whose name he didn't know, leaning in as if with sheer volume he might blast the bafflement off my face: "His fire is a holy comfort, Brother in Christ!"

But even this, too, was in its way familiar. Not simply the religious extremity, the way some people seemed to have looked too long at God as into the sun, so that everything they saw subsequently both was and wasn't that blaze; no, not simply this, but my father – who is after all a psychiatrist at a state hospital for the criminally insane – in the midst of it. Sitting in that living room in Mwanza, while my father prodded Clyde with questions the way a child might prod some sleeping beast, or when I lay sprawled in the hold with Chuck, less stunned by his torrent of talk than by the fact that my father, who could not have known how to fly this plane, was flying it, the sensation was not new. Here he was again, after all these years, wielding the storm we were in.

So it wasn't simply an imagined past that it seemed I was going back to during those five weeks in Africa, but an actual one as well. By day I might see hundreds of flamingos peel like a layer of skin from a lake, might be stopped short by a fish eagle's scream or flies jeweling the fresh head of a monkey in the market. At night, though, among the crocheted wall-hangings, the butter beans and sweet tea, the prayers so earnest and conversational it seemed you'd open your eyes and Christ himself would be presiding, I was back in my childhood, sitting quietly even if the adults talked of me, how I was feeling poorly, or what I'd be when I grew up, a preacher, like as not, for hadn't I wept and trembled in the church that day, look how I'd burned with His fire, when the Lord, praise be, had taken hold of my heart.

▼ ▲ ▼

I don't know what my father believes. He goes to church occasionally, I think, and at Christmas dinner, which is usually the only time I see him, prays with the same straightforward, unironic piety that he did in my childhood, when we went to church three times a week, recited Bible verses over breakfast, and described ourselves as "charismatic evangelicals." I know that just a couple of years before our trip to Africa, when he was bitten three times by a rattlesnake, then had all his vital signs shut down from the volume of serum needed to counteract the poison, he saw no white light, was visited by no ministering or delivering ancestral angel, as is the custom in our family. What he felt, he says, with whatever vestige of himself was still capable of feeling, was relief.

But he didn't die. He never dies – not from the cancer he's had, not from the broken back he suffered skiing. When the motor home he was driving plowed a vertiginous icy quarter mile through barbed wire, mesquite trees, and shocked cattle before rolling over and down an embankment, he hitchhiked home, saying he'd sold it, too damn big. When his small plane ricocheted off the runway into the fields, somersaulting shattered and wingless into all the papers in the area, he walked away unscathed. I can only imagine him, after the first, fierce curses, laughing.

I grew up with a notion of radical conversion, a sudden, sometimes ravaging call for which the only answer was your life. You must be born again. For most people this happened in puberty, and may be seen, of course, merely as one religion's way of trying to restrain the animal volatility and confusion of that time, the body's imperatives countered by God's. And for most people, too, it was a mild enough experience. The choir sang quietly, the preacher held out his hands, and people rose from their pews and gave their lives over to Christ – for good, usually, because most of the people I grew up with, though they had their human portion of sin and sorrow, lived and died equably inside their faiths. Though they might talk of being born again, the experience itself often seemed to have a pro forma feel to it.

Far more compelling to me, both then and now, were the ravishments. Though even in my most pious times I detested church, would often have to be disciplined for my insubordination during the sermons, on Wednesday nights when people stood up to give their testimonies, I was riveted by those trials of fire – the woman whose voice seemed as ripped and stitched as the scars she bore on her wrists; the man who, high on acid, was strapped by his "friends" to a bull, which whipped him so savagely his collarbone sheared right through his skin. Into such wounds – as I imagined it – the Lord entered. My favorite book, though it terrified me, was Nicky Cruz's memoir, *Run Baby Run*, about a young gang-member in New York to whom God came in the form of a blade. Torn in two, born again, he became a kind of missionary to Manhattan, which, pictured on the cover with steam spiriting out of an iron grate, red letters slashed in black, seemed to me then as boiling and pernicious a place as Hell itself.

My father has had the kind of life into which such a terrible intrusion ought to have come, which is the same kind of life from which faith often falls utterly away, but if either of these has happened, I don't know about it. "Why don't you just call him up and ask him," a friend once suggested sensibly when I was wondering about this. I thought about it, but my father and I don't "just call each other up," for one thing, and I'm also very skeptical about what I'd learn. What might he say? *I believe in a literal Heaven and Hell, that God sent his son Jesus to die on the cross for my sins and the sins of all humanity.* Too simplistic. *It's a metaphor, a story, a way of organizing and giving meaning to your life.* Too mild. *All religions are one religion, which is our urge toward transcendence; it is not the tale that saves us, but the telling.* Too intellectual. *I'm not religious, but I'm spiritual.* Too squishy. There are some silences, I think, that words only intensify.

What I know is that in my childhood we moved back to the tiny, parched, purgatorial town in which my father had been raised, because, he said, the Lord had called him home. But whether it was that same voice that sent him some years later storming through our lives and through his own, or some blind reaction to the fate that voice had wrought, I don't know. So little and so much of him left in me: his knee shaking next to mine during a sermon as if it matched my nervousness; his prayer – half grief, half fury – when he gathered the family around to tell us his own father had died in a fire; his hand steadying me the night of my conversion, when I was so filled and frightened by God that I fled the service deep into the bowels of that Baptist church, where he was the one who found me, he the one who stayed, and who knew what quiet to keep.

▼ ▲ ▼

We went across the Serengeti and back again, all eight of us in the SUV, hellish: even the elephants fled. We saw hyenas catch and kill a wildebeest, their snouts of blood; a cheetah's long line of dust like a fuse, then the little detonation of its quarry's death; endless vultures flapping and tugging at carrion as if to lift it into the sky. We saw warthogs with fierce, smashed faces and perpendicular tails, hippos like grounded clouds, the swiveling heads and barklike legs of ostriches keeping pace with the car, weird fruits of a maker's sense of whimsy. "I'm not that interested in the animals," Scott told me once when I'd interrupted his work to ask him the name of some child-sized stork picking through the trash, which at the time I took to be evidence of his general impercipience, but which I now suspect was meant to indicate mine.

We went to villages that were nothing but mud huts and misery, missionaries vanishing to administer drugs and doctrine, taking my father with them occasionally to treat a wound or simply to confirm that the body, in this instance, was not what needed treating. There were churches to observe or inaugurate, classes to teach, "witch doctors" to meet and, because a word from them could close the people's ears to Christ, appease. Dressed in tattered slacks, leisure shirts, and tennis shoes, these witch doctors weren't nearly as picturesque as I had hoped, though it was from one of them, Mindy confided to my father, that she'd bought the potion that purged her demon and reminded her of all that was lovable in Clyde.

We went to Arusha, Musoma, Singida, houses materializing in the unlikeliest evenings, with clean sheets, stocked larders, and doors to which we always had the keys. We went clear to Lake Tanganyika and the border of Burundi, all the way back across the country to Dar es Salaam, where my father and I took a little speedboat across the water to Zanzibar, a guide showing us the white-walled maze of the old town, the ribs of half-built boats being lashed together with what looked like palm bark, the grim asylum where they kept their mad. "You are not like him," the guide said at one point when my father had wandered off trying to find a way inside, which pleased me, because people often say the opposite. And then: "You don't trust."

And I didn't – not him with his honed English and ease; nor the mild illness I couldn't seem to shake; nor the wide-open, prairie-like landscape in which the evening light might coalesce into a lion, a rock relax into a crocodile, as one did once just fifteen feet from where my father, whom I didn't trust, was standing. "Son of a bitch," he said, delighted, backing up as quickly as he could on that snake-bitten foot, one chunk of which the doctors had not been able to un-blacken, and thus had cut away.

I didn't trust the simulacrum of small-town Texas life – partly because it was a simulacrum, and partly because it wasn't. I'd seen my share of people like Mindy, using God like a drug to both heighten and dull a reality that's too ordinary and painful to bear, and I'd seen my share of people like Chuck, who had turned his annihilating loneliness into a spiritual mission. I'd grown up with these tattered cornfields and clotheslines, this scorched earth a mile from Hell. I'd sprawled half my childhood on broad homey porches just like the one at Scott and Ellen's house in Shinyanga, under which their dog, which they had brought with great difficulty all the way from Texas, was killed by a black mamba the very day of their arrival.

Mainly, though, I had no faith in their deepest aims. Although most of the missionaries with whom I came into contact in Africa were doing genuine good, providing medicine, education, and comfort to people who otherwise would not have received it, and though as much of their efforts seemed to be directed toward general relief as toward proselytizing, they were there, finally, for the purpose of conversion. At all those little makeshift churches we went to, which were like my childhood services in every way but for the Swahili, when the call for converts went out at the end, and here and there a person rose, it seemed to me that they were merely substituting one superstition for another, simples and cures for cross and verse, the blood of a goat for the blood of the lamb.

I can't say exactly when my faith fell away. Perhaps it is – I am – still falling, for the issue hardly seems resolved. There are even moments, always when writing a poem, always when I am suspended between what feels like real imaginative rapture and being absolutely lost, that I experience something akin to faith, though I have no idea what that faith is for. It seems that a god possessed ecstatically, as mine was in my childhood, not by books but in my blood and bones, would make a hard departure. I can't find the scar, though, and I've done some serious searching. I've begun to wonder if doubt, like grief, is less one moment you can point to, one wound you can heal, than all the moments of past and future, memory and imagination, into which that doubt, that grief, has bled. I've begun to wonder if the god I knew so bodily and utterly in my childhood could ever be completely gone.

At some point, though, that whole visceral energy of image and language, that charge with which my childhood was both enlivened and fraught, became mere myth and symbol, as if the current simply went out of them. That it happened so easily, was so devoid of crisis, might argue that my faith had no real purchase on me; that I seem prone to periods of apparently sourceless despair might argue the opposite. At any rate, whether that loss is cause or effect, whether it has infiltrated my life in other ways or is merely one dimension of a wider loss, which I would call consciousness, the fact is I don't give myself over to much. I don't trust.

▼ ▲ ▼

The pictures I have of that time in Africa – all taken by my father, and thus all missing him – are mostly of animals, many of which are in compromised conditions. Whether that's some tendency of his eye, or whether these are the ones I kept, and thus the tendency is mine, I'm not sure. Here is a giraffe with a hole in its throat (what could have reached that high?), here a hyena snarls toward us with a ruined leg. In the river in far western Tanzania where that crocodile came to life near my father there are many other crocodiles, thirty or so, each picture a livid mix of water, welted bodies, and the wide wreck of the baby hippo being devoured.

There isn't a single picture of a missionary. There isn't a white face among these photographs but for mine, dressed in a motley assortment of borrowed missionary clothes and bought African ones, a living emblem of confusion. What I do have, though, are several pictures of individual Africans outside of one of the ramshackle churches we went to, all of them ragged, beaming, newly saved. Again, my father's eye or mine, I couldn't say. It would be like my father, caught up in the excitement of the event, to promise to send such pictures back to their subjects as mementos of the experience. It would also be like him to forget such promises the minute the moment was over, because my father, for both good and ill, is a man who lives entirely in the present tense.

There we differ. I have in the years since that trip periodically retrieved these pictures and stared at them, just as I sometimes do with the handful of family photos I own, and with the same sense of obscure purpose in which there is no trace of nostalgia. And though I must have spent a good deal of time in Africa trying to see animals, now it's really only these pictures of people that compel me – the young man about the age I was at the time, smiling with his mouth but not his eyes, which are, as I see them, at once black and blazing, utterly focused and utterly elsewhere; or a girl much younger, who seems tensed, readied, as if the moment she must have exploded into were just under her skin. So closely I look at them, as if within each brow were my own memory's flint and tinder, in every face a latent flame.

"I want the one rapture of an inspiration," wrote Gerard Manley Hopkins, who, as it happens, was both poet and priest. *To inspire,* meaning both to take in breath and to take in spirit, to be awakened by and to the creative force of one's own mind, by and to all that lies beyond. I think of my grandfather – stern, stone man – lying on what he thought would be his deathbed, visited, the story goes, by an angel of such radiant life and love his sight was blazed away for days. Impossible to believe, impossible not to. I think of my great-grandmother, unaware that I, decades after that day in church when her chest began to bleed, am in the doorway, a child. Her robe is open, and she is leaning into the mirror as if listening to it, with one hand touching her scars.

▼ ▲ ▼

The illness that seemed to have been hovering over me all month – *the shadow of the wing of madness,* Baudelaire might have called it – finally struck. We were back in Nairobi. My father had gone for a walk. I fell into a deep sleep, then woke with ruined eyes, my body a seethe of heat, my mind on fire. The missionary who drove me to the hospital, a veterinarian, diagnosed me with malaria, telling me that everyone got it at some point or another and that I shouldn't worry. What I felt, though, was not worry or fear at all, but something closer to relief, as if all the anxiety I'd felt over the past weeks (years?) had finally acquired a physical form, as if whatever it was I suffered from could be named, and what could be named, cured.

But it wasn't malaria, nor was it any of the other half-dozen easily identifiable diseases the doctors tested me for upon arrival. I was placed on a cot in a long row of cots, all of which, judging from the sounds and sense of urgency, were full, a thin scrim of material pulled around my bed, which made the light seem soiled, all the people shades. At some point my father showed up, but I was gone by then, fevered into what he later told me he feared was "dying sick," my own moans no more real to me than the sounds of the other patients, the doctors coming and going, or my father praying over me, which, he said, he continued to do all night long.

I don't know what happened or didn't happen in that moment I called conversion in my childhood. Maybe it was one of our more urgent services, the preacher pounding the podium, a kaleidoscopic

burn of faces, some hymn so consuming and familiar it seemed my
whole body sang. Maybe the frenzy was all and only mine. Whatever
the circumstances, though, if some tear truly occurred in the mem-
brane between my existence and existence itself, my mind and
God's, it seems to have sealed utterly. Aside from my father's hand on
me in that church basement, I remember nothing of the experience,
feel nothing for it, though Proust would say that's the strongest evi-
dence of strongest memory, which is not memory, in fact, so much as
latent, living sensation, buried in the body, waiting to break out and
be life again.

"A loss of something ever felt I," Emily Dickinson wrote, who
could never quite bring herself to call that "something" God,
though she sensed the source of that loss was as early as her earliest
memories: "Too young that any should suspect / A Mourner walked
among the children." If I could trace my own losses back, could read
my life by blood and bone, would there be a single source? Do I want
that charge again, or the time that it enlivened? Is God merely a syn-
onym for gone?

Near dawn the fever broke. By nine I was out of the hospital, by
noon at the airport, and shortly after that, though I would be de-
tained for twelve hours by immigration officials in England who
feared contagion, on my way home. The illness had subsided by the
time I landed in San Francisco, or not so much subsided as simply dis-
tilled into a concentrated, constant, ringing headache that, despite a
battery of tests and remedies, persisted for the next two months and
has recurred ever since, as if my brain were a bell that God, running
out of options, sometimes strikes.

During the worst of it I found myself going to church on Sunday
mornings for the first time since high school. It was hardly a con-
scious decision, and I think it distressed the woman I was living with
at the time only slightly less than the illness itself. I closed my eyes
during the prayers, mumbled along with the hymns, and listened as
attentively as I could to the sermons. But every time, though none of
these churches was similar to the one I'd grown up in, and though I
was there in good faith, if not *in faith,* I became the same hive of
nerves I was in childhood, wanting it only to be over.

Finally, after the service had started one Sunday in a large cathedral, while the organ poured out its sounds of stone and gold, and the sunlight streamed through stained glass, saints ablaze, I found myself sliding out of the pew, walking not down the aisle toward the altar but up, out the door, into the brightness.

I drove up in the hills and found a place to sit, for no reason, I think, other than to avoid going home before I was expected, and thus avoid the silent questions. A hawk dipped and drifted lazily over me like a piece of ash above a fire. The wind laid its long body down in the tall grass as if to rest a moment, then rose. And I thought not of God, nor of my pain, but of that loud, lumbering transport plane that once had ferried men to Hell. I thought of Chuck, frenziedly emptying his confessions into me as if he himself were near a reckoning, and of my father in the pilot's seat, turning with a look of cunning and conspiratorial joy to show me that he was in control of this thing, and then, as he lifted his hands from the wheel, and with a look of stranger elation, that no one was.

2001

The Limit

I don't understand anything... and I no longer
want to understand anything. I want to stick to
the fact... If I wanted to understand something,
I would immediately have to betray the fact, but
I've made up my mind to stick to the fact.

DOSTOEVSKY, *The Brothers Karamazov*

I

I was fifteen when my best friend John shot his father in the face. It was an accident, I'm certain, and but for the fact that I'd dropped a couple of shotgun shells as I was fumbling to reload, the shot could have been mine. I sometimes wonder what difference that might have made.

We were dove hunting, catching them as they cleared the edge of the small tank on John's family's property outside of town. Surrounding the tank was a slight rise of brush before the fields, and John's father, a country doctor who shared a small practice with my father, had wandered off through the brush behind us to check the fence line. I was close to my limit that afternoon, which I'd never gotten, wearing one of those hunting vests with pockets big enough to hold a dozen or so birds. I remember the full feel of it, reaching in every so often to touch the little feathery lumps as they cooled. It was nearly dusk, my favorite time in West Texas, the light like steeping tea, shadows sliding out of things.

I'd been hunting for a couple of years. It seems odd to me now that I was allowed to have a gun, as my family's history was not a placid one, and I myself was prone to sudden destructive angers and what my grandmother called "the sulls." I have more than one vivid memory of being in my bedroom as one of these angers subsides, books and clothes scattered on the floor, a chair and dresser overturned. I take the shotgun from under my bed and pump a shell into the chamber – roughly, so everyone in the house is sure to hear. No one comes. No one ever comes. I set the stock on the floor, lean my chin on the top of the barrel, stretch my arm down toward the trigger I can't quite touch, and wonder if this is something I'll grow into.

Theatrics, that gun aimed at my parents more than myself, with a kind of calculated malice that, twenty years later, makes me wince. My mother was terrified of guns. That my brother and I weren't allowed to have toy guns as we were growing up, yet both got shotguns as gifts in our early teens, is ironic, I suppose, though in that flat world of work and blunt fundamentalism in which I was raised, where in grade-school county history lessons I learned the virtues of a man who had slaughtered three of the seven white buffaloes known to exist, and where one branch of my family had spent their happiest years in a town called Dunn, it has only a sad sort of retroactive irony.

My mother's abhorrence of guns was something more than the expression of a delicate feminine sensibility. Her own mother had been murdered in front of her and her two brothers when she was fourteen. The killer was her father, about whom I know only that he was compulsively itinerant, almost certainly manic-depressive, and for the month or so prior to the act had been living apart from his family. He walked in the back door one evening and killed his wife as she was cooking dinner, waited while his children ran out into the fields, then lay down beside her in some simulacrum of spent desire and shot himself in the head.

This was just a story to me, less than that, really, since it wasn't so much told as breathed, a sort of steady pressure in the air. I don't remember it ever being mentioned, and yet I also don't remember a time when I didn't know about it. It had more reality for me than the night in my infancy when my father, who was also given to the sulls, went into his room and didn't come out for several months, for I have no memory of this and didn't learn of it until after I'd left home; but less reality than the aunt, Opal, who had committed suicide before I was born. Supposedly, the whole extended family had conspired for a time to create their own private climate of calm, eradicating all hints of darkness from their lives like a country rigidly purging its past, steering conversations toward church and children, hiding the knives. It was hunting, as one might imagine, that proved most difficult in this regard, though Opal's husband was very careful to make sure their two sons kept their guns "hidden" under the beds, the shells all locked up in a little chest to which he had the only key. It seems not to have occurred to anyone that they might simply stop hunting and get rid of their guns. It was Texas. They were boys.

My family was so quiet about these matters that I thought they were something we were supposed to be embarrassed about. I learned early and no doubt too well that only certain kinds of violence were acceptable, both as topics of conversation and as actions. I loved the story of the uncle who, frustrated by a particularly recalcitrant cow, slammed his fist into its skull so hard that the cow dropped immediately to its knees like some ruined supplicant. I loved my immense, onomatopoeic uncles, Harley and Burley, who'd storm into town after months on offshore oil rigs, the nimbus of gentleness around each of them made more vivid and strange by their scars and hard talk, the wads of cash they pulled from their pockets like plunder.

And though I was mildly, reflexively disciplined by my father after the one truly serious fight I had growing up, when I was consumed with an anger that still unnerves me and continued to beat a cowboy I'll call Tom even after I'd broken bones in my hand and every blow was doing me a lot more damage than it was doing him, I was alert to the tacit masculine pride. Even the principal who meted out our corporal punishment for fighting on school grounds whipped our backsides with a kind of jocular aggressiveness that amounted to approval.

But anything that suggested madness rather than control, illness rather than health, feminine interiority rather than masculine action, was off-limits. Or perhaps not so much off-limits as simply outside of the realm of experience for which we had words, for I don't remember *resisting* discussing these things, really, or having them deflected by adults. Later, when I would begin to meet other young writers, who like myself generally had more imagination than available experience, the events of my family's history would acquire a kind of show-and-tell exoticism, little trinkets of authenticity brought back from the real world. That it wasn't a real world, not yet, that it had no more reality for me than what I read in books, didn't seem to matter too much at the time.

Now it does. At some point I stopped talking about my family's past and began reinventing it, occasionally in what I wrote, but mostly just for myself, accumulating facts like little stones which I would smooth and polish with the waters of imagination. I chose them very carefully, I realize now, nothing so big that it might dam up the flow, nothing too ugly and jagged to be worn down into the form I had in mind. Psychoanalysis is "creating a story that you can live with," I have been told, and perhaps that's what I was doing, though in truth I think I wanted less a story I could live with than one I could live without, less a past to inhabit than some recreated place I could walk finally, definitively away from.

The bullet hole between my grandmother's shoulder blades, then, and the way she crumples faster than a heartshot deer. I can see my grandfather stepping away from the door, can see the look in his eyes which, I know, is meant to assure his children as they back slowly out of the room that he is as baffled and saddened by this as they are, that they needn't be afraid, that he would never, never hurt *them*. He walks heavily across the room, steps over his wife, and, in some last gasp of that hopeless hardscrabble sanity his children will inherit and pass on, turns off the stove so the dinner won't burn, then lies down beside her on the floor.

I can see my Aunt Opal, too, gathering the laundry, humming something, deciding at the last minute to wash the coats. She is not beautiful but there is something of the landscape's stark simplicity about her face, a sense of pure horizon, as if what you saw were merely the limit of your own vision, not the end of what is there. As she shakes out her husband's coat, a single forgotten shotgun shell falls out of the pocket onto the floor. I can see the dull copper where the light dies, the little puckered end of the red casing.

Lately, though, more and more, it's John I see, standing stolid and almost actual in his boots and hunting vest, lifting his shotgun to his shoulder and laughing as I fumble to load mine. He is physically very similar to me but at ease in his body in a way I'll never be. He does not yet inhabit that continuous present that precludes remorse, but already he is all impulse and action, whereas I am increasingly deliberate, increasingly interior. There is some inner, inarticulate anger we share, though, and recognize in each other. When John's begins to slip out of control, the results for the people around him will be immediate, palpable, and utterly disastrous. My own implosion will be no more noticeable to the people around me than something I've imagined.

The gun that goes off in my ear now is a fact. It is muted by all the intervening years, by all that has happened, both internally and externally. Still, the authority of its report surprises me, as does the strangely muffled shout that seems to occur at almost exactly the same time, as if the dove, which once again John has not missed, which as I look up is plunging downward, had a human cry.

2

I don't want to kill myself. I never have, though for a time not too long ago the act emerged in me like an instinct, abstractly at first, and with a sort of voluptuous, essentially literary pleasure (Nietzsche: "The thought of suicide is a powerful solace; it enables a man to get through many a bad night"). Gradually the thought became more painful as it became more concrete, more dangerous as it became more familiar, more alienating as it became more my own. I thought of it as a kind of cancer in my mind, because eventually no matter what I was doing – teaching a class, sitting at a dinner party, trying to write, waking every hour of every night to check the clock – *that* was what I was doing, attending to that slowly clarifying imperative that beat itself out inside me as steadily and ineluctably as my own pulse.

I told no one. I couldn't. On the couple of occasions when I'd made up my mind that I would tell friends what was happening, my heart began to race, I had difficulty breathing, and I simply had no language for what I needed to say. Also, even during the worst of it, I always doubted the validity of the feeling, suspected that, like the impersonal stories I used to tell about my distant familial history, it might just be a bit of disingenuous self-dramatization. Despite the fact that I've had relatives on both sides of my family commit suicide; despite my knowledge that my father has resisted the impulse all his

life, and my sister has twice attempted the act, I suspected I might be
faking, using the thought of suicide as a way of avoiding the more
mundane failures of my life. I wasn't going to tell anyone until I was
sure. But how does one prove such terror is real except by committing
the act?

My father knew, not definitively, perhaps, but with something like
that visceral sense by which an artist comes to recognize the flaws
in anything he's made. Our relationship is as fitful as ever – we go
months without talking to each other – but there is more ease be-
tween us now, more forthright affection and trust. I think this has
more to do with him than me. During the fifteen years or so when our
relationship consisted of little more than holiday exchanges of infor-
mation, he endured a divorce, bankruptcy, the loss of his medical
practice, the death of his second wife, divorce again, back surgery, an
almost fatal rattlesnake bite, a heart attack (from the volume of
serum given to counter the snakebite), cancer, a plane crash, alco-
holism, the estrangement and self-destruction of his children, and no
doubt several other calamities that he's managed to keep secret. It
was a run of luck that would have mellowed Caligula.

During the approximately six months that I was – what to call it? –
thinking, sinking, we talked on the phone twice. On both occasions
he asked me, out of the blue, and with a sort of mumbling quietude
that I've begun to recognize in my own voice at emotional encroach-
ments, "Do you ever think of doing away with yourself?" That's just
the way he said it, "doing away with yourself," which led me to make
a snide, annihilating comment about the linguistic imprecision and
general uselessness of psychiatry, because in his late forties that's
what my father had become, a psychiatrist living on the grounds of a
state hospital, where suicide was as ubiquitous and predictable an im-
pulse as hunger, where even the doctor whose place my father had
taken, whose office he used and whose bedroom he slept in, had
"done away with himself."

Some families accumulate self-consciousness in the way that
others accumulate wealth (and perhaps one precludes the other). A
man who eats and works and copulates all with same bland animal ef-
ficiency somehow sires a son who, maddeningly to the father, pauses

occasionally in the midst of plowing to marvel at the shapes in the clouds, or who sometimes thinks fleetingly that perhaps there is an altogether different order of feeling than the mild kindliness he feels toward his wife. He in turn has a son who has the impulse to be elsewhere – geographically, sexually, spiritually – but not the wherewithal to wholly do so, who lives the impulsive, appetitive lives of his own children in the fixed world of his parents, and destroys both. A person emerging from the wreckage of this – and many simply don't – is likely to be quite solitary, given to winnowings and adept at departures, so absurdly self-aware that he can hardly make love without having an "experience." He might even be, maddeningly to all concerned, a poet.

That I should have turned out to be a poet seems strange to me for all sorts of reasons – I don't relish poverty or obscurity, to name just two – but my background has never seemed one of them. Bookless though it was, my childhood, with its nameless angers and solitudes, its intimate, inexplicable violence, seems to me the very "forge and working-house" of poetry. Tellingly, my father, though he certainly never read poetry, is the one member of my family for whom my becoming a poet never seemed at all odd or surprising. I begin to understand this now. He knew – he taught me – love's necessary severities, how it will work itself into, even be most intense within, forms of such austere and circumscribed dimensions that, to the uninitiated, it might not seem like love at all.

I am eight years old. My mother has been scratched by the kitten we've had for a month or so, and there has been a flurry of panic and activity as she has had the beginnings of a severe allergic reaction and been rushed to the hospital. I don't know where my brother and sister are, or why I've come home with my father, or if my mother is all right. I'm sitting on the couch, staring at the television, though it's not on. My father is looking for something in a kitchen drawer, now he's back in the bedroom looking for something else. My face is boneless, ghostly on the black screen. I'm hardly there. He walks past me with the kitten in one hand and a hammer in the other, opens the sliding glass door to the porch, closes it behind him. I shut my eyes, will myself away.

It's eight years later. My father is having an affair. He and my mother are at the edge of what will be a nasty, protracted, ruinous divorce in which their children will be used as weapons. It's the middle of the afternoon on a school day and I'm stoned, maybe on speed as well, I forget. Some little argument cracks the surface of civil estrangement we've tacitly agreed upon, and out of that rift all the old anger rises. I begin to curse at my mother in a way I've never done before or since, now I break something, now something else, and she's scared enough to call my father at the hospital and leave the house until he rushes home.

They come in together. I am sitting in the living room, seething, waiting. My father stands over me and quietly – guiltily, I realize, the first flaw in his hitherto adamantine authority – asks me what is going on. I tell him I'm ashamed of him. I call him a liar. I curse him in the harshest and most profane terms I can muster. He hits me open-handed across the face – hard, but with a last-minute hesitation in it, a pause of consciousness that seems to spread like a shadow across his own face and, as he sinks into a chair, is to this day the purest sadness I have ever seen.

I stand up slowly. I am vaguely aware of my mother yelling at my father, of my sister in the doorway weeping. I am vaguely aware that our roles have suddenly and irrevocably reversed, that he is looking up at me, waiting for what I'll do. I hit him squarely between the eyes, much harder than he hit me. He does nothing but cover his head with his hands, doesn't say a word as I hit him again, and again, and again, expending my anger upon a silence that absorbs it, and gradually neutralizes it, until the last blow is closer to a caress.

That was the end of my childhood. My father moved out within a month or so, and in the same time I gave up drugs, began the exercise regimen that I've maintained for twenty years, and started assiduously saving for the tuition for my first year of college, to which I was suddenly determined to go, and which I would choose entirely on the basis of its distance from Texas. Once there I sometimes went months without talking to any member of my family, whose lives seemed to me as dangerously aimless and out of control as mine was safely ordered and purposeful. I began to read poetry, which I loved most of all for the contained force of its forms, the release of its music, and for the fact that, as far as I could tell, it had absolutely nothing to do with the world I was from.

And then one night John killed a man outside of a bar. I'd kept up with him somewhat, had been forced to, in fact, since in a final asser- tion of physical superiority he'd ended my lingering relationship with my high-school girlfriend by impregnating her. I knew that he'd gone to work in the oil fields, and that he was deep into drugs. Our friend- ship had fallen apart before this, though, a slow, sad disintegration that culminated in a halfhearted, inconclusive fistfight on a dirt road outside of town. I forget the reason for the fight itself, and anyway it wouldn't be relevant. What we were trying to do, I think, was to for- malize the end of something that had meant a great deal to both of us, to attach an act we understood to a demise we didn't.

My mother called to tell me about it. John had gotten in an argu- ment with a stranger that escalated into blows. They had been thrown out of the bar by bouncers and continued the fight in the street. In front of some thirty or forty people John had slowly and with great difficulty won the fight, beating the man until he lay on his back gasp- ing for air. And whether the pause I've imagined over and over at this point is something that came out in the trial, or whether it's merely some residual effect of my friendship with John, my memory of a de- cent and sensitive person to whom some glimmer of consciousness must surely have come, what happened in the end is a fact. At nine- teen years old, with his bare hands, in front of a crowd of people who did nothing, and with a final fury that must have amazed that man who was only its incidental object, John destroyed him.

Hanging up the phone, sitting there in my dorm room of that pre- posterously preppy college fifteen hundred miles away from my home, it all came back, the guns and the fights, the wreckage of my family, my friendship with John, the wonderment in his voice in the hours after that hunting accident when he kept saying, *I shot my fa- ther, I shot my own father,* as if he were trying out the thought, trying to accommodate it in his consciousness.

I did what I always do: I went for a run, thirteen miles through the hills of Virginia, much farther than I usually ran, but without diffi- culty, my heart a steady *thump-thump-thump* in my chest. It was not release. It was the same thing as my precipitous decision to get out of Texas, no different from what poetry would be for me for years, until I would finally find myself back home one day, living on the grounds of that state hospital, collecting facts. It was what suicide would have been the final expression of: flight.

3

Dr. Miller's face was obliterated. He walked out of the brush across from us and around the edge of the tank with the hesitant precision of someone making his way across a familiar room in the dark. Amid the blood and loose bits of skin there were clumps of pellets cauliflowering his cheeks and the sockets of his eyes, distorting his forehead and throat like a sudden, hideous disease, his dark shirt darker down his chest. His lips, too, were so misshapen that it was hard at first to understand the directives he was giving us, though he spoke calmly, deliberately, with the same West Texas mix of practical necessity and existential futility that no crisis could ever shock my own father out of.

He drove. I don't remember there being even a moment of discussion, though both John and I had our licenses by then, and though Dr. Miller had to lean over the steering wheel to see, wincing as the pickup jolted over the ruts and stones. I was sitting in the middle of the seat, John at the door. I kept trying not to look at Dr. Miller, kept thinking that his breaths were shorter than they should have been, that I could hear blood in his lungs.

There were two gates before we got to the road. At the first one, John simply leapt back in the truck as it was still moving, leaving the gate unlatched. Dr. Miller stopped, turned his head like some sentient piece of meat toward us, and said, "Close the gate, John."

At the second gate, after John had gotten out of the truck, Dr. Miller said without looking toward me, "You didn't fire that shot, did you?"

Could it be, in life as well as in writing, that our deepest regrets will not be for our lies, but for the truths we should not have told?

"He didn't mean to," I said, the words spilling out, "it was an accident, we thought you were in the south pasture, we didn't hear you, we –"

"It's my fault," Dr. Miller said peremptorily, putting his hand on my knee. "I know that."

About halfway through the ride John began to weep. He was leaning over against the door, and as his shoulders trembled up and down, it seemed years were falling away from him, that if he were to reach out it would be with a hand from which all the strength was gone, if he were to speak it would be in the voice of a child. I looked out at the fields that had almost vanished, darkness knitting together the limbs of mesquite trees, accumulating to itself the crows and telephone poles, the black relentless pumpjacks that, when John and I spent the night out here, beat into our sleep like the earth's heart.

Dr. Miller drove himself straight to my father, who was still at the office. My father registered no more alarm for Dr. Miller's injuries than Dr. Miller himself had done, though my father did, I noticed, immediately and carefully touch my face, my shoulders and arms, as if to ensure himself that I wasn't the one hurt.

John and I waited in my father's office. I sat in my father's chair behind the desk, John in the chair across from me, looking out the window. This is when I remember him saying, "I shot my father, I shot my own father," not to me, and almost as if it were a question, one that neither I nor anyone else could answer. Not another word was said. I sat there watching the clock on the wall across from me, willing it to go faster, faster.

To be a writer is to betray the facts. It's one of the more ruthless things about being a writer, finally, in that to cast an experience into words is in some way to lose the reality of the experience itself, to sacrifice the fact of it to whatever imaginative pattern one's wound requires. A great deal is gained, I suppose, a kind of control, the sort of factitious understanding that Ivan Karamazov renounces in my epigraph, *form*. When I began to spiral into myself and into my family's history, it was just this sort of willful understanding that I needed. I knew the facts well enough.

But I don't understand, not really. Not my family's history and not my childhood, neither my father's actions nor his absence. I don't understand how John could kill someone, or by what logic or luck the courses of our lives, which had such similar origins, could be so different. I don't understand, when there is so much I love about my life, how I could have such a strong impulse to end it, nor by what dispensation or accident of chemistry that impulse could go away, recede so far into my consciousness that I could almost believe it never happened.

It did happen, though. It marked me. I don't believe in "laying to rest" the past. There are wounds we won't get over. There are things that happen to us that, no matter how hard we try to forget, no matter with what fortitude we face them, what mix of religion and therapy we swallow, what finished and durable forms of art we turn them into, are going to go on happening inside of us for as long as our brains are alive.

And yet I've come to believe, and in rare moments can almost feel, that like an illness some vestige of which the body keeps to protect itself, pain may be its own reprieve; that the violence that is latent within us may be, if never altogether dispelled or tamed, at least acknowledged, defined, and perhaps by dint of the love we feel for our lives, for the people in them and for our work, rendered into an energy that need not be inflicted on others or ourselves, an energy we may even be able to use; and that for those of us who have gone to war with our own minds there is yet hope for what Freud called "normal unhappiness," wherein we might remember the dead without being haunted by them, give to our lives a coherence that is not "closure," and learn to live with our memories, our families, and ourselves amid a truce that is not peace.

I hear my father calling me from what seems a great distance. I walk down the hall of the office that has long ago been cleared out and turned into something else. But here are my family's pictures on the walls, here is the receptionist's window where my sister and I would play a game in which one of us had some dire illness that the other, with a cup of water, or with some inscrutable rune written on a prescription pad, always had the remedy for. And here is John, small and terrified, walking beside me.

Dr. Miller is sitting up on an examining table, his face swathed in gauze, his shirt off, revealing a sallow, soft, middle-aged body. Its whiteness shocks me like a camera's flash and will be the first thing

I'll think of when, within months, John tells me that his father has left for another woman. We stop just inside the door, side by side. My heart seems almost audible.

"Well now," my father says, smiling slightly as he looks to the table then back to us, "did you boys get your limits?"

Dr. Miller laughs, and John moves toward him.

He is all right. Everything is going to be all right. I stick my hand in my pocket full of cold birds to feel how close I've come.

2000

II

A Piece of Prose

O f all the many and mostly noble reasons why a poet might turn to prose, there is one which is often primary, personal, and only occasionally conscious: it staves off the silence. If, as Thomas Mann wrote, a writer is someone for whom writing is more difficult than it is for other people, a poet is someone for whom writing – in his poems, I mean – is more difficult than it is for other writers. At least it seems this ought to be the case. To write a real poem is to be made aware at once of the singularity of words and their precariousness, their "propensity to come off from reality," as Czeslaw Milosz puts it. For anyone who has been made so aware, the time between poems can become a time of some peril, of encroaching unreality and increasing confusion. It can seem like silence is steadily claiming everything.

Prose can be an antidote to this, at least for a while. Though I don't feel that critical ability inevitably accompanies a poetic gift, nor that all poets bear a kind of *a priori* burden to produce criticism (those who do usually know who they are), I have little patience for people who see the application of critical intelligence as somehow inimical to poetic creation. It's true that a poem can't be an illustration of an idea, that a too scrupulous attention to one's own means and modes of creation can result in paralysis. Something like this seems to have happened to Coleridge, but it's hardly an inevitability. Ideally, the two activities should be at once intimate and separate.

"Periods of poetic activity usually end with critical awareness," Cesare Pavese writes, and the articulation of this awareness can be a way out of it, a way into whatever new and different work lies ahead. The poetry of a poet-critic is always of paramount importance, for himself, obviously, but also in a way for his audience, even if that audience is unfamiliar with the poems. The worth of a poet's critical awareness will have been determined by the truth and intensity of the poetic activity that preceded it, the depth to which he descended in his poems. (Accomplishment is usually but not necessarily an issue: it's possible to come up empty-handed but greatly changed.) The poet's own emphasis will be somewhat different. Criticism will be valuable to him only insofar as it charts the waters where he's been, enables him to move away, and equips him for the next descent.

But prose can also be mere evasion. Silence is not some negative state with regard to poetry but is in some way part of its very nature, the element out of which, with great pain, it emerges and to which, with what can sometimes seem an almost greater pain, it tries to return:

> As all the Heavens were a Bell,
> And Being, but an Ear,
> And I, and Silence, some strange Race
> Wrecked, solitary, here –

Enduring silence is no small part of poetry's discipline, acquiring the patience to wait, knowing when not to write. There is a kind of frenetic production that conceals an essential indolence, and a writer can be at the same time prolific and mute. Prose that is written *merely* to stave off silence, then, serves roughly the same function as booze or excessive exercise. It's merely a busier, less efficient oblivion.

Don't ask me where the balance lies, somewhere between a statement once made by William Matthews – "one job of a poet is not to fall silent" – who seems to miss the point, and the late muteness of Ezra Pound, who impaled himself upon it: "In the end, silence overtook me." Not to fall silent, then, and yet to feel it, to bring something of its pure potential and finality into one's work and self without being overtaken by it: there's the goal. For me, for now, prose helps.

2

Style is not an infallible guide to the value of a poet's prose and opinions, but it's the least fallible. That's Auden, or almost, who was himself an exemplary prose stylist. By "exemplary" I mean two things.

His prose has the sort of authoritative yet intimate air that is evidence of issues engaged at a primary level, which is to say, in his own poems. The second thing is at once simpler and rarer: it gives pleasure. One ought not expect that the style of a poet's poems and prose will be indistinguishable, but I do think it's fair to expect that some of the aesthetic elements that lead to distinction in poetry – metaphorical intelligence, a sense of linguistic rhythm, enough wit and wide life to suggest that some whole person is addressing you – will make itself felt in the prose. It's going too far to hope for a prose that could, like a poem, compel and even almost convince simply by the way it sounds, but I like a writer who at least *tries.*

There are dangers in this. A writer as good as Seamus Heaney can have you thinking some lumpy, lugubrious translation of an Eastern European poet is ringing in your inner ear and setting your moral soul on fire. I don't mind this. We reveal ourselves much more deeply – both in terms of taste and character – in our enthusiasms than in our censures. The lapses passion causes are never altogether ignoble. Love, even if misguided, even if its object has been supplanted by an ideal, is always distinguishable from the cold, clinical efficiency of mere need. It's the difference between a wrongheaded but right-hearted affair and – more on this when I talk about reviewing – prostitution.

Criticism is easier to write than poetry, but it shares a first imperative of that more exacting art. Poets, so long as they are poets, never lose their sense of language as a living thing, their ear for it in the air of their own time. They use language only so long as they are living it, discovering in its historically specific depths and inflections the same small set of truths that every other poet has labored – and lived – to discover. It's all in *how* you say a thing.

Criticism is different, in that it does matter precisely *what* is being said, and good insight can occasionally survive bad style. Geoffrey Hill's criticism is an example. There are brilliant things packed away inside the knotted prose, but getting at them can be a bit like cracking a husk coincidentally with your tooth: that's a tough nut to savor. There are, I think, more examples of good style surviving bad judgment. Think of Eliot on *Paradise Lost,* Johnson on the Metaphysicals, Yvor Winters on almost anything. We read these pieces less for

their perceptions than for the lively, momentarily misguided minds
at work in them, for their *styles.* Being right won't save you. Judicious
dullness is like a good job of embalming: the subject is cleaned up,
tastefully presented, recognizable, and dead.

"Writers themselves usually make the best critics," the poet Anne
Stevenson has written, "because, even when wrong, they care so
much about writing well." My experience as a poet makes me want to
agree immediately with this. My experience as a reviewer gives me
some pause. When John Hollander begins a sentence, "Before we avail
ourselves of these texts," this is one reader who knows immediately
that he's not going to be around long enough to avail himself of these
texts. That's a joke, of course, but just barely. John Hollander's book
The Work of Poetry is probably the most meticulous and comprehen-
sive of the twenty or so books I read through in preparation for this
essay,* and I certainly learned things from it. But there's a stuffiness
to his style, some main charge missing. Similarly, although James
Longenbach has some solid things to say about the legacies of Mod-
ernism in *Modern Poetry After Modernism,* and though his prose is
always clean and readable, his tone is that of someone who can't stop
looking over his shoulder. With his careful qualifications, his endless
good sense, his empty term-paper rhetoric ("his strategy... helps to
insure the future health and diversity of American literature"), he
sounds less like a poet than a valedictorian.

Which raises the question: what exactly *should* a poet's prose
sound like? There are random answers among the books I read
through. It may have the dense, impacted quality of Christopher
Middleton's (some tough nuts here), the reach and richness of Derek
Walcott's essay on Lowell. It may have the autobiographical elegance
of J.D. McClatchy's essays on reading and writing, the passionate
economy of the title piece in Donald Justice's book *Oblivion,* the
moral seriousness of Mary Kinzie's *The Cure of Poetry in an Age of
Prose.* In prose as in poetry, there is perhaps only one definite re-
quirement for a vital style: it must make a reader feel that something
is truly at stake.

*These books are listed in the Notes.

The higher the stakes, the better, more durable the work. Patrick Kavanagh wrote of "dabbling in verses" until they became his life, suggesting an idea of the poet as someone who one day wades into the shallows of words and later discovers, with what is half elation, half pure panic, that the deepest currents of his life are running through them. The way one tries to reconcile that latter discovery with that initial play will be one's style. It is a reconciliation that, for the poet, must never quite occur, for the moment style becomes completely conscious, the moment it becomes applied rather than discovered, it becomes a manner.

This burden is eased considerably in the more forgiving medium of critical prose, in which one needn't reinvent an achieved style, but it isn't altogether gone. If you find that your life is in your poetry, or that you can somehow only get to your life *through* your poetry, it follows that the ideas you have about poetry will demand a similar sort of scrupulous attention to language as language. When Yeats agonizes in his *Autobiographies* over the difficulty of achieving a great prose style, he is attesting to the relationship between his poems and his prose, his language and his life. A poet's prose engages and emerges out of this relationship, this difficulty, and the style that is its means of doing so will be imprinted with the deepest currents of a particular mind, a particular life. Or not.

3

Thus far I have been talking primarily about what I would call impractical prose, the origins of which are more internal than external, bound up with the poet's feeling for his own gift rather than with his feeling for his or poetry's place in the world. Such prose may be prompted by its occasion, but it won't be determined by it. Letters can sometimes fall in this category (Rilke, Keats, Crane), as can reviews. Eliot's famous essay on the Metaphysicals is in fact a commissioned review, though the book in question is clearly little more than a catalyst for ideas that had long been emerging in Eliot's mind. The one evaluative sentence comes almost as an afterthought.

Practical prose is almost always more ephemeral, if for no other reason than the impermanence of the books themselves. Practical criticism is a sort of oil in the engine of the literary world. It's what poets with prizes, houses, and big reading fees have learned either to avoid or practice very cannily. It's what fills the back, usually terminally boring pages of literary magazines. It's what everyone – *everyone* – disparages for being too timid, too political, too exclusive, too incestuous. Discovering you have some ability for practical criticism is like being a prospector discovering you can crack rocks on your skull. Eventually other prospectors begin to bring you rocks, for which you charge a nominal fee. No one's happy when you point out there's no gold inside, as you must almost always do, and in those rare instances when you do discover a vein of the real thing, none of its benefits accrue to you. The only definite permanent result of practicing such a talent is a massive headache.

But practical criticism can be even more important than other kinds. It can serve as a cleansing element when that aforementioned engine's begun to sputter and spew pollution, the air contaminated by habit and unconscious conventions. Great poets aren't breathing that air, but good ones are, and the health of a literary culture is in some ways more contingent upon its good poets than its great ones. One need only read through a period piece like the *Morrow Anthology of Younger American Poets,* a sort of *Golden Treasury of Suburban Verse,* to see what can happen when the practical critical intelligence is in a kind of generational abeyance. History will dispense with even the most massively wrongheaded of our monuments, but it's a slower erosion than people think. When a good practical critic like Geoffrey O'Brien goes after the Morrow anthology, he exposes the soft rot at the center of some of our assumptions, and thereby helps to hasten a necessary decay.

For a number of years, William Logan was the best practical critic around. I sometimes disagreed with his judgments fiercely, but *that* I so fiercely disagreed, that his prose provoked such a response, is what made him the best. Most criticism is like most poetry: it simply leaves you indifferent. I've seen Logan's name bring bile to the lips of the gentlest spirits, and there is no doubt that gratuitous rancor is a weakness in his work. But for breadth of intelligence, an incisive style, and pure passion, the reviews he wrote in the late eighties and through the nineties are tough to match.

Good reviewing always has an edge to it. "Passions face both ways," Logan writes, and it's telling that the title of his book is *All the Rage,* that Mary Kinzie's collected reviews are called *The Judge Is Fury.* Anger, when it's the good anger, when it's for the faked emotion or failed technique (the same thing, usually) that is a deep violation of life, can hone and enhance taste. Something of the same kind of self-dissatisfaction that leads to the finding of forms in poetry – you want an order that you are not, a peace that you can't be – can lead a critic who is primarily a poet to seeing that quality in other work, and often the purest, most convincing praise is laced with an element of, if not anger exactly, at least insufficiency, self-dissatisfaction, a critic's sense that someone else has done something that he could not. It's only when one's anger is for the "literary world," when its origins are personal and mercenary, that it becomes debased, one's energies short-circuited, and the calibrations of taste distorted.

One ought to inhabit the role of reviewer without relishing it. Part of what makes Fred Chappell's prose attractive – besides the wit, readability, and sharp opinions – is his unease over the entire enterprise and his part in it. This keeps him alert, for the most part (he has a soft spot for Southerners), saves him from the boilerplate praise of most contemporary reviewers; the clichéd thinking of critics who use phrases like "bearing witness" or "subversive" or "taking risks" with the sort of gestural imprecision that ought to be anathema to a poet; the bland personality-pieces that conflate the person and the work, amiability and accomplishment.

Good reviewing is mostly the province of the young, whose occlusions can amount to a kind of strength. The cheerful broad-mindedness that can be attractive in a person, a bloodhound ability to sniff out the good in the smelliest circumstances, can ruin a reviewer. Young poets usually have some sort of passionate focus rather than range. They will miss much, will make outlandish mistakes, but when some book falls within the range of taste they have acquired, which has been largely determined by their own work, they will nail it. And it just so happens that, since major shifts in a culture's poetry are also usually the province of the young (the Romantics, the Modernists, etc.), most of what is truly innovative and new in poetry, whether it's some subtle change in the way conventions are being inhabited or a more radical assault upon those conventions, will occur within this range.

Innocence can also help. The poetry world being what it is – so small, so self-contained, so far removed from *the* world – a poet who isn't a hermit is going to suffer, both professionally and personally, from the sharpness of his opinions. Young poets may know this, but they know it as young smokers know that cigarettes cause cancer: it's pure abstraction. They'll fire from the hip for a while, partly just for the flair of it, but mostly because of a genuine, healthy contempt for complacency and the idea of a "career" in poetry. If this isn't quite the case in the la-la land of workshops and blurbs, it ought to be.

I'm not at all sure what causes or enables some poets to persist. Whatever one thinks about Logan and Chappell, or other midcareer poets who have continued to write balanced reviews of contemporary books (Dana Gioia, Sandra M. Gilbert, Mary Kinzie, Bruce Bawer), there's something admirable in this persistence. Admirable, that is, so long as one trusts the motives behind it, the sense of necessity, even almost of moral responsibility, to which both Logan and Chappell allude. Less generous motives are not difficult to imagine. It's easier to make a name for oneself as a reviewer than as a poet, though anyone who would value this lesser recognition is probably not a real poet anyway. Then, too, there are always those who are keen on accumulating "power" in the poetry world, and reviewing may be just one more means of doing so. One hardly knows what to say about this. Wielding power in the poetry world is roughly the equivalent of cutting a wide swath through your local PTA.

Public reaction may in the end be one of the strongest incentives, and not a base one. Poetry is lonely. Publish a poem in some conspicuous place and the response is not likely to be overwhelming, not likely to even *be* a response. Publish a review or essay that is at all partisan or passionate in that same place and you'll get some letters. One of these will be from someone who is clearly quite intelligent and thoughtful, and will be very gratifying. Another will come from someone you

suspect has broken off from society, who likely wrote you while on a
break from building his bomb shelter or foraging for dung beetles.
And then you'll get the rare, cherished one that could go either way,
like the letter I once received from some mad rancher down in South
Texas who objected to a review I had written. "Christian Wiman!" he
screamed in a letter to the editor. "What is this, a joke? Some sort of
right-wing temperance group?" He was pronouncing it *Christian*
women, you see. I sent him a bottle of bourbon.

4

The scope of a poet's prose will tell you at once something of his own
and his culture's perspective of poetry's place in the world. One of
the most consistent qualities of the books I read through while think-
ing about this piece was modesty – tonal modesty, yes, a certain leveling
stylistic diffidence, but even more than that a modesty in the range of
subject matter they address. The three books by non-Americans –
Walcott's *What the Twilight Says,* Milosz's *Road-side Dog,* and
Middleton's *Jackdaw Jiving* – make for a sharp contrast, as all of
these writers are more ecumenical, more political, more historical
than their American counterparts, who, when they do range away
from specific treatments of poems or issues relating to poetry, tend to
do so in the direction of personal experience.

American poets, except in the rarest instances (Adrienne Rich),
and then usually only with regard to a very specific issue, don't be-
come public intellectuals in the broadest sense of that term. It's
tough to become a public intellectual when your public thinks of you
as extraneous, even faintly ridiculous, but even when a poet does
seem to have acquired something of a public forum – our poets laure-
ate, for example – there's little effort to speak to broader cultural issues.
The enclosed focus of most contemporary American poetry, which
often seems to have resigned itself to the fact that its only readers are
other poets, seems to obtain for our criticism as well. It's difficult to
imagine a book like Milosz's *The Captive Mind* or Octavio Paz's *The*
Labyrinth of Solitude being written by a prominent American poet.

I mean that mostly by way of observation rather than criticism.

Some of the strongest writing in these books I've read occurs when criticism merges with autobiography, and combining the intimately personal with the critical may be a particularly American strength. (Tellingly, this is precisely where Walcott's writing becomes weakest.) I have already mentioned McClatchy in this regard, whose autobiographical essays are at once personal and impersonal, directly confessional but very cannily crafted. C.K. Williams's compelling essay in *Poetry and Consciousness* on why he no longer reads many novels, which digresses and then focuses on what form means in a poem, is another good example of this balance.

The example of poets becoming pundits is not always, or even usually, a good one. As it happens, of the three books by non-Americans that I mentioned, only Milosz's seems to me compelling in this sense, as cultural commentary, as wisdom. American precedents aren't too promising. We could live without the sophisticated hatefulness of Eliot in *After Strange Gods,* the streetcorner rants of Pound on money. And yet all of these examples – Walcott and Middleton included – suggest an idea of what the poet's place in the world might be, and thus by extension what poetry's place in the world might be. The reach is greater, whatever has been successfully grasped, and it's hard not to see the narrowed scope of contemporary American critics (including this one) as a diminished thing.

The recent rash of technical manuals on prosody is almost certainly a symptom of this attenuated scope. These manuals are by and large a salutary thing, I guess. After the train wreck of broken-prose confessionalism, there seems to be a general heightened emphasis upon technique, an understanding that, for the best poets, technique is coextensive with feeling, and that many of the elements associated with traditional technique must be mastered if poetry is to remain a serious art. Still, there's something disappointing in the fact that one of our most prominent poets of the moment, Robert Pinsky, whose first book of opinionated and partisan prose, *The Situation of Poetry,* remains interesting and useful, has produced a mild, rudimentary book on the sounds of poetry. There's something frustrating in watching so many well-established poets expend so much energy explaining dipodic meters, synaloepha, or the evolution of the pantoum. Yeats, at the death of Swinburne, declared himself King of the Cats. The battle now seems to be over who will be King of the Teachers.

This pedagogical inclination can sometimes disguise narrowed focus as enlarged scope, can substitute range of reference and taste for range of passion and experience. Part of becoming a poet is realizing that, as those shallows in which Kavanagh spoke of dabbling begin to deepen, the currents they contain are not simply of one's individual life, but of life itself, of reality beyond one's own. It is this awareness that informs the work of the truly great critics like Heaney, Eliot, Coleridge, and Dryden, and that I find missing from so much contemporary writing about poetry, which is frequently merely explanatory, concerned with *how* rather than *why* one ought to read particular poems, locating them in literature rather than life. Close readings have their uses, can anchor a criticism that has become too impressionistic and vague. Witnessing a powerful mind limit itself to the literary elements of a text can be fascinating, and yet there is for me always something a bit appalling about it as well, like watching a spider that, limb by limb, line by line, sucks the life out of some poor fly.

But there's a much subtler kind of pedagogical withdrawal. A recurrent refrain within these books I've read is the necessity for broadmindedness, a rejection of aesthetic exclusivity, a plea for openness with regard to what poetry can be, or what it needs to be at any given moment. "I don't think any particular imperative – that poetry must become more difficult, more accessible, more formal, more disjunctive, more self-conscious – is ever very useful," Longenbach writes, largely in response to Eliot. It's a statement that on its surface seems pleasantly equanimous and hard to disagree with, a reformulation of negative capability, of sorts, in that for Longenbach the ideal for both the poet and critic seems to be that capacity "of being in uncertainties, Mysteries, doubts, without any irritable reaching after fact & reason." I think this is wrong, or at least oversimplified.

Poetry arises out of absence, a deep internal sense of wrongness, out of a mind that feels itself to be in some way cracked. An original poem is a descent into and expression of this insufficiency. Criticism, when it is written by a poet who understands the urgency involved in making poems, is usually either a careful delineation of the depths entered (Heaney), or an equally careful attempt to recast them somewhat in order to make them more manageable (Eliot). In either case, in terms of taste, historical understanding, and a feeling for what is *necessary* in poems, the criticism is going to be pitched in one particular direction. We might say that often the critic in a man must choose sides, *precisely in order that* the poet in him can go on stealing secrets from the enemy. You spend years sealing up the gaps in your uncertainty, shoring fragments of fact and reason against your ruins, all the while praying that in rare moments some ghost of that good unknowingness – call it spirit, call it the unconscious, call it God – will slip back in to save you from your best efforts. Negative capability is a good and necessary thing, but you can't *plan* on it.

Poetry, insofar as it is written by those bundles of accident and incoherence that are individual poets, demands imperatives, whether it's Eliot formulating his ideas about impersonality, difficulty, and tradition while writing his personal, aurally immediate, and altogether original poems, or Milton deploying dogma as a sort of defensive strategy against the real feeling and passion of *Paradise Lost.* Indeed, strong critical beliefs can serve roughly the same function as dogmas, which only those whose lives are as blithe and formless as their poems will dismiss out of hand. The poet can't ever embrace either, that's probably right, but the critic can and often must on his behalf. So while it's generally true that at any given moment it's not necessary that poetry be more difficult, more accessible, more formal, more disjunctive, more self-conscious than the poetry of the past, there's a way in which, for anyone whose concern is for the here and now, for the poems that are possible for us at this particular moment, this is a useless sort of truth. It's the long view of the scholar, not the immediate, urgent anxiety of the poet.

5

Poetry's origins and courses are mysterious and, if it is to avoid becoming mechanical, merely an imitation of literature, must remain so. It ought to come as easily as leaves to a tree, Keats said, by which he meant, I think, not that it ought to come necessarily with ease but that there should be something natural about it, that it should be both a poet's life and life itself occurring somehow in language. This is why at the onset of a poem, when most possessed by it, it can seem like greatness is possible. It may not be possible for *you,* and coincidental with this immensity of potential may be the most corrosive awareness of inadequacy, but there is some greatness inherent in the act itself.

Reality doesn't need us. A poet knows this, and then, in the midst of a poem, when reality streams through the words that would hold it, doesn't quite. W.S. Di Piero, probably the most consistently compelling and idiosyncratic prose writer among contemporary American poets, writes of that moment when one realizes that one's "attempt to write poetry, with all its halting correctiveness and will toward coherence, is of no consequence to the starry sky." And yet it was the starry sky that occasioned the poem, perhaps, that seems to be not simply its subject but somehow *in* the poem, of it. It is a calling, we say, trying to explain this need to make things the world can do without, as if the plain givenness of reality could ever be a call, as if a poem could ever be an answer.

Prose is an altogether different order of experience, more public, less mysterious, less ultimately rewarding. I'm not sure it makes much sense to speak of "greatness" in critical prose, and the only call you're likely to get is on the telephone, some editor asking you to write something. And yet I've found it impossible to talk about prose without talking a great deal about poetry, for a poet's prose is intimately bound up with that original calling.

It can occasionally, in certain limited ways, be even more satisfying. Prose can provide a poet with a means of direct self-discovery and articulation that poetry, with its impersonal formal imperatives in which personality and selfhood can seem to be annihilated, cannot. Poetry, feeding on singular instances of consciousness and psychological urgencies, can't afford to become a habit, and the will to remain vigilant to its occasions can be exhausting and self-destructive. Prose can afford to become habitual, without much damage to either the poet or his prose. There can be great comfort in this, both in terms of surviving the silences I've mentioned as well as satisfying a puritanical desire for work, work, work. In the end, though, when the work is done, any poet who is at all a poet knows it for what it is, which is something considerably less than the real work, mere means, a very careful sort of public appearance, a bit of money, maybe, a bit of a headache, probably, a piece of prose.

1998

Finishes: On Ambition and Survival

The way a poet thinks about the relation of poetry to his life will have a great deal to do with the kind of poetry produced. There is a world of difference between the poem-a-day routine of Dickinson, which allowed for many slight and casual pieces, and the sonnets Hopkins said he had "written in blood," between the seemingly limitless fluency of Auden and the precarious austerities of Hart Crane. It's oversimplifying matters considerably to think of this difference as merely one of relative emphasis on process and product, as if for Auden and Dickinson it was the act of writing that mattered, whereas for Crane and Hopkins it was the finished work. The "supreme question" that James Joyce said we must ask of any work of art – "out of how deep a life does it spring" – is answerable to the same degree in the best work of all of these poets. But the distinction is not altogether without value. Poets devise various means of surviving their silences, their *essential* silences, I should say, because for some poets this involves keeping up a steady skimming sort of hum, treading water while waiting for stirrings from the deeper reaches. For others the time between poems can be considerably more difficult to endure, and the painstaking way they work over each poem is not unlike a never-quite-converted person reaching to remember as the god withdraws, doubt like silence seeping back in.

Often a change from a poetry of consuming singularity to a poetry that is more observational, steadily occasional, and perhaps reportorial occurs within the career of a single poet. John Berryman, who for a number of years was obsessed with writing one perfect poem, eventually "relaxed" into what was for him the more natural, accumulative method of the first seventy-seven *Dream Songs*. Robert Lowell, by contrast, who described his young self as "burning to believe that each finished poem would be my last," eventually burned out in a blast of powerful but largely undirected energy he called "fourteen-liners." Each poet's change in style reflects a change in his perception of the relation between his poetry and his life. Although in certain obvious ways the later work of these poets is more ambitious than the early work, which began to seem limiting and claustrophobic to both of them, there is a sense in which their development may be seen as an attenuation of ambition. At some point, as the poems and years begin to pile up, not finished but abandoned, the perfect poem that once seemed possible seems increasingly less so, and poets who find themselves alive and writing in middle age may, like Lowell and Berryman, come to speak of the passion that animated their early search for one perfect work with some of the willed forgetfulness or distancing irony of the survivor.

In his fourth book, *North,* Seamus Heaney writes in the title poem:

> Compose in darkness.
> Expect aurora borealis
> in the long foray
> but no cascade of light.

The lines are cast as a directive to the poet himself, a kind of dream-voice arising out of a history that is at once cultural and, especially in the context created by the surrounding poems of *North,* personal. Using the provisional terms that I've suggested, these lines situate Heaney on the side of poetry as process, art for the sake of life rather than vice versa. They express faith in the idea that, though no one poem ever brings the longed-for "cascade of light," there is a promise of revelation in the life devoted to practicing the art. But *because* the lines are cast as a directive, implicit within them is the suggestion that their message is one of which the poet needs to be reminded. Heaney has written elsewhere that a poet ought to think of his poems as stepping-stones, a metaphor that, like the lines from "North," contains a notion of destination, of poems as means. Few poets can match the disciplined attention that Heaney pays out poem by poem, and I don't think that in either of these instances he is suggesting that the extent to which poets give themselves over to each individual poem is in any way diminished by a broader view of the relation of poetry to one's life. He is not, like a pop psychologist, adjuring himself to value the effort over the achievement, nor is he offering up in the face of defeat a shallow, pot-at-the-end-of-the-rainbow optimism. The emphasis is on the poet's *expectations* of what each finished poem will do for him, and there is a diminishment in this regard. The lines from "North" would run the risk of sounding a bit self-satisfied and even sententious were it not for their exhortative, self-incriminating quality. As it is, there is some built-in resistance to them, some hard and still-contested self-knowledge, as if the poet once thought, perhaps at times is still inclined to hope, that one perfect poem might save or change him. *My hope was just that pretty would save me.*

For a young, ambitious poet, this sort of broad perspective is likely to be met with impatience or, if it comes from an older poet whose poems bear no more sense of urgency than any other daily habit, disdain. Young poets who have read widely often will imagine themselves delivering a knockout punch, writing one poem that is so perfect that the whole world of their reading will be forced to make a place for them. It goes without saying that for most poets this ambition extends to the world of their living as well, in which they crave a fame somewhat less lofty than that found in the eyes of all-judging Jove. Nevertheless, in the absence of this first compulsion, the latter is not likely to lead to work that will survive in the ever-eroding soil of topicality or personality in which it is rooted. This one work on which the poet sets his sights may be, but certainly needn't be and in fact probably shouldn't be, a long poem. Keats, taking aim, setting himself to the sort of dogged Miltonic work for which his gift really wasn't suited, wrote his bloated *Endymion.* Lowell took eight years to forge "The Quaker Graveyard in Nantucket" into its final form, but Lowell's poem is no less ambitious, and to my mind much more successful, than Keats's. Both poets were setting their sights primarily on Milton, whose own early efforts culminated in "Lycidas," an idealization of the intensity and integrity of the young poet's ambition, which, Milton seems to suggest, is in an odd way authenticated by the poet's early death.

Because the ingredient of great poetry which most young poets lack is either life experience or the sense of self needed to fully inhabit their experience, the perfection that they imagine themselves

Yes!

achieving will usually be one of form and style. Though this formal perfection will not necessarily involve traditional metrical forms, it does seem likely that, for those poets of what Robert Lowell, speaking of Allen Tate, called "high formal imagination," traditional forms will for at least a while be the context within which formal individuation occurs. (William Carlos Williams, though not a poet of high formal imagination, does seem to me to be meeting this challenge on his own terms in his early work, which bears everywhere the pressure of the iambics that are being resisted and subtly revised, unlike most contemporary free verse in which the only technical resource is the line break.) "Lycidas" and "The Quaker Graveyard in Nantucket" are great poems (*Endymion* is not, so I'll drop it), but their greatness inheres in their respective realizations of form, in the way each individual talent unsettles its influences even as it takes its place among them. Milton hardly knew Edward King, whom he was ostensibly elegizing in "Lycidas," and the poem is mostly an occasion for Milton to lay out his own literary ambitions with the sort of lyric exuberance that (unfortunately) he eventually learned to resist. And for all of the rhetorical pyrotechnics of "The Quaker Graveyard in Nantucket," for all of its grave meditating on death and will and divinity, the poem is primarily a celebration of sound, a long tide of rhythms in which Lowell, teetering on the brink of meaning, romped around in everything he had read. The ostensible passions of both poems, their apparent subjects, feel staged, supreme fictions within which each poet could blaze away with the one passion that was at that time manageable: the passion for poetry. It would be simplistic and inaccurate to say that either of these poets in their early work *lacked* feeling. Like the early work of many poets – Eliot, Bishop, Crane (most of Crane, I think), Rilke in the *New Poems,* Plath – the respective forms of "Lycidas" and "The Quaker Graveyard in Nantucket" don't enact feeling so much as withstand it. Such poetry may be quite moving, but in the attentive reader's experience of the poem there is always a kind of baffled detachment that mirrors the poet's own, a sense that there is a great deal of life that, though left out of the poem, is nonetheless exerting great pressure at the poem's edges, a cultivated indifference and distance that the poem at once preserves and laments. Poetry at

such times is like a diving bell in which the young poet descends into
an element in which he or she otherwise couldn't survive. And like
that diving bell, the poetry must not leak.

The image of the diving bell suggests an urgency to the discovery
of form which is sometimes overlooked or, unfortunately in the case
of most poets, outgrown. Harold Bloom has pointed out that the fin-
ished poem of a great poet is not the resolution of the anxiety felt to-
ward his or her literary ancestors but an *achieved anxiety*, a form
within which the struggle between the poet's ambition and the past's
delimiting achievements is enacted. Thus the cramped rhapsodies of
a poem such as *The Bridge* don't just recall Whitman, who is the
strongest poetic presence ghosting that poem, but change the way we
read the earlier poet. Bloom's sense of this inter-textual struggle that
occurs in the making of any truly new work is particularly acute, but
I think he at times runs the risk of making the poet's work into a
purely literary phenomenon, of abstracting from that bundle of acci-
dent and incoherence the poems that fit so neatly into ideas of influ-
ence, as if the poet's only thought were to secure a prime plot in the
cemetery of literary history. But there are always other, earlier con-
cerns driving a poet toward form and fame.

John Ruskin, whose comments on visual art are often immediately
relevant to poetry, writes in *Sesame and Lilies:*

> the more beautiful the art, the more it is essentially the work of
> people who *feel themselves wrong;* – who are striving for the ful-
> fillment of a law, and the grasp of a loveliness, which they have
> not yet attained, which they feel even farther and farther from
> attaining the more they strive for it.

There is a sense in which all art arises out of injury or absence, out of
the artist's sense that there is something missing in him, something
awry or disturbed. It's often assumed that this initiating impulse be-
hind a work of art is discoverable within the events of the artist's life.
Although this is sometimes superficially the case, the sense of wrong-
ness that Ruskin is describing is a more pervasive, less easily isolated
cause, some original injury that, for someone whose devotion took a
similar form as Ruskin's, would be something like a fall from grace,

a sense of separateness and incompletion underlying the existence of every work of art. This is an essential distinction to make. It is imperative to note that this sense of wrongness is not synonymous with "suffering," that Ruskin is not making misfortune into a kind of renewable resource out of which a work of art is fashioned, a mistake that has left the lives of many poets of our own time clearcut and completely quiet. Such a distortion led a poet as intelligent and formally imaginative as Berryman to the morbid assertion that the "luckiest" artist was the one who experienced the severest suffering short of death, which is to make one's suffering into an idol and to pervert the experience of creating art into a misguided martyrdom.

Ruskin's sense of wrongness is an abstraction, a conviction, in both senses of that word, deep-held and never quite definable. It isn't somehow added to or replenished by the experience of actual suffering (which, as anyone who actually suffers knows, may prevent the production of art entirely), nor is it ultimately diminished by the achievement of art, though for a time it may be entered and withstood – the diving bell descending. Art – or, to be more precise, form – is not only what enables artists to experience this sense of wrongness at all, which is their deepest being and will possess them one way or another, it is their only hope of wholeness and release. A genuinely felt form, one that is itself meaning and not merely a bearer of meaning, is not some ready-made vessel within which the poet descends into experience. Even for young poets, even when working with "traditional" forms (which must be remade in the artists' own image to *be* living forms), it is recreated with each descent; moreover, it must be done when the poets are already *on their way down,* so to speak, dreaming the diving bell into being around them. The coming on of a poem is like the first burn in the brain of the unprotected but still descending diver, and though it cannot last, a finished form is the only possible relief for the pain its inspiration engendered.

Ruskin's idea was not original. It is hinted at in the work of some of the Romantics, from Keats's defeated Saturn in *Hyperion* to the unnamed griefs of Byron's heroes, and it's since that time that distortions of the idea have become so dangerous. As with most other ideas, though, Shakespeare was there early on. Hamlet, anxious and self-incriminating at the outset of the play, trying to work his unspecific sense of wrongness into a specific action, to give it *form*, is the very embodiment of Ruskin's idea of the artist. The final death scene, wherein Hamlet's release is compromised by all that has been left unsaid, all of the "things standing thus unknown" that keep his deed from being definitive, exemplifies the Tantalus-like striving that is not only the life spent making art but also, for the poet obsessed with one perfect work, the life of each individual poem. That Hamlet dies after his final inadequate act – a death that, it should be noted, is considerably less glossy and idealized than the one lamented in "Lycidas" – is also important and, as will become clearer, not at all metaphorical.

The notion of a formal alleviation of pain is more explicit in Donne's poem "The Triple Foole":

> I thought, if I could draw my paines
> Through Rimes vexation, I should them allay,
> Griefe brought to numbers cannot be so fierce,
> For, he tames it, that fetters it in verse.

It's important to notice that the relief Donne anticipates inheres in the difficulties of craft and not in the mere expression of his grief. As it happens, in fact, the very clarity and beauty with which he manages to "fetter" his grief turns out to be a falsification of it, a lovely affront to the injury out of which it was made:

> But when I have done so,
> Some man, his art and voice to show,
> Doth Set and sing my paine,
> And, by delighting many, frees againe
> Griefe, which verse did restraine.

The perfection others find in the poem is not available to the poet, whose grief is freed by the final form, which, while it was being painstakingly found, had kept the grief at bay. Donne attributes the impermanence of the poem as a place of refuge to the admiration of others, but in Ruskin's terms what comes leaking back into the finished form is all of the life and grief left uncontained by art, particularly by an art that is thought of primarily as a means of restraint and protection.

I am interested in this sense of wrongness, and the formal feeling that is intimately related to it, particularly as it pertains to poets at an early stage in their writing, well beyond apprenticeship certainly, perhaps even already writing the best poems they will ever write, but with the bulk of life yet to get through. This is the stage that Richard Wilbur was referring to when he said, "One does not use poetry for its major purposes, as a means of organizing oneself and the world, until one's world somehow gets out of hand," and it's what Keats was referring to when he wrote, "I must think that difficulties nerve the Spirit of Man – they make his Prime Objects a Refuge as well as a Passion." For a poet at this time an individual poem can begin to seem a point of repose somewhat more permanent than Frost's lovely but limited "momentary stay against confusion," or Heaney's stepping-stones. And the farther fall into the blithe irony of Auden – "Loud hymns that were the royal wives of silence, / Now you are art and part of our confusion" – can seem positively unbearable. Form for such poets, their refuge and their passion, is the dreamt calm at the center of the things that have begun to "get out of hand," and a perfect form, which would give them some permanent position from which to take hold of life, seems always almost within reach, the analogue to the impossible act that would have delivered Hamlet entirely from his own guilt and anxiety.

The problem is that for most young poets the difficulties of form, though not removed from life, are not yet the difficulties of life itself, are insulated from the pressures and strangeness of varied experience, and form remains to some extent impervious to the changing nature of the element in which it is embedded. This disparity between the world and the forms by means of which it is apprehended frequently manifests itself in the too-exclusive attention and submission to talent, which is at once the young poet's greatest strength and most debilitating weakness, from the preening prettiness of early Wilbur or Keats to the overimposing crenellations of early Lowell. Though Wilbur is right that one doesn't really begin to write poetry that matters until encountering some chaos, whether external or internal, most young poets write less to organize life than to keep its chaos at bay. The aptness of Bloom's ideas on influence notwithstanding, what young poets of high ambition and equally high anxiety know is that to make a place for themselves in the world of their reading they

must make a place for themselves in the world. That is to say, the fight
to join the canon *one carries around in one's head* (that seems impor-
tant to emphasize), which for anyone who reads widely and discrimi-
natingly will be made up primarily of the dead, is first of all a fight to
stay alive.

This rather obvious paradox opens onto a knottier, more trou-
bling one. Many poets have written of the fear they feel when finish-
ing a poem that they will never write another. This can seem pretty
grand and romantic for those poets whose "publications" pour out of
them at a steady, tepid pressure, but there are certainly some who,
"burning to believe that each finished poem will be their last," one
day wake to discover that they've succeeded, and that the fear is
something more than they had bargained for. If a poet is writing to
forestall an immense and unspecific sense of "wrongness," creating
poems in which the pressure of this sense is withstood, *and* this poet
also genuinely fears that each finished poem will be the last, he is
caught in a potentially fatal dynamic. In time the pressure of experi-
ence left out of one's poems increases, the descent becomes more
precipitous, and it becomes more difficult to find forms that, like
Donne's in "The Triple Foole," even temporarily restrain that pres-
sure. And if poets imagine one work which, in its invulnerable perfec-
tion, will resolve these conflicting tensions once and for all, what
exactly are they imagining *beyond* this one perfect work? Perhaps an
end to the pain of creation, to the harder pain of their ever-widening
silences, words unspooling easily and steadily out of them into
something done. Maybe they dream of the numb fame of cocktail par-
ties and conferences, or of a change in their nature which, like the
speaker in Yeats's poem "Words," might enable them "to throw poor
words away" and be "content to live." But underlying all of this, I
think, the search for one perfect work is a search for a permanence
implicit in the very idea of perfection, for some undiscovered country
beyond all pain and change where the poet will become somewhat
more historical than he intended, or knew that he intended. To
search for one perfect work, to believe in such a thing, is to crave
something absolute, an absolution, and the fear some poets have that
they will never write another poem is also in an inescapable sense

their most profound desire. One perfect work might heal whatever wounded them into words in the first place, and then the need to write poems, which by this time is all raveled up with the need to live, will be gone. The rest is silence.

I remember the stunned sense of discovery and foreboding I had when, after having been away for a number of years and learned the literary sense in which God's finger "touches" the ordinary person into the artist, I walked into my family's small graveyard plot in West Texas. Chiseled on a headstone there is what turns out to be a common inscription on tombstones throughout the South: *God's finger touched him and he slept.* Inspiration is thus inextricably linked with expiration in this phrase, a connection that poets from Shakespeare ("This thought is as a death...") to Keats ("Darkling I listen...") to Lowell ("this open book... my open coffin") have had to come to terms with long before any literary theory linking death and writing was around. I have always thought Keats's statement that poets are the "least poetical thing in existence" has a deep ambivalence about it that usually goes unnoticed. Besides the self-dramatizing swagger of a young poet reveling in his own uniqueness, there is a suggestion of isolation, a sense of a deep sadness that the poet can never be either fully centered in his own experience or wholly at home in the lives that he imagines. Eliot's description of writing as an "extinction of personality" intensifies Keats's confusion unmistakably, and I think that some of Eliot's more notorious critical pronouncements having to do with the objectification and impersonality of the artist, which have recently been seen as merely an elaborate screen for Eliot's own emotional timidity, ought to be read at least in part as Eliot's attempt to define this ambivalence that Keats was getting at, the ambivalence that most serious poets ultimately feel for their gift, which they wish would once and for all change them, or heal them, or just leave them to the unmediated life which they imagine words have led them away from.

This ambivalence, this dual movement, the sense of loss that is inseparable from the fulfillment of form, is at the heart of the creative experience, or at least the creative experience as it exists for those whose work is words. We say that the artist gives life to his characters, and indeed he does, but the life that he gives them is his own. A poem is said to save experience from "the wreckful siege of battering days," and this too is in a sense true, though what enables this truth is the form from which the poet falls away the minute it is found, and the poem that may seem so inevitable and even immutable to a reader is no peace the poet knows. No poet escapes this condition, I suppose, except by escaping poetry, which many poets manage to do, of course, even as they continue to publish at a steady pace. But for young poets for whom words won't quite be the world, who feel themselves slipping into the relentless instants that follow even their most inspired achievements, whose grief is less the grief of life than grief for the fact that art is not finally the highest end of life – the painful desire for silence that is at the heart of articulation can be particularly acute, either because it is not understood and therefore, like an amnesia or repression, disabling in essential ways, or perhaps worse, because it is understood all too well:

> I think the loathed minutes one by one
> That tear and then go past are little worth
> Save nearer to the blindness to the sun
> They bring me, and the farewell to all earth
>
> Save to that six-foot-length I must lie in
> Sodden with mud, and not to grieve again
> Because high Autumn goes beyond my pen
> And snow lies inexprest in the deep lane.

That "again" in the second stanza of this short poem, "Moments," by Ivor Gurney is a poignant reference to all of the poems that the poet has written before, as well as a lament for the imminent failure – "inexprest" – of this one. Gurney wrote the poem when he was in his early thirties, fighting off the insanity that eventually overcame him. It has none of the equanimity and promise of Heaney's lines from "North," nor does it have that poem's confidence in the mind's ability to find repose in a passionate attention to the details of immediate experience ("Keep your eye clear / as the bleb of the icicle, / trust the feel of what nubbed treasure / your hands have known"). For Gurney it's precisely the inability of language to articulate and arrest experience, to fix him forever in an instant, that is the source of his anguish. Or at least it's the source to which he has access, for one doesn't need biographical information to sense that the anguish underlying this poem is less about the elusiveness of "high Autumn" than the untraceable pain that needs to simplify deliverance into a linguistic possibility, less about the world of leaves and snow than the lonely enclosure from which that world is observed, the word-windowed center of a dead silence in which the poet found himself suspended.

It will be evident that I am speaking here of a certain kind of poet, one for whom the experience of consciousness – the consciousness of experience – is so threatening that, for a time at least, it is borne only by a kind of formal armor. It is borne, though, not evaded, otherwise the poetry will be mechanical and what is known as "academic." Very good poetry may be written by a poet writing out of the diving bell, but there are definite limits to such poetry, and I don't think it can be sustained. "Silence augmenteth grief, writing increaseth rage," Fulke Greville wrote in his elegy to Sidney, a line that could aptly be applied to those young poets for whom silence is unbearable and their own increasingly "finished" achievements increasingly inadequate. Then there is Sidney himself:

> But harder judges judge ambition's rage,
> Scourge of itself, still climbing slippery place,
> Holds my young brain captiv'd in golden cage.

Poets who don't manage to find a way out of their own formal defensiveness, their own uninvolved inventiveness and immaculate talent, will eventually end up in captivity, stalled there in the tiny unwatery world of the diving bell, perhaps panicking, perhaps mistaking the waning of inspiration for the coming on of a severer discipline, but in any event running steadily out of air.

What seems clear, then, is that if poets beyond the first flush of their own formal successes, which as I have noted will inevitably also be failures, mean to continue to write real poems, they must move beyond a poetry written solely because they "feel themselves wrong." The passage I quoted earlier from Ruskin continues:

And yet, in still deeper sense it is the work of people who also know that they are right. The very sense of inevitable error from their purpose marks the perfectness of that purpose, and the continued sense of failure arises from the continued opening of the eyes more clearly to all the sacredest laws of truth.

This is the context in which to read Heaney's lines from "North," in which the "aurora borealis" is roughly analogous to Ruskin's sacred laws. Both are as yet unrealized, but they are not merely illusory expectations; the promised revelation is implicit in the work at hand. Which is to say: the craft that is adequate to one's own deepening experience will be somehow poised between the injury or absence out of which it emerges and the restorative truth toward which it aspires.

But if the diving bell is dangerous to one's life, surviving the diving bell is often the end of one's art. Most formally imaginative poets, if they live long enough, eventually relax into what W.S. Di Piero has termed "efficient mastery," a habit of writing that lacks the risk and range of real craft as well as the focusing danger of the diving bell. Frost, who felt more acutely than most the confusion that a felt form stays, became in much of his late poetry an efficient master. Others come readily to mind: late Wordsworth, Tennyson, Robinson, acre after acre of Browning being wise. Di Piero contrasts this efficient mastery with a "passion for form," which I understand to be a continual engagement with the refractory actual, a refusal to force varied experience into *any* of the preexisting forms of the imagination. It's this passion that must be both sustained and changed within the fully developed craft. To attend to a passion for form when one is young, to make of one's pains a few poems that are, as Louise Bogan said that minor poetry should be, "hard and durable," is a significant accomplishment. To sustain this passion into the changes of middle age and beyond, refusing to relax into mastery, is a much rarer, greater thing.

And indeed Heaney's career is nearly exemplary. If the work since *Seeing Things* has begun to tilt a bit too heavily toward Truth, begun to seem the work of a poet who no longer feels himself at all wrong,*

---

*I would draw an exception for *District and Circle* (2005), which seems to me a return to form for Heaney, and splendid.

many of the poems from the four books immediately preceding that one are perfectly poised between the sense of wrongness out of which they emerged and the half-glimpsed wholeness and rightness they in their formal accomplishment afford. That is to say, there are poems from these four volumes – *North, Field Work, Station Island, The Haw Lantern* – that seem to me about as good as lyric poetry gets. Gone, mostly, is the need to announce their own legitimacy, the long arm of self-consciousness keeping the world at a long arm's length. Gone, too, is some of the sheer strut and verbal flourish which mar some of Heaney's early poems (including some of the poems from *North*), the sense that talent was occasionally on parade rather than in harness. Here is "The Harvest Bow" from *Field Work:*

As you plaited the harvest bow
You implicated the mellowed silence in you
In wheat that does not rust
But brightens as it tightens twist by twist
Into a knowable corona,
A throwaway love-knot of straw.

Hands that aged round ashplants and cane sticks
And lapped the spurs on a lifetime of game cocks
Harked to their gift and worked with fine intent
Until your fingers moved somnambulant:
I tell and finger it like braille,
Gleaning the unsaid off the palpable.

And if I spy into its golden loops
I see us walk between the railway slopes
Into an evening of long grass and midges,
Blue smoke straight up, old beds and ploughs in hedges,
An auction notice on an outhouse wall –
You with a harvest bow in your lapel,

Me with the fishing rod, already homesick
For the big lift of these evenings, as your stick
Whacking the tips off weeds and bushes
Beats out of time, and beats, but flushes
Nothing: that original townland
Still tongue-tied in the straw tied by your hand.

The end of art is peace
Could be the motto of this frail device

That I have pinned up on our deal dresser –
Like a drawn snare
Snipped lately by the spirit of the corn
Yet burnished by its passage, and still warm.

The poem has an equable, utterly accomplished feel to it, a pleasing sense of formal fulfillment and completed experience. With that last line one hears Yeats's box clicking shut, his sign that a poem had wholly realized its final form. I think it would be a mistake, however, to believe that the poem has reached the peace it posits as the end of art. The "original townland" is still "tongue-tied" in the harvest bow, what was lost is still lost, whatever the child in the poem needed said is still unsaid. But whereas for Gurney this rift between word and world, between fleeting experience and the forms with which the mind seeks to apprehend it, could only be painful and frustrating, a helplessly and hopelessly temporal existence the only ease for which was death – Heaney makes this distance and absence into the animating energy of his poem. Indeed, as the first line of that last stanza implies, it could not be otherwise, for if the end or aim of art is peace, an art that reaches its aim ends or dies. If art originates in an attempt to heal or right a sense of wrongness, then an achieved peace renders art unnecessary and irrelevant, a splendid ornament.

This "failure" of Heaney's poem is not only thematic but formal. Consider, for example, what a very different poem "The Harvest Bow" would be if its rhymes were not so oblique: *bow/you, rust/ twist, corona/straw,* etc. It is as if we are given an intimation of an utter formal fulfillment which the poem can't provide and we can never know, a certain peace but not the peace that passeth understanding. The poem seems to me a great one not only because of the rich memory-life it recovers as living language but also because of its unaverted acknowledgment of the physical *goneness* of that life, the forbidding distance implicit in its revelations, its refusal to falsify experience by mastering it. The form of the poem, like the harvest bow itself – both culminations of a lifetime's craft – is a sort of "drawn snare," still warm from its encounter with the living memory it has failed to change or save.

Save. The word recalls others that have arisen unintentionally but, I am beginning to believe, inevitably in this essay: *conviction, conversion, absolution, deliverance.* The religious tenor of the list reveals little more than my own inclination and upbringing, I think, but the sense they give of a life outside of art, the sense that art is *for the sake of* something besides either itself or the self, is perhaps less limited in its application. If self-preservation is the motive force behind the work of many young poets, perhaps developing beyond this involves an effort to preserve something besides the self, giving oneself over to something outside of oneself, whether it's Lowell making his "fire-breathing manic statement" against the war, Milton pamphleteering himself to the brink of the gallows in the years before seclusion and *Paradise Lost,* or some much more local love like Keats (*solid* Keats) tending to his dying brother. Such a commitment may not enter the verse as subject matter at all, or may enter it only obliquely ("Where youth grows pale, and spectre-thin, and dies"), just as specific sufferings may have little to do with what drives one to write poems in the first place. I am struck by the fact that in the last lines of his last play Shakespeare has Prospero – the consummate artist, for so long islanded by his art – say that any possible relief now lies beyond the reach of his art:

> Now my charms are all o'erthrown,
> And what strength I have's mine own;
> Which is most faint; now, 'tis true,
> I must be here confin'd by you,
> Or sent to Naples. Let me not,
> Since I have my dukedom got
> And pardon'd the deceiver, dwell
> In this bare island by your spell;
> But release me from my bands
> With the help of your good hands.
> Gentle breath of yours my sails
> Must fill, or else my project fails,
> Which was to please. Now I want
> Spirits to enforce, art to enchant;
> And my ending is despair,
> Unless I be reliev'd by prayer,
> Which pierces so that it assaults
> Mercy itself and frees all faults.

> As you from crimes would pardon'd be,
> Let your indulgence set me free.

How different this is from the utter interiority, balked feeling, and self-destructiveness of Hamlet. Contrary to the contemporary cliché that makes the act of writing poetry indistinguishable from the act of praying, prayer in this epilogue is relegated to a higher, or at least later, status than art. It isn't unrelated to art, by any means, for it is only through his art that Prospero has reached this point, but prayer is on the other side of art, so to speak, an ultimate articulation toward which poetry is always tending. And unlike the speaker in Donne's poem, Prospero's "project" fails if it does not please, if it is not adequate and true to the needs and experience of a world outside the self. To attain Ruskin's latter understanding of art as a sense of rightness and wholeness, or to share Heaney's hopefulness in the revelatory possibilities of an eye-to-the-ground attention to one's work, requires an acknowledgment that the world is the reality within which the work occurs and has its meaning, not some alien place within which its formal purity is contaminated.

But lord knows such a commitment won't always ensure better poetry. Poets may manage to attain either a good-sensed and giving existence or a rabid activism (they aren't necessarily mutually exclusive), may eat their oat bran every morning or shout loudest on the picket lines, only to find that it was in that consuming, solitary, self-destructive search for perfection that their words had force. It's a hard fate, but it is one. Berryman, "staring down the intolerable years / to the mild survival," feared it was his, and he whipped his life into a frenzy his late lines could do little more than helplessly mimic. Lowell feared it too:

> Sing softer! But what if a new
> diminuendo brings no true
> tenderness, only restlessness,
> excess, the hunger for success,
> sanity of self-deception
> fixed and kicked by reckless caution...

But up through *Near the Ocean,* from which this passage is taken, Lowell managed to keep his formal imagination responsive to his own volcanic energy, keeping his lines lean and seething even as he made them accommodate some of the bulk and brute usualness of all the time one has to get through between poems. Eventually, though, the time between poems became the poems for Lowell, and his passion for form fizzled into fourteen-liners, the steady, predictable kicks of someone in deep water keeping himself afloat. Such a falling off happens to most poets, of course. If they live past the point at which they realize that no perfect work is going to save them, they rot into the respectability of late Wordsworth, the prolific efficiency of Tennyson or Robinson, the counterfeit "immediacy" of Lowell or Berryman. Rare is the poet like Bishop, who sustained the high quality of her verse throughout her life, or Yeats, who remade himself in old age. Even rarer, perhaps, are the ones who, realizing that real poetry is over for them, refuse to stave off the silence with any idle sound they can manage. So it is worth remembering and respecting a poet like Yvor Winters, who, when asked late in his life by Donald Hall when he was going to write more poems, replied – painfully, accusingly – when he had something more to say.

Heaney's lines from "North" have to do with survival, with reconciling the singularity of ambition with endlessly recurring days and diffuse experience. Because what seems evident is that if poets find themselves writing because they "feel themselves wrong," and find that only through the achievement of form can they hold off (but never quite take hold of) what threatens them, then eventually they are going to run out of will and resources. "Unlike writing, life never finishes," Lowell wrote as a grand old public poet of unsinkable reputation and shipwrecked standards. Only it does finish, of course, in a final silence which all one's poems, all those high-finished boxes clicking like coffins shut, both impeded and implied. The difficulties of form, which if clung to beyond a certain point turn what was defense and refuge into an inescapable cage, must become the difficulties of life itself, one's craft adapted to and altered within what Keats called "the van of circumstance," one's passion for poetry transformed – but not attenuated, never relaxed – into a passion for life.

Because at some point the diving bell metaphor is not just inadequate to one's experience but positively dangerous. At some point the pressure builds, the right words won't come, and all the unsung life begins to leak into the tightest lines. Then the poet feels what Hart Crane must have felt long before he finally leapt into an actual ocean, after his four years of fighting with *The Bridge* and feeling the air of inspiration running out on him – the water taking him in.

1995

An Idea of Order

An anecdote, first of all. A few years ago I had an argument in a series of letters with a friend. The argument was instigated by a poem I had sent her, which she thought was emotionally compelling but formally anachronistic. She meant her response to be strong praise with a slight caveat. I understood it as slight praise with a monumental objection. Our subsequent exchange centered on the meaning of form in a poem, and whether or not a poem whose form felt, as she put it, as if it could have been written eighty years ago could have any primary relevance for its own time. I argued that it could not. Even factoring in my obstinacy and fragile ego, I still believe I was right; not with regard to my own poem, perhaps, to which I was as blindly attached as most poets are to things they have just made, but rather in the general argument that ensued. I still feel that the form of a poem, no matter how "traditional," must make its claim as a living thing, its expressive capacity somehow adequate to contemporary experience. To say that a poem is formally anachronistic is, for me, to say that it's not much more than a curiosity.

I don't think my friend's beliefs are at all anomalous. Many poets and critics now almost automatically distrust any work that exhibits formal coherence, stylistic finish, and closure. Occasionally they simply dismiss such work as naive or reactionary. At other times, and probably more damagingly, they either subtly devalue or patronize the work in question, praising the craftsmanship of the poems in such terms as make it clear that this is not "important" poetry. The hardcore version of this argument goes something like this: because our experience of the world is chaotic and fragmented, and because we've lost our faith not only in those abstractions by means of which men and women of the past ordered their lives but also in language itself, it would be naive to think that we could have such order in our art. A poet who persists in imposing order upon our uncertainty is either unconscious, ironic, or irrelevant. Even among many readers and writers who wouldn't altogether accept the premises of this argument, and who are often completely open to traditional forms, there is still a widespread tendency to distrust any form that seems too intact, to assume that it somehow distorts or evades the mental climate we inhabit. The range of such work is limited from the outset, the argument goes. It can't speak to us with the immediacy or intensity of an art whose refusal of finish and closure more obviously accords with our experience of contemporary life.

There are a couple of different assumptions underlying such a conclusion. The first is that in order to be truly important the form of a work of art must somehow express something of the times in which it is created. With this I agree. It's why my response to my friend was so vehement. The second assumption, though, is that the form of a work of art expresses reality by imitating it. Our experience is fragmented and partial, therefore the forms with which we apprehend that experience must be similarly fragmented and partial. Yvor Winters termed this the "fallacy of imitative form," but Winters's alternative was genuinely reactionary. He thought of a good poem as one in which uncertainty had been forcibly eradicated.

What I am interested in, and what I want to focus on here, is a kind of closure that compromises itself, a poetry whose order is contested, even undermined, by its consciousness of the disorder that it at once repels and recognizes. I believe there is no necessary contradiction between some of the ambitions and anxieties informing the work of a poet such as John Ashbery – "The forms retain a strong measure of ideal beauty / As they forage in secret on our idea of distortion" – and the best work of some poets who work in what are called "closed forms" and whose poems exhibit no conspicuous stylistic opacity. I would even go one step further: I believe that it's sometimes precisely in those works that exhibit the greatest degree of formal coherence, the greatest sense of closure, that a reader may experience, and thereby more likely endure, the most intense anxiety and uncertainty.

Because most of our ideas about formal instability and fragmenta-
tion derive from the Modernists, probably the best place to begin is
with a reluctant one like Frost. Frost was in much of his work simply
a dull period poet, sighing into formal and intellectual conventions as
into warm bathwater. In his best work, though, he was as attuned to
his own time as Pound or Eliot. There is a shift of cultural conscious-
ness between two superficially similar poems such as Thomas
Hardy's "The Darkling Thrush" and Frost's "The Most of It." It isn't
that the former presents the natural world as a source of possible con-
solation for the speaker, attributing some "blessèd Hope" to the
bird's song at the end of the poem, whereas the latter is more obvi-
ously ambivalent about this. Both poems seem to me at their cores
equally skeptical. The difference has more to do with the arrange-
ment of the world with regard to the respective speakers. In "The
Darkling Thrush," the entire natural world is made into a metaphor
for human life:

> The land's sharp features seemed to be
>   The Century's corpse outleant,
> His crypt the cloudy canopy,
>   The wind his death-lament.
> The ancient pulse of germ and birth
>   Was shrunken hard and dry,
> And every spirit upon earth
>   Seemed fervourless as I.

Much of Frost's work arises out of the same assumptions and em-
ploys the same technique, of course, but not "The Most of It." Hardy
has fallen away from those poets who saw in the world the workings of
God, but he can still see in the world the workings of his own mind, is
still comfortable with a metaphor that links the two. Frost is fallen
somewhat farther. He can't quite see the world in relation to himself,
can't avoid his suspicion that the world and the terms with which he
apprehends it have nothing to do with each other. In "The Most of
It," the edge of uncertainty is the edge of the mind:

> He thought he kept the universe alone;
> For all the voice in answer he could wake
> Was but the mocking echo of his own

From some tree-hidden cliff across the lake.
Some morning from the boulder-broken beach
He would cry out on life, that what it wants
Is not its own love back in copy speech,
But counter-love, original response.
And nothing ever came of what he cried
Unless it was the embodiment that crashed
In the cliff's talus on the other side,
And then in the far-distant water splashed,
But after a time allowed for it to swim,
Instead of proving human when it neared
And someone else additional to him,
As a great buck it powerfully appeared,
Pushing the crumpled water up ahead,
And landed pouring like a waterfall,
And stumbled through the rocks with horny tread,
And forced the underbrush – and that was all.

Something has been severed here, some sense of connectedness with the world and life, of the universe as a place that can be described or understood or – as with Hardy – at least suffered in human terms. The feeling isn't by any means forgotten, but it exists as a limb exists for a man who no longer has it, some phantom tingling telling him what is gone. There's something subtler than a simple disjunction between form and subject matter going on in this poem. That is one way to enliven traditional forms, sometimes a very powerful one, as Thom Gunn's *The Man with Night Sweats* attests. I also mean to distinguish the effect of Frost's poem from the poetry of such deliberately clenched and defensive poets such as Winters or J.V. Cunningham. Both of these poets were acutely conscious of the chaos outside of the mind, but this anxiety expresses itself in their forms only as an exclusion. Some poets survive as turtles survive, by pulling their extremities in.

Frost was more ambitious, and consequently more vulnerable. Look at Frost's poem one way and it seems to be saying that the world did respond to the self, if in an ambiguous form. Within that word *unless* is a whole world of hope and possibility. Change the angle slightly, though, and the poem is saying exactly the opposite. Nothing ever came of what he cried but this buck, which, in human terms, is nothing. The concluding phrase contains a similar sort of apparently mutually exclusive meanings; it can be read as a brusque dismissal or as a kind of transcendental claim: that was *all.* The poem is at once an assertion of connection with the world and a recognition of existential isolation. It straddles these two possibilities, and it does so *formally.* The rhymes reiterate the voice that is the mocking echo of the poet's own. Each seems to answer a cry that comes before it, but it does so with such unvarying regularity that it suggests itself as *merely* an echo. The effect would be quite different if even one of the rhymes was off. Stylistic roughness or overt formal distortion would have the paradoxical effect of *diminishing* the uncertainty and anxiety in this poem. It would seem as if life had definitively answered. In a very real sense, the tension between the closure of "The Most of It" and the uneasy feeling which that closure creates is an example of, to use a word that is often used to justify merely incoherent art, dissonance.

"The Most of It" is one of Frost's momentary stays against confusion. It aims in art at a calm and coherence that its writer lacked in life, and it's interesting to consider the poem in light of an essay that Auden once wrote on Tennyson. In the essay Auden criticizes poets who attempt to use poetry to fulfill needs that can only be properly fulfilled outside of poetry – through direct action, religious belief, personal relationships, or some other area of "life." The point is well-taken. Poets who confuse art and life often make a mess of both. But there are dangers as well for poets who accept too readily Auden's clean distinction between art and life. They may become esoteric. They may become emotionally and technically glib. They may become late Auden.

Most artists make art precisely because they feel some sort of absence or incoherence in their lives. It seems not simply inevitable but necessary that the art they produce in some way seek to contain or heal whatever is missing or wounded or wrongful in them. For those poets whose confusion in life inclines them to closure in art, the key to avoiding Auden's criticism and example lies, I think, in the kind of self-contested quality that I find in "The Most of It." This is obvious enough when the surface of the poem is disrupted, so that there is a pronounced disjunction between the sense of closure and the effort it took to get there, or between the finish of art and the roughness of life: early Lowell, Bunting, Hart Crane, Hopkins. It is less easily perceived when the surface of the poem is completely clear. "The Most of It," for a moment at least, seems to be the order in which it can't quite believe. Its closed world of metrical regularity, of rhymes that confuse answers and echoes, is a kind of refuge from the flux and profusion of a world for which it can't keep itself from reaching. Both its aspiration and its doubt are part of its form, as are its effects of seeming at once compensatory and comfortless.

Among those poets inclined to closure and finish, perhaps this distinction may be drawn. There are those who seek to replace whatever they have lost in their lives, and there are those who seek in their art a form within which their loss may be felt. The former will be either a clenched, occasional poet like Winters and Cunningham, or the sort of poet of whom it is said, "He lives for his art." He may be great, as Rilke was great, but there will be about the work a palpable sense of separation and enclosure, something of what the art critic Edgar Wind called "an emotionally untainted sense of form." The latter kind of poets – and the poets I'm talking about in this essay are the latter kind – will usually have some sort of deep ambivalence about the value and efficacy of poetry itself, and this ambivalence *will make itself felt formally*. They are also enclosed in a kind of cell, but from beyond the wall on which they practice their half-learned language of taps and scratches there sometimes comes something like an answer, something that, in their better moments, they can almost believe is an "original response." The wall is poetry. Life is on the other side. The wall is what separates the poet from life, but it is also the means by which life is apprehended and understood.

The figure is Simone Weil's. The tenor of her metaphor is grander – "It is the same with us and God. Every separation is a link." – but the idea of isolation and communication as coextensive is the same. Weil found a language for a kind of belief that had outlived or otherwise lost its object, and in my attempts to explain to myself why I experience a certain kind of closure and formal coherence in poetry as both fulfillment and deprivation, presence and absence, she is one of two or three prose writers who have been very important to me. Another is Proust, whose *In Search of Lost Time* is a monumental effort at formalizing loss, at making a place in language wherein the past can *be* lost instead of simply forgotten and unfelt. My deepest sense of this book, though much of it is comical and ironic, is of abiding sadness. Its source is less in the specific characters and events themselves than in Proust's constant consciousness of his own failure, his inability to fully recreate and retain whatever it was that made his losses "life": "But to release that fount of sorrow," he writes in *Within a Budding Grove,* "that sense of the irreparable, those agonies which prepare the way for love, there must be – and this is, perhaps, more than a person, the actual object which our passion seeks so anxiously to embrace – the risk of an impossibility."

I'm trying to describe a similar effect in form, one arising from a belief or need that has outlived or lost its object, a formal coherence whose reach exceeds its grasp:

> The garden of the world, which no one sees,
> Never had walls, is fugitive with lives;
> Its shapes escape our simplest symmetries;
> There is no resting where it rots and thrives.

That's the last stanza of Richard Wilbur's "Caserta Garden," a poem that, in this last stanza at any rate, expresses more compellingly the inadequacy of language, indeed of all human ordering, than anything that I have read by the Language poets. The poem is itself one of the "simplest symmetries" that the world escapes. It wants to be the rest or "stay" which it admits does not exist beyond its own borders, but by such an admission it makes those borders at least partially permeable. Its strength inheres in the balance it maintains between a consciousness of its limitations and the assertion of formal order it makes in the face of them. Like "The Most of It," "Caserta Garden" has the poignancy of impossibility about it.

One might compare these two poems, and particularly "The Most of It," with a contemporary poem that has a similar theme but more relaxed form. I take A.R. Ammons's poem "Gravelly Run," in which Ammons seeks to know the self "as it is known / by galaxy and cedar cone," to be in a direct line that runs from Hardy and Frost. Ammons's poem, though, ends much less ambiguously than "The Most of It":

no use to make any philosophies here:
    I see no
god in the holly, hear no song from
the snowbroken weeds: Hegel is not the winter
yellow in the pines: the sunlight has never
heard of trees: surrendered self among
    unwelcoming forms: stranger,
hoist your burdens, get on down the road.

"Gravelly Run" is a poem that is certain about the mind's inability to be certain of anything beyond its own borders. It gestures toward the order from which Frost's poem has fallen away, but the nerves are now even more numb, both the expectations and anxieties diminished. This difference expresses itself formally. Although Ammons's poem is clearly "formal" in its way, cohesive in its sounds and shape, it does not have the kind of symmetrical urgency of "The Most of It" or "Caserta Garden." There is no sense of impossibility about it, of some abstract order articulating itself with a kind of beautiful futility in spite of what the poet knows, or doesn't know. I don't mean for this distinction to be necessarily a qualitative one; "Gravelly Run" is a splendid poem. The point I want to make is that there are effects available to traditionally formal poems that aren't available to other forms, and that one of these effects has to do with an *intensification* of the uncertainty and even open-endedness that we normally associate with looser forms. "To crave and to have are as like as a thing and its shadow," Marilynne Robinson has written; "and when do our senses know any thing so utterly as when we lack it?" Both "The Most of It" and "Caserta Garden" shadow an order that they suggest does not exist. Their forms make us feel physically this lack, at once easing and intensifying our perception of the disorder that is the reason for this lack. The disorder of "Gravelly Run," by contrast, is an idea.

    The poems that I have discussed so far are not really "contemporary." "The Most of It" was first published in 1946, "Caserta Garden" in 1947. Ammons's poem is more recent, and it raises the question of whether faith in the mind's ability to find meaning in the world hasn't eroded to such an extent that the comparison is unfair or irrelevant. I want to look now at a couple of contemporary sonnets which I believe accomplish effects similar to those of the Frost and Wilbur

poems, while being very much of their own times. I want to reiterate
that the effect I am describing has to do with getting something of
contemporary *consciousness* into the form, which may have nothing
to do with the details of contemporary life – quatrains crammed
with brand names, colloquialisms, and such. I'm after something
more subtle, powerful, and, I think, more lasting.

Here is Marilyn Nelson's "Balance":

> *He watch her like a coonhound watch a tree.*
> What might explain the metamorphosis
> he underwent when she paraded by
> with tea-cakes, in her fresh and shabby dress?
> (As one would carry water from a well –
> straight-backed, high-headed, like a diadem,
> with careful grace so that no drop will spill –
> she balanced, almost brimming, her one name.)
>
> *She think she something, stuck-up island bitch.*
> Chopping wood, hanging laundry on the line,
> and tantalizingly within his reach,
> she honed his body's yearning to a keen,
> sharp point. And on that point she balanced life.
> *That hoe Diverne think she Marse Tyler's wife.*

This poem draws a thematic line – between aesthetic beauty as a
source of power and beauty as power's object – which it walks in form.
The sensuous descriptions of Diverne elicit our admiration for her
even as they "hone" our sense of the historical context in which they
occur. This is no ordinary courtship. Marse Tyler can rape Diverne if
he chooses. The form of the poem elicits a similar sort of troubled ad-
miration. I have said that "The Most of It" and "Caserta Garden"
draw their strength from their consciousness of their own limitations
as forms. Although "Balance" isn't as directly self-referential as ei-
ther of those poems, I think its techniques – the italicized speech of
the other slaves rendered in perfect iambic pentameter, those lines
juxtaposed with the language of the educated poet ("metamorpho-
sis," "diadem") – make it impossible to ignore the context in which it
was written: a contemporary African American woman employing a
form that is the product of a culture that has traditionally excluded

and exploited African Americans. (The form itself has no inherent political meaning, but that doesn't mean that a poet's treatment of the form can't give it a political meaning. And when a poet inhabits a form as uneasily as Nelson does in "Balance," calling deliberate attention to this uneasiness, I don't see how this dimension of the poem can be avoided.) It's simplistic to say that Nelson is "subverting" the form, as it is to say that she is submitting to it. The poem contains both possibilities. The stakes aren't as immediately high for Nelson as they are for Diverne (though anyone who has found that her confusion in life finds both expression and alleviation in form knows that the stakes are indeed high), but the line between power and powerlessness, control and chaos, is being walked by both of them. I take the slant rhymes of the first twelve lines to be a kind of conscious wobbling. The final full rhyme – coming after the explicit, coarse sexual reference in the last line and the revelation that this is a white man watching a slave (without the "Marse Tyler," this would be unclear) – is a very qualified sort of control. The form is both finished and painfully insufficient, locked but volatile.

"Balance," then, is a good example of what I mean by a kind of closure that compromises itself. There is a discrepancy between the finality with which the poem concludes and the possibility of disorder which it contains. The disorder that threatens the formal order of "Balance" is more cultural and political than epistemological (though it is inevitably this as well), but the discrepancy between the two is roughly analogous to the distance between the echoes and original response of "The Most of It," or between the formal self-containment of "Caserta Garden" and the formless world that is its subject. I have come to think of this discrepancy as a kind of space within the form itself, a core of air that isn't order and isn't disorder, some absolute emptiness that the form can neither eradicate nor fill. Engineers know that some structures are sturdier if some give is built into them, that sometimes a frame that's hollow rather than solid will bear a greater strain. Perhaps a similar principle applies to the forms of some poems.

In the last sonnet of Seamus Heaney's elegiac sequence to his mother, "Clearances," (and, in a more unequivocally positive sense, in his essay on Larkin) something like this space becomes the poem's subject:

> I thought of walking round and round a space
> Utterly empty, utterly a source
> Where the decked chestnut tree had lost its place
> In our front hedge above the wallflowers.
> The white chips jumped and jumped and skited high.
> I heard the hatchet's differentiated
> Accurate cut, the crack, the sigh
> And collapse of what luxuriated
> Through the shocked tips and wreckage of it all.
> Deep planted and long gone, my coeval
> Chestnut from a jam jar in a hole,
> Its heft and hush become a bright nowhere,
> A soul ramifying and forever
> Silent, beyond silence listened for.

Christopher Middleton has written that most poetry, even great poetry, tends to perpetuate clichés, and we might reduce the cliché behind this poem to something like this: "She's gone but will live forever in my heart." There's something more complicated going on in the poem, I think, something having to do with the form and its relation to that final line. To listen for a silence requires contrast. A silence that is "listened for," then, is everything outside of sound. It is what surrounds the words we use, the poems we write. A silence that is "beyond silence listened for," it follows, must be a silence that is imperceptible. It is either the complete absence of sound, or it is some stillness inside of sound itself, some final silence haunting all our words, all our poems, something not dissimilar from the silence that Wittgenstein was referring to (or trying to refer to) when he said, "Whereof one cannot speak, thereof one must be silent." Heaney's poem tries to speak of this annihilating silence, tries to make it *mean.* That in some ultimate sense he fails is part of that meaning.

To understand what the form of Heaney's poem has to do with this meaning, a comparison with another contemporary poem might help. In Robert Hass's well-known "Meditation at Lagunitas," the speaker addresses the problem of language's referentiality and "truth" directly, wondering if, since the word *blackberry* has no definitive denotative capacity, "a word is elegy to what it signifies." Recognizing the corrosive effect of this premise upon language and, if one believes that language is the only means by which we secure our experience, upon life, the speaker eventually offers up with equal parts helplessness and tenderness the details of a remembered relationship:

> Longing, we say, because desire is full
> of endless distances. I must have been the same to her.
> But I remember so much, the way her hands dismantled bread,
> the thing her father said that hurt her, what
> she dreamed. There are moments when the body is as numinous
> as words, days that are the good flesh continuing.
> Such tenderness, those afternoons and evenings,
> saying *blackberry, blackberry, blackberry.*

Like Heaney's sonnet, and like the other poems I've mentioned, "Meditation at Lagunitas" is conscious of its own inherent limitations as a piece of language yet persists in trying to make meaning in the face of them. Unlike those other poems, though, which counter their consciousness of disorder with an urge toward some ideal order in their forms, the tension between order and disorder in Hass's poem is merely a matter of competing assertions. It's like Ammons's poem in this respect, except that Ammons recognizes the world's unknowability and says in effect: "Get over it." Hass, like Heaney, can't quite get over it, but he has nothing to counter his doubt but the fact of his own deep feeling, nothing to offer up against the inadequacy of language but a piece of pretty writing. There is consequently a softness at the center of the poem. Heaney's poem contains the same sort of competing literal assertions ("Utterly empty, utterly a source"), but there is an austerity about it, some deeper meaning, and deeper emptiness, in its form. Though it is more rough-hewn than the other poems that I have looked at, it nevertheless aims at the abstract order of a sonnet, making itself into a space analogous to the one that is the poem's subject. The poem admits that there is nothing to hold, and holds it. "Grace fills empty spaces," writes Simone Weil, "but it can only enter where there is a void to receive it."

Whatever one thinks about the religious implications of that sentence, there is a kind of faith that a poet had better not lose. It is a faith in the mind's ability to find meaning in a world that exists independently of itself, and a concomitant faith in language to serve as a means of doing so. In the absence of this, poetry can only be at best a diversion within life; at worst it is a complete evasion of it. Yet even for those poets who manage to retain such faith, who in their better moments believe in the value of poetry and in its capacity to formalize some fragment of living reality, the prospect of spending a life trying to articulate sweet sounds together ought to be fraught with doubt and uncertainty, some unshakable sense that, in the face of real suffering and chaos, poetry may be irrelevant. It is this tension that keeps talent alive.

It is also this tension that keeps forms alive. The least satisfying forms are those that are the most satisfied with themselves. Edward O. Wilson has written that there are always two kinds of original thinkers, "those who upon viewing disorder try to create order, and those who upon encountering order try to create disorder." Those who merely imitate the order they see around them are ornamentalists. There are pleasures to be had from such work, but they are the pleasures of amenities. At the same time, formal distortion is interesting and meaningful only when it occurs in a poet for whom formal coherence seems a real possibility. (This is what distinguishes Ashbery from his imitators. It is also what distinguishes Ashbery from Ashbery.) It requires no great talent to imitate chaos, or to illustrate the inability of the mind and language to make meaning. Those who do so, as Wallace Stevens suggested, are simply exacerbating our confusion:

> This structure of ideas, these ghostly sequences
> Of the mind, result only in disaster. It follows,
> Casual poet, that to add your own disorder to disaster
>
> Makes more of it.

I have not intended this to be an argument in favor of a "return to traditional forms." Much of the self-satisfied metrical poetry I read makes me nostalgic for Dada. I have focused on these forms for the sake of clarity and economy, and because they seem to provoke the strongest animus. I do feel that, whether one writes in traditional forms or free verse, it's probably time to get beyond this automatic resistance to finish and closure in poetry, that the idea of form as somehow more authentic if rough and unfinished has itself become something of a convention. If one's experience of life is truly confusing and chaotic, and if one's feeling for the inadequacy of language is something more than an academic idea, perhaps the proper response is either silence or coherence. Not the kind of coherence that eliminates uncertainty, not the kind of closure that congratulates itself, but something sharper, some only momentary peace which, because it comes with a consciousness of its loss, is also pain.

My friend thought that to write in traditional forms was to cleave to a vanished past, to insulate oneself and one's work against one's own time. I have tried to make a case for them as bearers of contemporary consciousness, though I do admit that one can't use these forms without referring to the past. So long as it isn't merely a sentimental attachment to the antique, I think of this reference as a strength. I also think that there is a sense in which to work toward some ideal order is to claim a connectedness with the future as well as the past, that a poem may foreshadow formally a time in which one's world and mind will – and I'm paraphrasing Marilynne Robinson here – be made whole. To reach for is not to grasp. Simone Weil writes that "we must believe in a God who is like the true God in everything, except that He does not exist, since we have not reached the point where God exists." I think perhaps the poems that I've been talking about in this essay were written by poets who believed utterly in an absolute formal coherence that – and this was *part* of their belief – did not exist. To experience such forms is to experience both consolation and provocation. It is to come into a place of language that is easeful and unchanging and will not let you forget the fact that it is not a place. It is to be given an image of life that you have lost or long dreamed of, to hear as sound something of the farthest sorrows that you are, and to know in that moment that what you've been given is not enough.

1998

Fourteen Fragments in Lieu of a Review*

There isn't much literature there couldn't well be less of. A four-hundred-page anthology of sonnets? It takes a real aberration of will to read straight through such a thing. Another man might win an egg-eating contest, with similar feelings, I would imagine, of mild shock, equivocal accomplishment, obliterated taste.

▼ ▲ ▼

What is a sonnet? Careful, because if this anthology is a reliable guide, your definition needs to include some poems that have neither meter nor rhyme and aren't fourteen lines long. The editor, Phillis Levin, states that her own working definition was that a poem "act like a sonnet," which must have meant that it lay quietly on the page when notified of its inclusion, because there are some contemporary poems here that have in common only ink and English. One would have to have retreated to a pretty narrow existence to work up much indignation over this, and I can certainly see why an editor would want to show how contemporary understandings – or misunderstandings – of the sonnet have evolved. I would say, though, that the sonnet isn't as flexible a form as this anthology suggests; relax its strictures too much, and its very particular formal effects are lost. A few of the contemporary American examples of the sonnet – by Billy Collins and Louise Glück, for example – are more interesting as commentaries on the tradition than as extensions of it; which is to say, not very interesting.

* *The Penguin Book of the Sonnet.* Edited by Phillis Levin. Penguin, 2001.

▼ ▲ ▼

The sonnet treats experience rather than enacting it. There are exceptions – the opening of *Astrophil and Stella,* much of Hopkins, Marilyn Nelson's "Balance," Gwendolyn Brooks's lovely "the rites for Cousin Vit." These poems attempt in their forms to contain or reiterate the reality they address. Usually, though, a sonnet combines emotional urgency with intellectual distance, or, perhaps more accurately, *manages* an emotional urgency *by means of* an intellectual distance. Most poets flock like moths to the flame of experience, and most of them melt there. Some given technique won't keep you from getting burned, but sometimes it's the only way of telling yourself – and others – what the flames felt like.

▼ ▲ ▼

A minor poet needs to fall deeply in love with his own limits. A major poet can't ever quite commit to them. What you feel in the work of Louise Bogan, J.V. Cunningham, Edna St. Vincent Millay are the edges of intelligence and talent being burnished, made definite and durable. What you feel in the work of Frost or Stevens is a mind surprising itself into regions it both invents and is. A minor poet who strays from the gift to which he's wed for life becomes gassy and diffuse, like Robert Penn Warren or James Dickey. A major poet who decides to settle in the suburbs of his gift becomes pinched and conventional, like late Frost or Wordsworth. In general, the sonnet is better suited to minor poetry. Except for Frost, almost all major poets who have worked extensively in the sonnet have done so in a series, which amounts to a different form.

▼ ▲ ▼

What an exacting art poetry is. There are fine novels that aren't very well-written (*Sister Carrie, The Idiot*), great novels in which nothing much happens (*In Search of Lost Time, Mrs. Dalloway*), books that survive their own sinkhole endings (*The Mill on the Floss, All the King's Men*). Poetry is less forgiving. If Iris Murdoch was too confidently categorical, had pulled her philosopher's hat a bit too tightly on her head, when she asserted that there was no such thing as a bad poem because bad poetry simply wasn't poetry, there's still an abstract kind of rightness to the remark. There's little margin for error in poetry, and in the sonnet there is virtually none. When you come across one that begins with "The world will burst like an intestine in the sun," it's like watching a diver bang his head on the board: you just hope he doesn't hurt himself further on the way down.

▼ ▲ ▼

The only antidote to contingency is an addiction to it. This is how I explain to myself my love for a poet like James Schuyler, who fulfills none of the formal expectations I have for poetry. He gave himself over not so much to the making of form as to a constant unmaking of it, as if a form could be constantly self-thwarting, defined by its own dissolution. The sonnet is the very antithesis of this. However chaotic its subject, however singular its technique (but remember: too singular and it's not a sonnet), it resists contingency. In a time marked by constant change, then, by lack of fixed beliefs and absolute loss, can the sonnet be anything other than pastiche or light verse? Of course it can, since form in art derives more of its energy from resisting reality than imitating it. (This has always been true: Ralegh and Jonson and Shakespeare might very well have believed in the order and balance of their world and their places in it, but they wrote poems because they couldn't *feel* these things.) This resistance is, or should be, stiff with the sonnet, but in the end such resistance is merely a matter of degree. Strictly speaking, there's no way to imitate contingency, no way to create a form in poetry (or any art) that doesn't resist it. Schuyler's fluid, apparently unfixable forms are, finally, an illusion, since they exist as definite, unchangeable shapes on the page. Something similar could be said of the opening sentence of this paragraph, which you can't wholly assent to without in some way draining of its meaning.

▼ ▲ ▼

Levin points out in her introduction that there seem to be virtually no notable sonnets from the Augustans, a fact which she attributes to their propensity for deductive rather than inductive logic: their poems are proofs of preexisting conclusions. It's an astute point, and angled in another way casts some light on the contemporary sonnet. "If you want to achieve something in business," Schopenhauer writes, "in writing, in painting, in anything, you must follow the rules without knowing them." The particular vice of the Augustans was that they always knew exactly which rules they were following: no technique could ever become instinctual. We, on the other hand, tend to resist the idea that there are rules, that technique must be internalized before it can be individualized. The result is surface distortions of a form rather than the groundswells of an original style.

▼ ▲ ▼

How many contemporary writers will tell you over dinner that God is dead and yet can't seem to keep his ghost out of their work. The sonnet has always been a form for devotional purposes, precisely because of its combination of strict rules and unknowingness: hottest and highest is the flame we dream. I've been struck, though, by how persistent the religious impulse is in the poems of this anthology, even if it's nothing more than the word *God* gauzing some unspeakable abyss. It could be an editorial rather than cultural symptom, I suppose, but I doubt it. Can Absence be a god, or have we made an idol of our emptiness? Will the future hear these songs as praise or blame? "I believe in my / Abandonment," Geoffrey Hill writes in one of the best poems in this entire book, "since it is what I have."

▼ ▲ ▼

Most poets since the Modernists claim not to aim at particular forms. Ecstasy affords the occasion, expediency determines the form, and all that. (Apparently, this wasn't always the case; you get the sense some Romantics wrote sonnets like fussy gunslingers, looking each other dead in the lorgnette.) I've heard a poet say to a student, "This poem is trying to be a sonnet," which is to say, I think, that not only is there some very particular reaction between reality and consciousness to which the sonnet is catalyst, but there is some kind of faith needed to release oneself into this discovery. (You could substitute any form, even "organic form," for the sonnet.) Faith in what? "If you don't believe in poetry," Wallace Stevens, that would-be heathen, once wrote, "you cannot write it." But what is one believing in when one is believing in poetry if not this correlation between reality and consciousness and form? And if you can believe in this...

▼ ▲ ▼

Is there some art that owes its strength to, is in some terrible way authenticated by, an act? Are there some poems life brands into being? "I was surprised to find how light I felt / With most of the back of my head missing," begins a moving sonnet by Joe Bolton, a young poet who, not long after writing those lines, committed the act he imagines in them. "Oh, should a child be left unwarned," Frost wondered, "That any song in which he mourned / Would be as if he prophesied?" Awful thought. Art is not life, and life is not art, but they face each other like two jagged matching cliffs that look as if they were once together, but with a long, long fall between them now. Some poets live and die all on one side, some on the other. A few become so nimble on the tightrope of their talent they can seem to dance that division away. And some, like Joe Bolton, come to consciousness with that line like a wire cutting into their hands, all of eternity tugging under them, and it's hard to tell if the poems they write out of such urgency are a means of holding on, or trial runs for letting go.

▼ ▲ ▼

Some days, although we cannot pray, a prayer
utters itself. So, a woman will lift
her head from the sieve of her hands and stare
at the minims sung by a tree, a sudden gift.

Some nights, although we are faithless, the truth
enters our hearts, that small familiar pain;
then a man will stand stock-still, hearing his youth
in the distant Latin chanting of a train.

Pray for us now. Grade I piano scales
console the lodger looking out across
a Midlands town. Then dusk, and someone calls
a child's name as though they named their loss.

Darkness outside. Inside, the radio's prayer –
Rockall. Malin. Dogger. Finisterre.

▼ ▲ ▼

Americans love mixed tones. It's often nothing more than a thoughtless and fake reflex – the easily digestible pap of pathos and irony in the recent movie *American Beauty,* say, which is a sort of glossy visual equivalent of a trend in contemporary American poetry. But this collision and confusion of impulses does produce some of our most notable poetry, whether it's Stevens or Ashbery or Berryman. This, perhaps, along with a penchant for scope rather than focus, is the main reason why contemporary Americans don't seem particularly good at the sonnet, which is rarely amenable to mixed tones; or why, when they do produce good sonnets, they don't sound especially "American" (Wilbur, James Wright, Hecht, etc.). The wry terror of Bolton's sonnet is an exception. R.S. Gwynn's oddly buoyant "Body Bags" also comes to mind, though it's not in this anthology. Whether this explanation is accurate or not, though, most of my favorite sonnets of the second half of the twentieth century seem to have been written by non-Americans such as Seamus Heaney ("Glanmore Sonnets," "Clearances"), Paul Muldoon ("October 1950"), Geoffrey Hill ("Funeral Music"), Eavan Boland ("Heroic"), George Mackay Brown (preposterously not included), Patrick Kavanagh (where is "Inniskeen Road"?), Tony Harrison (whose best poem, "Bookends," isn't included), and Carol Ann Duffy, who wrote the poem – "Prayer" – I quote above.

▼ ▲ ▼

How rare it is that difficulty or obscurity is somehow so integral to a poem that it's part of the poem's achievement (and in prose, perhaps never). The sensation you get when coming into the lyrical clearings of Shakespeare or Frost – or, to a lesser extent, into an individual poem like "Prayer" – is of suddenly being able to breathe much more easily and deeply, looking around you at the whole scope of earth and sky instead of keeping your eyes trained carefully on the unpredictable ground where you are walking. And yet there are also styles that earn their agonies. Wyatt, Hopkins, Geoffrey Hill – these are some narrow and rocky passages, but you know there's no other way to get where they're going.

▼ ▲ ▼

Balzac in *Lost Illusions* talks about "temperaments who are perfectionists to the point of morbidity." I know the feeling. The sonnet can seem particularly attractive to such a temperament, because it gives such a definitive click to that box Yeats equated with finished form. (A friend once told me that all she could hear in this image was that very expensive sound of a very expensive car door clicking shut.) Mere virtuosity can be compelling, though perhaps less so in an art that one practices, and probably not at all for one whose art has come to seem a means of staying alive. Contested technique, that's what one learns to recognize and trust most deeply, the tightrope quivering with balance or panic. And yet no artist inclined to ideals and absolutes (many aren't) outgrows them, not utterly. Proust said that what initiated and sustained all the massive work of memory and imagination of *In Search of Lost Time* was "the thought of perfection," and it's possible to read every sentence of that book like the words to a lyric poem: as both devotion to and desecration of that thought.

2001

Poetry in a Visual Culture

It's National Poetry Month again. The spirit wilts a bit at the thought. Not that the attention to poetry isn't a good thing, but that such stark marketing measures are necessary. Is there a National Visual Art Month? A National Novel Month? The ludicrousness of the idea is telling: if poetry were truly integrated into this culture, we wouldn't need a month to proclaim its importance. National Poetry Month is a late lifesaving gesture, like those paddles applied to a patient whose heart is failing. Sometimes such measures are necessary. National Poetry Month has had some salutary effects, and I'm all for *anything* that makes poetry more a part of the culture, part of life. But it's hard not to see the designation as a symptom of illness rather than health.

Does the illness belong to the culture or to poetry itself? I'm inclined to lay the blame on the former: it's this fat country whose heart is failing. Poetry is those paddles, not *the* antidote by any means, but one step in the right direction. That's not to say that poetry itself couldn't do with a bit of a jolt, something – and it may simply be some*one,* some great poet – to shock us out of the bad habits that develop when any art has either abandoned hope of an audience, or begun pandering to it. But the range of poets in this country is so wide, the kinds of poetry so various, that it's difficult for me to believe that just about everyone couldn't find *something* useful and meaningful to his or her own life. The country isn't listening, though, not really. And in the rare cases when poetry does come to its attention – National Poetry Month, say – it can't hear.

Poetry, like all the fine arts, even when they are apparently "public" in their orientation, is predicated on the existence of an inner life. It assumes not only that humans have such a thing, but that it can be shared. It assumes, moreover, that this transaction of interiors is integral not only to the life of the individual but also to the life of the culture. These assumptions are rarely explicit in the work (though sometimes they are: Yeats's "Easter 1916," Auden's "September 1, 1939"), and they usually remain unconscious in the mind of the poet. But to try to say something about life, even if it's only your own life, in the language we all use, to publish the result or even to hope for one reader – this is a communal gesture.

Increasingly, though, the "language we all use" in this country isn't language. I spoke recently with a junior high school teacher at a public school in Manhattan. She said the toughest, most dispiriting part of her job was coming up with lesson plans that took into account the brevity of her students' attention spans, which meant *always* having a strong visual component. This probably won't come as a surprise to readers of *Poetry,* but I would suggest that the phenomenon is probably also to some extent *true* of readers (and editors) of *Poetry.* Ask anyone how they're doing these days, and the most frequent response will be some form of "busy" or "tired." We all feel that there is somehow less time than there once was (a feeling borne out by statistics on increasing work hours), and the feverish need we have to fill every hour of every day with measurable tasks and accomplishments suggests the same sort of erosion of memory and imagination that makes those schoolchildren impervious to anything that is not visual.

To change from word to image as the primary means of representing experience radically changes both an individual's and a culture's relation to time. Words, even when one uses them unconsciously (and perhaps especially then) are inflected with history and contingency. They are both enlivened and compromised by all the different meanings and associations they have accrued. Their effect is at once interior, in that there are inevitable, ineluctable differences in specific meaning as a word moves between one mind and another, and exterior, in that words are how we have historically formulated and understood our common experience.

Images, by contrast, cannot escape the present tense. Their strength is precisely this "presentness": no memory can ever be as complete as a photograph, no book or poem can ever be as consuming

as a movie, and no culture can ever be as uniformly unified by lan-
guage as they are by an image. But this is the chief weakness of im-
ages, too: that they have no interiority, no depth or density, that the
way in which they bind us is so *uniform*.* Memory is a much more
complicated phenomenon than the abstracted visual experience
that images reduce it to. So is history. Consider how different our ex-
perience of 9/11 would have been – and would be now – if we had not
all watched it on television. I suspect it would have been considerably
less intense. I also suspect, though, that previous generations' expe-
rience of national tragedies, though perhaps lacking the *immediate*
intensity of our experience of 9/11, were more fully integrated into
the country's consciousness, more comprehensively imagined and
therefore remembered, though people had nothing but words from
which to imagine the events.

Is it possible that the nature of human consciousness itself is
changing? That as our abilities advance in one direction – visual stim-
uli, information assimilation, efficiency – other capacities atrophy
and die? Many of our oldest ways of understanding our world –
myths, singularity and consistency of place, depth of engagement be-
tween successive generations – are being lost, are perhaps already
lost in any culturally significant sense. Whether our reliance on – and
submission to – the image is a cause or an effect of these changes, we
now live in a world that seems almost *designed* to eradicate the inner
life. When a real poem falls on such soil, how is it supposed to take
root?

That's not a rhetorical question – at least not for those of us who
are poets, editors, teachers, or avid readers of poetry. One frequently
hears the argument that, since poetry has existed in every culture we
know, it will certainly survive in future ones. There may be a scrap of
truth in this, but it's a misleading sort of truth. A culture might
evolve or devolve to the point where its poetic impulses and appetite
are completely satisfied by pop songs and advertisements. Poetry as

*Here and elsewhere I'm not referring to art images, which certainly do have
depth, interiority, etc., but which have no more purchase on our collective
imagination than poetry does.

we know it in twenty-first-century America *can die,* will die without a committed audience that is larger than its practitioners, and those of us for whom the art is important must ask ourselves hard practical questions about its survival. Have we strayed too far from the techniques of poetry that have traditionally made it pleasurable and memorable? Should our content be more public? Should poems be as "accessible" as the daily paper? Must they in some way adapt to the dominance of the image? What in the world *is* a poem? But there is an earlier and more urgent question which all of these practicalities beg. *Should* poetry survive? What is the point of persisting with this art at this time?

We pay lip service all the time in this country to the idea of "the individual." We credit our notions of democracy and equality to the fact that we are a nation made up of individuals. But the great bulk of our experience, from where we live to what we eat to what we wear, comes from the top down. It is institutionalized, generic, and monolithic. This is nowhere more true than in our aesthetic experience, which is dominated by movies and television, and which, more often than not, is designed to make all the rest of our experience seem much more authentic and various and enjoyable than it is. Think of all the advertisements urging you to "be yourself" or "do your own thing." Think of all the movies in which one character's independence of spirit is packaged for collective consumption. The *idea* of individualism is on sale in this country. We buy it en masse.

One of the great sustaining pleasures of poetry is the experience of a *truly* individual voice. One of its paradoxes is that this experience of another's individuality is a powerful way of discovering and confirming one's own. This rarely happens consciously, as if one looked up one day from reading Robinson Jeffers and proclaimed, "I am!" Nor does it happen collectively. The widespread attention paid to Auden's "September 1, 1939" after 9/11 illustrated another of poetry's powers, to articulate and galvanize collective feeling. But this is different from – and in a fundamental way secondary to – the intimate, solitary engagement with poetry that I'm describing.

That act is about consciousness. Those of us concerned with the fate of poetry tend to emphasize its "relevance" to life, and indeed one of poetry's great strengths, which has been too often forgotten or even denigrated by contemporary poets, is to make direct, succinct, and comprehensive statements about life – Auden's "We must love one another or die," for example, or Yeats's "Too long a sacrifice / Can make a stone of the heart." But the greatest power of poetry for this particular country, at this particular moment in history, may be simply this act of preserving some aspect of truly individual consciousness in a culture bent on obliterating it. That is to say, poetry's deepest value for our lives may consist precisely in how *unlike* life it is, at least unlike this welter of images and uniformity and busyness that we are now calling life.

Why does this matter? Pascal once said that all the troubles of the world could be traced to man's inability to sit alone with himself in a room for an hour. Imagine what he would say about us, who cannot sit still long enough to read a poem. I've never been very convinced by the cause-and-effect argument regarding art and life, at least not in terms of subject matter – that witnessing moral dynamics in novels will make you more moral, for example, or that watching violent movies and video games will make you more violent. The greater effect, both good and bad, seems to me one of *form.* A person whose mind adapts to the dominance of the image might come to think of his life as occurring in that same present tense. This can make one unfit for the crises of one's life, which require deep memory and a sense of futurity. It can also make one capable of the most ruthless and ultimately self-destructive actions.

And what is true of an individual is true of a culture. That we turned so ingenuously and spontaneously to the Auden poem after 9/11 suggests that, as a nation, there is some hope for us. We retain a need for collective expression with some historical depth and imagination to it, and we retain some residual sense of what true consciousness is and how we might share it. However, that we turned away from that event so quickly and, I would argue, so utterly; that we allowed our lives to be flooded by the same busyness and insipid entertainment; that even the wars ignited on our behalf came to us replete with jump cuts, mood music, and sterilized narratives – this suggests that the moral health of this country, the situation of that patient on the table, is dire.

Don't get me wrong. Poetry isn't going to "save" us, not as a culture and not as individuals. Art sharpens but does not alter reality, and in any event there are certainly other forms of art that both induce and require genuine consciousness. Poetry, though, with its distilled and durable language, its aural immediacy and layered meanings, and its brevity, may be the best tonic for our times. Too many of our marketing efforts for poetry tend either to overestimate its effects – Harold Brodkey saying that if everyone in the world read poetry there would be no more wars, for instance – or to underestimate them, as when we dumb poetry down to a level that essentially precludes the kind of deep engagement with language that I've been describing. The true power of poetry is at once smaller and greater.

National Poetry Month? By all means, let us rejoice and be glad in it. But let us also remember that the power of poetry accrues individually or not at all; that the most effective preservation and promulgation of poetry in the culture may begin with a solitary engagement with a poem that you find difficult and off-putting but somehow enthralling, vital; that this act can have concentric societal effects beyond those that can be measured by marketing tools or poetry popularity contests. Let us remember, amid all the hoopla of National Poetry Month, apart from all its hucksters and detractors, that in the end we go to poetry for one reason, so that we might more fully inhabit our lives and the world in which we live them, and that if we more fully inhabit these things, we might be less apt to destroy both.

2004

In Praise of Rareness

Every time we print an issue of *Poetry* that has more prose than poetry in it, we get at least one letter of complaint. These complaints vary in tone and temperateness, but inevitably there are sentences that run something like this: "Given the nature of your journal, and given its very name, what's with all the prose? Couldn't you use those pages for more poems? Shouldn't *poetry* be your emphasis?"

Well, yes and no. Yes, poetry should be (and most definitely is) our emphasis; but no, that does not necessarily translate into publishing more of it. In fact, I think a strong case can be made that the more respect you have for poetry, the less of it you will find adequate to your taste and needs. There is a limit to this logic, of course, or else Plato would be the patron saint of the art. But still, an overdeveloped appetite for poetry is no guarantee of taste or even of love, and institutionalized efforts at actually encouraging the overconsumption of poetry always seem a bit freakish, ill-conceived, and peculiarly American, like those mythic truck stops where anyone who can eat his own weight in rump roast doesn't have to pay for it.

Reading through old literary journals is not an activity I would ordinarily recommend, but it can be instructive in this context. People who know the history of *Poetry* usually point to a couple of indisputably high moments: the first under Harriet Monroe, who published the early work of just about all of the major Modernists; and the second under Henry Rago, who was on the whole more eclectic and adventurous than Monroe. It's interesting, then, to look at a couple of memorable issues from those times.

In June of 1915 Monroe, in a now-famous story, took the advice of *Poetry*'s foreign correspondent, Ezra Pound, and printed the first published poem of T.S. Eliot, "The Love Song of J. Alfred Prufrock." The

other contributors of verse in that issue include Skipweth Cannell,
William Griffith, Georgia Wood Pangborn, Dorothy Dudley, Bliss
Carman, Arthur Davison Ficke, and Ajan Syrian, all of whose work
sounds pretty much like this:

> O leaves, O leaves that find no voice
> In the white silence of the snows,
> To bid the crimson woods rejoice,
> Or wake the wonder of the rose!

Just over forty years later, when Rago was editor, Sylvia Plath made
her first appearance in the magazine with six poems that, though not
representative of Plath at her best, nevertheless practically blaze with
radiance beside the poems of Lysander Kemp, Louis Johnson, Edith
Tiempo, William Belvin, August Kadow, etc., etc.

My point here is not to illustrate how badly most poetry ages, nor
to present some sort of long perspective by which to judge a con-
temporary journal. Because one generation's treasures are the next
generation's jokes does not invalidate the earlier meanings people
may have found. It's quite possible that for many people those now-
indistinguishable poems alongside "Prufrock" provided just the
provocation or consolation they needed on a bad day, or caused them
to look at their immediate world not, lord knows, with new eyes, but
at least with old eyes, at least to look. (And in fact the general reaction
to "Prufrock" was decidedly negative.) Time is the ultimate test of
art, but it is not the *only* test of art. It is possible for a work that will
not survive its own time to nevertheless speak truly to that time. For
us, coming across passages like those I've just quoted is like discover-
ing some foul, furred thing at the back of the refrigerator: one's
whole spirit winces. But for someone somewhere they were once
fresh. What happened then is happening now, I guarantee you. It is
the bliss and curse of being alive.

But that's a digression. The point I want to make here has to do
with the *prose* in these issues, which in both cases remains surpris-
ingly fresh, readable, even relevant. In the 1913 issue there is a
memorable, sharply worded piece by Ezra Pound, which, ironically,
fulsomely praises the utterly forgotten poetry of T. Sturge Moore. In

the issue edited by Rago, there are excellent reviews by Thom Gunn and Charles Tomlinson, as well as an astute piece on verse drama by William Meredith. This tendency is borne out by other back issues of *Poetry* (issues old enough to allow for some perspective, I mean). The poetry is pretty much a steady backdrop of competence for the occasional and (now) unmistakable masterpieces. The prose is surprisingly consistent in its quality and appeal.

Does it follow from this that prose is the more durable art? Of course not. No one is reading that prose I just mentioned, nor is there any particular reason why they should be. Critical prose exists solely for the sake of the moment in which it is written. Its function is either to bring to light some work from the past that has been neglected or misunderstood for the sake of enlarging and refining contemporary consciousness, or to help readers know what contemporary works to read and how to read them. The bulk of the critical prose that survives is written by famous poets, and it survives only because the poetry of these people has survived. There are a few exceptions to this, but in general aiming at eternity with critical prose is like praying to a potato. You may very well get God's attention, but probably only because He likes a good laugh.

Is prose simply easier to write than poetry? Again, not necessarily. Prose can be damnably difficult to write, but it's been my experience that one can always will oneself to write it. Right now, for instance, because I am busy and lazy in equal measure, I am bashing these sentences out hurriedly before the issue goes to the printer. I think we can all agree that what I am writing here is not, let us say, for the ages. But perhaps at least a majority of us can also agree that it is written in perfectly adequate prose. All sorts of useful things may be written in perfectly adequate prose: editorials, history, philosophy, theology, even lasting novels. But there is no such thing as a perfectly adequate poem, because a poem into which some strange and surprising excellence has not entered, a poem that is not in some inexplicable way beyond the will of the poet, is not a poem.

The truth is, sometimes poetry is almost embarrassingly easy to write. There are the famous stories: Keats writing "Ode to a Nightingale" in a single morning, Coleridge channeling "Kubla Khan," Milton essentially taking dictation from God (or perhaps the Devil, because that's who came out looking better) while writing *Paradise Lost*. But besides these instances, just about every poet admits to some simultaneous feeling of helplessness and unaccustomed power in the writing of his best poems, some element of mystery. This is the chief "difficulty" in poetry, in fact, at least for those of us who are poets, that it comes so infrequently, that it remains beyond our wills.

Anyone involved with the institutions of poetry would do well to remember this. With all the clamor in this country about the audience for poetry, a veritable barnyard of noise into which I myself have been known to bray, we shouldn't lose sight of one of poetry's chief strengths: how little of it there is. I don't mean how little there is in the culture, but how little there is at any one time that is truly excellent. Poetry's invisibility is deplorable and worth fighting. Its rareness is admirable and the chief source of its strength. Indeed, I sometimes think that if we honored its rarity more, poetry's invisibility would be less of a problem, or at least we might define the notion of visibility differently. Seamus Heaney has noted that if a person has a single poem in his head, one that he returns to and through which, even in small ways, he understands his life better, this constitutes a devotion to the art. It is enough. And in fact I find that this is almost always how nonspecialists read poetry – rarely, sparingly, but intensely, with a handful of high moments that they cling to. The emphasis is on the memorable individual poem, and poetry in bulk is rarely memorable.

All of this ought to have implications for the writer of poems as well. If poetry is so rare in the world, if so much of it is dross, just think how much rarer it must surely be in your (our!) own work. There is nothing wrong with thinking of poetry as a process, with developing a way of writing that allows you to churn out verse. Nothing wrong with it, that is, unless you give up all attempt at discrimination and insist on publishing all of these efforts. It may not be the case that anyone who is writing a book of poems every two or three years is writing too much, but he or she is almost certainly publishing too much. The great thing about writers like Larkin, Hopkins, Bishop, Bunting, Eliot, Herbert, Justice, and Bogan is that they demanded more from their work than anyone else did, and their discipline and dissatisfaction are now our pleasure.

What might all this mean for a literary magazine? Thirty years ago George Dillon and Hayden Carruth, who were then editors of this magazine, created a firestorm when they published an issue that had a mere eleven pages of verse in it. They explained their actions by saying that there simply weren't enough poems on hand that merited publication, and that to have lowered the bar of admittance would have been to lower the prestige of the magazine. It's impossible to know whether or not they were justified, because it's impossible to recover the material from which they were choosing. My suspicion, though, being familiar with Carruth's work as an anthologist and critic, and having edited this magazine myself for several years, is that they were. I also suspect that it was not at all a denigration of poetry, but an exaltation of it.

2006

In the Flux That Abolishes Me

Sometimes at *Poetry* we get manuscripts from dead people. I don't mean the living dead, though we get those too. I mean the dead dead, who are by this point either singing with choirs of angels or sitting in the eternal workshop that is Hell, but in any event have no access to stamps. The manuscripts come to us by way of the poet's friends or family, who are occasionally following some last directive of their loved ones but more often acting on their own. They want to honor or understand all those hours that John or Mary or Sam or Jane insisted on solitude and silence. They want it to mean something.

One's heart would have to be frozen over to mock either this poetry or these posthumous efforts. It's true that we haven't yet found anything to publish in these submissions, but it's also true that we owe the entire work of great poets like Emily Dickinson and George Herbert to family and friends – and, later, editors and critics – who preserved and promoted it. If art's survival is sometimes so precarious, so dependent upon the whims and resilience of the first people to come across it, just think of what we must surely have lost.

But there's another reason to be respectful of these poems, particularly if you yourself are a poet and harbor any sort of public ambitions for your work. It is very difficult to predict what the readers of the future will choose to preserve, but one thing is certain: they won't choose much, and they will think we chose badly. Indeed, even if you are a well-known poet reading these lines, even if your Upper East Side castle is packed with prizes and undergraduates fling their undergarments during your readings, the chances are good that you and your work will lie down in the dust together. It may take a little bit longer than it did for John or Mary or Sam or Jane, but the final effect is the same.

That's the downside of a life spent trying to write poems. The up-side is that no one believes in the downside, not really, not wholly, and not at all in the moments that matter most, when one discovers a poem that seems to speak right through the centuries, or when a new poem of one's own lights a fire in the mind. What is one believing in then?

> The mind has suddenly become a great soundboard, echoing far beyond its accustomed range into its own vast borderlands, where lost paradise and hoped-for heaven have betaken themselves; and we are shaken by a cosmic wind, and know ourselves for creatures of a far greater range than we are commonly aware of.

That's Ruth Pitter, an English poet who lay down in the dust in 1992, and whose work, it seems, survives in the minds of fewer and fewer people every year, most of them poets. Still, it *does* survive, precariously, tenaciously. Does this not seem like a very impressive survival? Does it seem cruelly inadequate that, out of all those hours these poets spent in solitude and silence, and given all the life they sacrificed for the sake of their work, only a handful of poems, maybe nothing more than a stanza here and there, persist in the consciousness of a later generation? "This is a great and beneficent catharsis," Pitter writes, "and poets know that to have composed even a few lines that will have this effect on even a few readers is a sufficient achievement. This I take to be our chief aim and justification."

And the others? John and Mary and Sam and Jane, whose work will advance no further in death than it did in life? Were their labors not "justified"? You might as well ask that question of Robert Carleton Brown, Lydia Huntley Sigourney, William Watson, each of whose work, famous in its day, now rots unread in a few old anthologies. In fact, while you're at it, you might ask the question of any figure, living or dead, whose work means most to you, for the truth is, in some ultimate sense, we are all in this together, singing and suffering the same fire of time that will, you can be sure, one day devour the work of William Shakespeare. ("And yet, and yet," Pitter writes, "some bird / Carols within that fire; warbling it woos, / Like the three children walks warbling in flame; / Nests in the flame, in the flux that abolishes me.") If it's eternity you're after, verse isn't going to get you there.

That's little comfort, I realize, but the dead don't need comfort. And for the living who seek in poetry some justification for their lives, or seek to justify the lives of those they loved, there is only one consolation, which is at the same time meager and immense: poetry is either a calling or not, its own reward or no reward, for the world can't ratify what God demands. This is true for the poet whose first publication leaves him at once tingling with joy and weirdly ravenous, and it is true for the grizzled figure with five Pulitzers whose day is ruined by a scathing review in, oh, let's say *Poetry* magazine. It is true for the ones who work all their lives with no thought of publication or readers, and it is true for those who, coming across these manuscripts in desk drawers or in shoe boxes, sort through them, bundle them up, and send them to us.

Not that we say any of this in our responses to this last group, of course. No, that would be presumptuous, and in any event sometimes there is more civility and honesty in the generic language of rejection. "We have been very glad to read these poems," we say, by which we mean that it is a good thing for survivors to send such work along to editors, because who knows what might happen, and it is a good thing for us to have our hopes awakened, our complacencies tested. "These poems have moved us," we say, meaning the blunt fact of them, the failure of them, the reminder they give of how much human endeavor, in human terms, comes to naught. "But we're not going to be able to use these poems at this time," we conclude, and mean exactly that, for who knows, perhaps one of these manuscripts will not be burned or buried but instead preserved, passed along to the poet's children, then to his children's children. Perhaps one of these very bundles will make its way into our offices again in a hundred years, when we shall all be changed.

2006

III

Fugitive Pieces (1)

The world no longer rises to our occasions. In Shakespeare not only is individual crisis societal crisis, but human drama is cosmic drama: "The heavens themselves blaze forth the death of princes." The suffering of individual characters is mirrored by, or answered by, the suffering of the world. When these two anguishes come to a head, when a king's storm becomes the sky's, when beasts begin whelping in the streets of Rome, the resolution is imminent. This correspondence between the inner world and the outer world contextualizes suffering, you might say, defines it in terms of place and time. And defining a pain, as any psychologist will tell you, is the first step toward resolving it.

Sometime in the nineteenth century things began to change. When Raskolnikov in *Crime and Punishment* finally goes to make his confession, after four hundred pages of high-pitched deliberation and moral anguish, the world to which he wants to confess, a squalid police station manned by a sergeant named "Gunpowder," is too chaotic and preoccupied to concern itself with him. There is the sense of an immense spiritual drama being unceremoniously deflated by circumstance, of there being literally no *place* for such suffering. The effect – which would become a signature effect of writers such as Beckett and Kafka – is at once comic and desolating.

But Dostoevsky was no Modernist. *Crime and Punishment* ends with Raskolnikov, locked away in a Siberian prison, being redeemed by Sonia's devotion, his own love for her, Christ. How I wish it didn't feel to me like a flinch. Though I love his intensities, his grand passions and their cosmic crescendos, there is a place in Dostoevsky (and indeed in much nineteenth-century literature) to which I cannot go. I feel strongly that the absence of belief – or, more accurately, the

absence of the possibility of belief – results in an attenuated litera-
ture, but I also feel that once this line has been crossed there is noth-
ing for an honest artist to do but note the plain facts of the earth to
which he's fallen. Patrick Kavanagh:

> No crash,
> No drama.
> That was how his life happened.
> No mad horses galloping in the sky,
> But the weak, washy way of true tragedy –
> A sick horse nosing around the meadow for a clean place to die.

> (*The Great Hunger*)

▼ ▲ ▼

And yet, and yet… just how far can such honesty – if it is that – go? To
what extent can art make suffering completely solipsistic and still re-
main art? At what point does an art in which both world and words are
drained of meaning become a vacuum of technique?

Cormac McCarthy's *Blood Meridian* is the closest thing I know to
a contemporary allegory, in that it's an allegory without referents,
without anything left to allegorize. It ends with the Judge, who is part
evil and part necessity and part pure genius, embracing and killing
the Kid, a cipher who is the only potential moral agent in the book.
After three hundred pages of brutal, beautifully described rapes, de-
capitations, genocide; after dozens of fabulous, nihilistic campfire
conversations during which the Judge articulates emptiness with di-
abolical eloquence, at one point slitting the throat of a child as casu-
ally as he'd clean a boot, at others wandering away in search of cave
drawings or old totems that he systematically "expunges from the
mind of man," the act occurs the only place it could: a toilet. Now
here's a book that refuses to flinch. It's brilliant, beautiful, truly great
in some limited way, but it also seems to me an art of exhausted moral
resources, and I can think of no other book that leaves me feeling
quite so cold and vacant.

Someone once suggested to me that the style or "form" of *Blood Meridian* serves as a moral counterweight to its theme. It's a familiar claim for twentieth-century literature, an accurate one, too, at least insofar as that for a lot of artists there is no means of moral assertion left except for style, a beautiful coherence of terrible material. I agree with Edgar Wind, though, that there are two levels on which we must react to a work of art. "We should judge it aesthetically in its own terms, but we should also decide whether we find those terms acceptable." And finally there is something about the aesthetic terms of *Blood Meridian,* as brilliant a book as it is, that I find unacceptable, something self-pleasuring about its style, some willful occlusion in the very clarity of its horror, a kind of – strange as it seems to say of a book like this – decadence.

One task of art is to articulate the missing links between the self and the world. Another task of art – a higher task, I would say – is to forge new ones.

▼ ▲ ▼

Corollary. At a reading, a poet whose work leaves me cold but whose mind and integrity I admire uses the phrase "poetry of consolation" with a kind of vehemence and contempt that immediately strikes me as too facile. Why should art not console? Doesn't the greatest art give us some means of dealing with the pain it forces us to feel? Isn't this the idea of catharsis? The phrase seems to me similar to Eliot's insistence that the poetry of his own time, if it was to be true to that time, had to be "difficult." Both ideas are legitimate, in a way, though in broader senses than either poet intended. I agree that poetry must be difficult, though that difficulty may have nothing to do with style (which is what Eliot was emphasizing), or may inhere in the very simplicity and transparency of a style – Frost, say, or Hardy, both of whom were writing at the same time as Eliot, both of whose work says something necessary and "true" to the time. And I agree that poetry must not *merely* console. (I think of Simone Weil's statement that the greatness of Christianity inheres not in the fact that it provides

a supernatural relief from suffering, but that it provides for a super-
natural use for it.) The soothing sort of verse that fills up our major
magazines, with its formal complacency and instant epiphanies
(add an anecdote and stir), has nothing to do with serious art. But to
react against this sort of poetry by saying that *all* poetry must not
console seems to me an embittered sort of impoverishment. Poetry is
larger than this.

▼ ▲ ▼

August Kleinzahler says in an interview that 90 percent of what he
writes comes out of direct observation. Richard Wilbur writes that he
has written only one poem in his life that proceeded directly from im-
mediate experience ("The Death of a Toad"). I don't think this
means that Wilbur doesn't carefully observe the world around him
and use those perceptions for his poems, or that Kleinzahler merely
notates what he sees. In order for a poem to be any sort of art at all –
and both of these poets seem to me real artists – there must be some
sort of catalyzing reaction between form and content, word and
world, which is to say that experience is always internalized. There
are varying depths of this internalization, though, varying degrees to
which a poet will inhabit, bridge, endure, ignore, enact (the verb will
vary depending on the poet) the separation between experience and
form, process and product, life and art, and one can see a sort of rift
in literary history between what I'll call, for simplicity's sake, poets of
observation and poets of culmination.

Whether one writes in free verse or in meter has nothing to do
with this distinction. Among those writers of observation are Ben
Jonson, John Clare, and Thomas Hardy (though what Hardy "ob-
served" was sometimes the working of his own mind), all tradition-
ally formal poets. Among those writers of culmination are Eliot and
Bunting, both of whom wrote largely in free verse. It's possible to
imagine all of the former, including Kleinzahler, saying of an experi-
ence that they got a poem out of it, and it's possible to imagine them
returning to a poem they have written to remind themselves not only

of the particular quality of an experience but what they felt about it. For the latter poets, the disjunction between a poem and the process by which it came into existence is likely to be much sharper, and if they feel their lives in their finished forms at all, they are likely to do so as a man might feel a severed limb, some momentarily concentrated, vaguely painful tingling in what once was, but never again will be, him.

▼ ▲ ▼

There are writers whose work has such an air of foreclosure about it, such a feeling of idiosyncratic completion, of a style being pushed in one direction as far as it can go, that one reads them with both despair and relief – despair at the futility of trying to imitate or learn something from them, relief at for once having this predatory imperative lifted. Eliot thought Milton was such a writer, the style so perversely evolved that a young poet could only be ruined by it, but then Lowell came along and made those inaccessible crags and cadences of Milton into something singular and strange. Eliot wasn't wrong, exactly, but he didn't note that choosing the writers one reads with this blend of despair and relief depends as much upon one's particular cast of mind, talent, and ear as on the writers themselves. "Properly speaking," Goethe writes, "we learn only from those books we cannot judge," but there's little consistency from court to court in this regard, and the learning that Goethe is referring to is not technique. What wonderful moments these can be, though, if you'll let them be, when you recover a kind of radical innocence and are once more merely a reader, a work purged of literature, infused with life.

▼ ▲ ▼

More and more what I want from the poetry I read is some density of experience, some sense that a whole life is being brought to bear both on and in language. It's not a quality one can counterfeit, nor do I think that age, breadth of experience, or a certain equanimity of tone – "wisdom," call it – are necessarily the issue. Keats was dead at twenty-six, no poet lived more narrowly than Dickinson, and would anyone really argue that the exalted nostalgia of Bunting's *Briggflatts* is "wise"? But the quality I'm talking about is everywhere in these writers. I would describe it as a recognizable complexity of experience culminating in a clarity of expression that is neither reductive nor summative, some sense that a fully inhabited life – be it brief, or narrow, or in some fundamental way thwarted – has been suffered into form. *Suffered* and *form* are the operative words here. "Technique is the test of a man's sincerity," Pound said, but he might have added that a feeling for the dimensions of human pain is the test of a man's technique. I should just say it straight out: I'm increasingly convinced that there is a direct correlation between the quality of the poem and the poet's capacity for suffering.

▼ ▲ ▼

Capacity for suffering. I mean to distinguish this from John Berryman's assertion that the luckiest artist is the one who experiences the greatest sufferings short of death, which seems to me absurd. What matters is not the extent of one's suffering, nor even that it have the sort of dramatic imprimatur that the world can recognize *as* suffering (an urge toward suicide, death of loved ones, war, etc.), but the extent to which one's experience of pain is internalized and, more importantly, transformed. Once again Dickinson is the great model. *That* she has suffered is clear from her poems, *what* she has suffered considerably less so. Indeed, you often feel Dickinson resisting the specificity of her own pain, which may be the most salient feature of this density of experience I'm trying to describe, a steadfast refusal to sink into what Wordsworth called a "treasured and luxurious gloom of choice." Late in James Baldwin's story "Sonny's Blues," when Sonny and his brother are having a conversation after having heard a gospel singer on the streets of Harlem, Sonny says: "It struck me all of a sudden how much suffering she must have had to go through – to sing like that. It's *repulsive* to think you have to suffer that much."

▼ ▲ ▼

The inability to write poems is one thing. The inability to maintain faith in poetry as a life's work quite another. Someone experiencing the former is like a thirsty man in sight of water. Someone experiencing the latter is like a man whose thirst water has ceased to slake. It's easy to mistake one condition for the other. The sweet relief you see glittering in the desert ahead of you may be only a receding haze of heat. The water that will no longer work on your deeper, more urgent thirst may be simply stagnant, brackish: what you need is something fresh. And yet both conditions are real, too, and both can be, in a spiritual sense, and occasionally even in a literal one, fata' ...u can die in sight of water, grown disillusioned one time t⌐ ⌐ perhaps merely too tired to move. And whether it is th⌐ ...a given life, or a life becomes somehow immune ⌐ ...⌐ properties, the effect is the same. The gleam go⌐ , or goes so far inside of them, goes so far inside ⌐ ...would take some last shattering for you to see.

▼ ▲ ▼

Recently I heard someone describing a poem as making absence itself into a perceivable presence and was immediately uncomfortable; not because of the offhanded ease with which he articulated the idea, but because of the realization of how many times I had done so. I respond most deeply to art that has, you might say, a hole in it, some stark vacancy that no perfection of form, or assertion of faith, or even density of experience can fill. Shakespeare in *King Lear,* Keats, Kafka, Dickinson, Paul Celan – one can think of many writers who fit this description, many works that seem both to circumscribe and mourn their source. But what was for these writers a harrowing, self-annihilating discipline is in danger of becoming for us a reflexive, disingenuous emptiness. There is a big difference between an art made in the wake of life, and an art that seems merely the result of life lived retroactively. The former is an elegy for the past, that it is so utterly gone, the latter a lament for one's self, that in some fundamental sense you *were not there*. Similarly, there is a big difference between the man who once had faith and now does not, and the man who has merely inherited the idea of losing faith. (Simone Weil: "He who has not known the presence of God cannot feel His absence.") There is some soft, static quality that's entered both our thinking and writing about the idea of absence. It's less a denial of grief than an addiction to it, less a gesture toward what has been lost than an idolatry of loss itself. It may be that this idea of making absence into a viable presence in one's life is like the earlier one linking artistic accomplishment with a capacity for suffering, which is to say, it only has validity in art so long as you sense that the artist never quite believes it.

▼ ▲ ▼

"What do you believe in?" I ask my students during a discussion of "Tintern Abbey" and "Sunday Morning," and the last half-hour of class is taken up with their hesitant, surprisingly sincere, even almost desperate explorations. We talk about how a poem might be a way of engaging this question, of clearing a space in one's consciousness where the question might at least be clearly asked. We talk about their own poems and what place they might have in this discussion. I quote Stevens: "If you don't believe in poetry, you cannot write it." I quote Keats, dying: "I feel the horrible want of some faith – some hope – something to rest on now – there must be such a book."

The rest of the day and all through the next I think about this conversation and the way a poem first occurs to me, which is almost always as sound, some deep weave of cadence and silence that hardly seems a part of me, and is most me, some music not made of words, yet which without words cannot be. I don't know where the impulse comes from, nor how it turns into words, nor what part of that impulse escapes them, as it always does. There is brute, blunt labor involved, which I don't mean to slight. But I do know that there is some part of this process that at least *seems* beyond my will and reason, some energy to which, if the feeling is going to find a form, I must submit. I haven't written a line of poetry in almost a year.

Walking into the next class I can tell immediately they've been talking. Before I've even sat down one of them leans toward me and says, "What do *you* believe in?"

▼ ▲ ▼

I don't trust anyone who doesn't grow weary of hearing his own voice. This, for me, is the difficulty of teaching – not the indifference of contemporary students (many aren't), not the time away from writing, not the tedium of explaining, explaining, explaining. No. The chief difficulty is the sound of your own voice, the assuredness that inevitably creeps in, the sheer volume of talk that, after a few weeks, you feel flabbing around you like a body gone bad. "If one wishes to avoid being a charlatan," Chamfort writes, "one must shun platforms, for if one sets foot on them, a charlatan one must be, otherwise the crowd will throw stones."

And prose is similar. How readily one can tell (especially one who has written prose) when tone has become a kind of vice. However austere it may appear, whatever its linguistic or personal or moral strictures, there is a tone one settles into with a sigh, an affliction to which reviewers and critics are particularly susceptible. "It is not true," Chamfort writes elsewhere, "that the more one thinks the less one feels; but it is true that the more one judges the less one loves."

▼ ▲ ▼

Patrick Kavanagh eventually disparaged his poem *The Great Hunger* because it was a tragedy, which he defined as "under-developed Comedy, not fully born." I think his terms are a bit imprecise, because I think tragedy is a higher form than comedy. Life is, finally, tragic: we will each of us lose whatever it is we most love. The greatest literature will always be that which emerges out of, and gives us some momentary means of bearing, this awareness. Still, I know what Kavanagh meant. It's something along the lines of the criticism that Walter Bagehot leveled at Milton in the nineteenth century, that the lack of humor and levity in *Paradise Lost,* because it unnaturally circumscribed human experience, limited the extent to which it could succeed as tragedy. This is the reason for the fool in *Lear,* which is surely as desolate a work as there is in English literature. We feel more intensely a fate and pain when obviating elements are included, when it gives us something of the complete texture of life, which is another way of saying that a work becomes great as it creates a means of withstanding the desolation it has depicted. This sort of breadth is probably a latent thing, though, inherent in one's talent. Or not: Kavanagh never again came close to being the writer he was in *The Great Hunger.*

▼ ▲ ▼

Milton: One of those people for whom it's impossible to imagine a childhood, or possible only to imagine a very odd one in which even his mother and father called him "Milton."

Hardy: A man who has been surprised by life so often that he will not, by god, be surprised by it in art.

Pound: An architect who, in the middle of the construction of his ideal design, falls in love with the scaffolding, decides this is what he wanted, this is what he'll keep.

Stevens: "I had an assignation with the spirit of man but I was weak and in love with the spirit of language and kept him waiting." (Carl Rakosi)

Niedecker: A sandpiper, that quick acuity, but in slow motion.

▼ ▲ ▼

At a radio station in Berkeley the first question the interviewer asks me is, "Are you a Neo-Formalist?" and the forcefulness and immediacy of my negative response catches both of us off guard. I babble something about the fallacy of the "Neo" part of the label, because there have been plenty of people working in form throughout the entire century, and about Seamus Heaney's exhortation to himself in *Station Island* to "Stay clear of processions" as an exemplary admonition to any artist. I believe both of these things. Many of the best poets of the second half of the twentieth century have written in both traditional forms and free verse, and the glue that binds any artistic movement, including Neo-Formalism, is mediocrity.

But there's something too familiar about this response, too pat, because the truth is that I *am* more drawn to poetry of contained formal expressiveness (which I don't think is limited to traditional forms, though it is more often found there) than to the sort of loose, discursive, anecdotal verse that has dominated contemporary poetry for decades, and I do think that Neo-Formalism provided, if not a corrective by example (because most of the poetry is bad), at least one of precept to the generic, self-obsessed free-verse poetry of the seventies and eighties. I agree with Ezra Pound that in general a poet of moderate talent is much better off writing in given forms than in free verse, and it's Neo-Formalism that has made this a viable possibility for many young poets. The bar has been raised somewhat.

I have long believed, though, that to be truly ambitious is to be alone. Wordsworth says that a poet must eventually forswear all aid and criticism of his work or his ability to discern what's real there, what is most and only himself, will become too debilitated to function. Aligning one's self with a group is not the same thing as seeking criticism, but there is a way in which such identification dulls this blade of solitude, makes it easier to believe in what you're doing, and thus easier to become complacent. I have quoted the letter in which Wordsworth says this so many times that the words sometimes seem to me my own, which is sharply ironic, of course. The dead are winnowed, as is the work by which we know them. How much easier is their company than that of the living, who have agendas and vanities and, even when they're great, even when they're Wordsworth, mediocrity coming constantly out of them.

Perhaps more than the association with mediocrity, then, this is why I was made uneasy by the interviewer's question, the fact that, right as I think I am about everything above, my answer revealed to me a stance that could become simply another kind of narrowing piety. Ambition, singularity, solitude – one could use such terms as a means of keeping one's self clean, staying above the fray. That's not what Wordsworth meant, nor what he did.

▼ ▲ ▼

Ambition and survival. An editor once told me, asking for a revision of a piece of prose I'd written, that the candid way in which I'd doubted my own abilities as a poet made her uncomfortable. Another once asked me to tone down the rage I'd written into a review of what I thought were complacently mediocre books. Both were right, in a way. In criticism as well as in poetry, it is our truest tones that most deeply betray us, when survival softens into abasement, or when ambition shrills into grandiosity. And yet both were wrong, too, perhaps not for their magazines, which they wanted within a certain range of decorum, but wrong for me and wrong about art in general. There is no middle ground. The egomania and the self-loathing and the rage of the young poet are all qualities that no artist can afford to completely outgrow. I'm all for disguises – the masks of Yeats, the magisterial pose of Eliot, the utter equanimity of late Heaney (if this is a disguise) – and I agree with Pascal that "one must have deeper motives and judge everything accordingly, but go on talking like an ordinary person." But I also believe that if the work is to survive it is at the height of accomplishment that one must feel one's failure most intimately, in the depths of self-doubt must burn with ambition's fiercest fire. It's not always pretty.

▼ ▲ ▼

What a difference there is, though, in both the public and private nature of poetic ambition since the seventeenth century. Milton could not only declare himself with authority within his work, beginning with a paean to poetic fame in "Lycidas" and on through *Paradise Lost,* which attempts to "justify the ways of God to men," but could be assured of a respectful social acceptance of that ambition. Contemporary poets, though their ambition may be every bit as consuming as

Milton's (though probably not as grand), realize pretty quickly that they inhabit a different world, a world that often doesn't even recognize poetry *as* ambition, certainly not one worth spending one's life on. Ram your head against this wall for a while, and you're likely to learn some gestures of protection, some means of deflecting what is of primary importance in your life into irony and indirection. The danger is that you become your defenses, the work gradually infected with the very falseness and frivolity you adopted to protect it.

▾ ▴ ▾

He sits down with another batch of books to review, takes a deep breath of air, and lets fly with all the freewheeling wit and long-accumulated contempt of a writer thwarted in major ways but thriving in minor ones. Publicly he defends himself by saying that it's a good thing to be offended by bad books, that art is to our moral soul as food to the body, and a steady diet of inferior stuff blunts the taste and rots the heart. We are a fat country in more ways than one, he says, and he's eloquent about the need for real art as antidote, real criticism as prescription. In solitary moments he's more likely to curse, not himself exactly, but his gift, the way acuteness and deficiency are in him so raveled with each other, that he could be given such clear vision of the heights to which he cannot rise. That both of these reasonings are true, that both in some proper context could be means for making criticism into its own noble and creative endeavor, that he is in some sense right about his country and himself – this is irrelevant. The explanations are, *for him,* specious, because he sees the world only through the lens of himself, because he is as single-minded, obsessed, and doomed as a wounded wasp, plunging its poison over and over into its own body.

▾ ▴ ▾

She storms into town amid the undergraduate awe and whisper-publicity that is an American poet's portion of fame. She has ideas about *everything,* which she doesn't so much aim as scatter wildly, a sort of constant covering fire by means of which she moves from event to event. A person of furious but wholly peripheral energy, she will visibly flinch if touched, though you're the one who's been scalded. Whatever center there is to her, whatever residual self amid all of this public passion and mesmerizing style, you're not going to see it. Literary squid: get too close and you'll get an ink of opinions in your face. By the time they clear she's long gone.

▼ ▲ ▼

A man who long ago learned to hold each act in light of the distant life in which he would repent it, who for years anticipated and even treasured, with a kind of half-conscious, terrible clarity, the self as it would emerge from the wreckage it created; a man grown equanimous and wise, devoid of ambition now but, what luck, replete with everything ambition brings – this house, these admirers, regret softened by renown, and this moment in which to gather his brood of wounds around him with an almost paternal pride, as a lovely elegiac light fills the room and all the intact past stands plain as a lawn. Spare me. A man can vanish into what he's done, give himself so utterly to his actions that he becomes, not the wise survivor crawling from the chaos of his deeds, but the smooth and empty shell they cast up. Who would believe this hollow noise is the sea?

1994–2003

Fugitive Pieces (II)

What are virtues in a person can be liabilities of poems. Diffidence, gentleness, satisfaction with one's self, a certain sort of immediate sympathy for the troubles of the world and of others: all these can keep a poem from rising above the merely pleasant. Frost once remarked that poetry was a way of taking life by the throat, but for so many contemporary poets it seems a way of taking life by the hand. Certain tactics become deadeningly familiar: the privileging of specific subject matter ("*Relate* to me," you can almost hear some poems cry); the primacy of personal experience and the assumption that language can contain it; the favorite foreign country that becomes a sort of grab bag for subject matter; the husk of anecdote cracked for its nut of knowledge; the serious intellectual and psychological issues that do a soft-focus fade-out into imagistic unknowingness; the ease, even pride, with which the poet accepts such unknowingness. Much of this poetry isn't "bad," exactly; you wish it were worse, in fact, because then you could more clearly explain to yourself why a large dose of it – a batch of books to review, say, or an hour spent browsing magazines – leaves you feeling not simply numb but guilty for that numbness, as if you were the only tainted thing in a world where everything was perfectly clear, perfectly pleased with itself. Intensity is the only antidote – of language, of experience, of ambition. In the presence of that intensity, all that is merely pleasant falls away.

▼ ▲ ▼

Peter Ackroyd in his biography of Blake wants to convince us that the poet was not the abstracted wacko of popular legend (lots of perfectly ordinary people love to watch "Faery funerals" under toadstools), nor an artist of purely visionary feeling, but finally more firmly situated in late-eighteenth-century London, more mired in his own time, than either Keats or Wordsworth. I think he's wrong. There is a sort of contemporaneity of event, of subject matter, that is different from, and lesser than, a feeling for the intellectual nerves of the time. Blake's "The Chimney Sweeper" (both of them) are the former; Keats's *Hyperion* and Wordsworth's "Intimations Ode" are the latter. This is what makes Keats and Wordsworth the greater poets. It's almost a mind/body distinction. Some poets attend to the latter – event, subject matter, etc. – in the hope of being absolutely contemporary, of "mattering"; other poets, greater poets, formalize the mind of their time; in some way they *are* that mind, a time's means of perceiving and enacting itself. (For a more recent example, contrast the meandering, mostly implicit anxieties of James Schuyler with the straightforward agony of Anne Sexton. The first occurs formally, often underneath the surface of poems with apparently trivial subjects. The latter occurs as theme. Schuyler is mind, Sexton is body.) Blake wasn't trying to "matter" or be contemporary; he would have despised the ambition. But when Ackroyd praises "The Chimney Sweeper" for this sort of topicality, it's simply the subject matter he's addressing. Certainly there are poems that manage to accomplish both of these ambitions, that are both the body and the mind of a time (*The Waste Land, Paradise Lost,* "Sunday Morning"), but I don't think Blake wrote any of them.

▽ ▲ ▽

On not reviewing a group of "nature poets." I once heard a painter say that he wanted in his paintings a feeling for nature but without the nature. What he meant by that, I think, was that he wanted the natural world but colored with his own consciousness, wanted his art to be at once of the world and his own mind, but not merely a mirrored image of either one. It's the difference between illustration and the creation of original forms, between representing or refining reality and enlarging it. It's the difference between sight and vision.

The distinction is useful for thinking about poetry as well. Among those poets who take the natural world as their subject, there are poets, and then there are nature poets. Poets are interested in consciousness and how the natural world might reveal it; personality is not the point. Nature poets are interested in using the world to dramatize the self; each poem is a showcase for the poets' own dewy sensibilities. For poets, the emphasis is on the poem as event: it's important that they write well and originally. Nature poets emphasize whatever event occasioned the poem: it's important that they be very sincere. Because poets feel acutely the foreignness of nature, and because they recognize both the appeal and the danger of that unlikeness, there is usually some reluctance or ambivalence that makes itself felt in their work. Nature poets can't walk across the backyard without tripping over an epiphany. Poets make you see the world with new eyes, as the saying goes, and they make you want it more, too, though in a complicated way, fostering alike by beauty and by fear. Nature poets make you indifferent to both nature and poetry. Poets – A.R. Ammons, say, or Lorine Niedecker, Marianne Moore, Gary Snyder, Theodore Roethke – are rare. You hardly ever get such books to review. Nature poets are everywhere. Sometimes if you've slashed your way through a batch of such stuff with some degree of feeling and taste intact, either Providence, or your editor, or your own sweet temper might decide that it's best for everyone concerned if you just move on.

▼ ▲ ▼

On rereading early Lowell. The image I keep having is of a man who has learned to make the sound of a leafblower with his lips. It's astonishing, beyond question, and worth seeing, but not exactly the sort of thing you want to linger over.

No. Too facile. Stupid reviewing tricks.

Though the authority of these early poems is almost purely technical, though all the historical and religious references feel like a sort of rodomontade, still, *what authority.* If I'm not as compelled as I

once was by the grand jagged fluency of "Quaker Graveyard," the sin-
uous ease of "Between the Porch and the Altar," or the sort of main
force musical prose of "Mr. Edwards and the Spider" and "After the
Surprising Conversions"; if now I can't read these poems without
thinking of how narrow the range is, how deflected the feeling, the
extent to which a life and mind had to be distorted and restricted to
write such lines, still, these poems have worn such deep tracks in my
mind that I find myself reciting them again for days like a kind of non-
sense spell, in awe of such technique, the sheer quality of the writing,
and remembering when I would have sold my soul to write like this.

▼ ▲ ▼

It seems inarguable that Lowell's reputation has declined radically
since his death. If young poets know his work today, they know only a
few mild, middle-period poems such as "Skunk Hour" or "My Last
Afternoon with Uncle Devereux Winslow" (but not usually "Waking
Early Sunday Morning," it seems, which may be Lowell at his best).
Occasionally someone has read the late poems, when, as Lizst said of
late Chopin, Lowell had begun to use his art "only to perform his own
tragedy for himself." If Lowell has influenced poets of my generation,
it is only in the most casual, least enduring ways – these endless, flac-
cid "fourteen-liners," for example.

This probably shouldn't be so surprising, and not simply because
there tends to be a concomitant reaction against inflated reputation
(and Lowell's reputation during his lifetime was definitely inflated).
For all of his "American" subject matter and pedigree, and despite
the fact that midway through his career he said he'd been influenced
by Williams and even Ginsberg, Lowell was in certain essential ways
a European poet, just as surely as Eliot was before him. Both have the
kind of plangent, factitious sadness of artists who choose their ruins,
rather than the real rage of someone simply coming to consciousness
among them (like, say, Faulkner). Both have the kind of automati-
cally elegiac tone that implies a presumption of cultural authority.
There is some element of falseness, of show, in the work of both,

which would be ruinous were it not for the absolute truth of technique each achieved. (These are all characteristics not of European poetry per se, but of Americans who aim at it.) They were monuments, both of them, long before they died. In Europe such figures might have been set in a square somewhere (this seems to have happened to Eliot in England). In America, they just get graffitied or smashed up.

▼ ▲ ▼

It's striking how consistently history produces and preserves complementary pairs of poets, and how influence sometimes seems not merely a matter of individual poets making individual choices, but almost a cultural phenomenon. Consider Lowell and Eliot again. Both were matched up with figures who were in obvious ways antithetical. In Eliot's case, this was Williams, and the stark difference in ambitions and temperaments went beyond the aesthetic to the personal, or at least Williams's attack on *The Waste Land* has a strong ad hominem quality to it. Lowell's complement was his friend, Elizabeth Bishop, whose poetry is characterized by reserve and exactitude, not raw energy and scope. I think it would be naive to assume that two such egos and ambitions wouldn't be competitive, but the competitiveness between these figures isn't really what matters, but what happened when the dust cleared. Lowell and Eliot won their battles, in that each was the towering figure of his lifetime, but each lost his war, for it's Williams and Bishop who have had the greater influence on subsequent American poets. On the surface it seems silly to say that one must choose between representative poets, but there is a sense in which, if you are yourself a poet, you do choose, consciously or unconsciously. These choices, whether it's between Eliot and Williams, Bishop and Lowell, or between other pairs such as Herbert and Donne, Dickinson and Whitman, are what literary history *is*. They are also the reason why literary history is never a fixed thing. My own choices? Eliot, Lowell, Herbert, and Dickinson.

▼ ▲ ▼

Plath: Those sounds coming from the dog underneath our porch that someone had fed meat and shattered glass. All afternoon into the evening, way back in the deep unreachable shadows. Then silence.

Dickinson: Tweezered immensities.

Rilke: Art whispering into Oblivion's ear, *I am so beautiful, I am so beautiful...*

Ashbery: The infinite absence between two mirrors.

Browning: A man who insists on petting a dog in the opposite direction that the dog's fur lies.

▼ ▲ ▼

I find contemporary memoirs, which I would distinguish from the contained essay organized to amuse or make a point, almost impossible to read. It isn't simply that so many people who write "literary" memoirs haven't had very interesting lives (and thus have to focus hard on one aspect of those lives, usually sexual), nor that I find it difficult to "believe" the stories told. Good writing can enliven the dullest details, and if craft is not the highest test of fact, it is of feeling. "No truth but the way to truth," Paul Tillich writes. Truth is fact. The way to it, at least when one's subject is one's own memory, is feeling. Thus it is quite possible (and common) for something to be true in a factual sense and yet false in an emotional or imaginative one, and vice versa.

But there are plenty of memoirs that are well-written, well-crafted, and it is often precisely these that give me the greatest difficulties, so what's the problem? I think it has to do with this relationship between fact and feeling, memory and imagination, and some very particular way in which memoirs refuse or elide the hard distinctions that art requires. Fact is not eradicated by imagination, but it is transformed. There is a sense in which memory is not simply the material out of which art is made but the price it exacts. You lose yourself to find yourself, as Christians believe, though the self you find, if you're an artist, is different from the self who suffered. "My memory is not loving but inimical," Italo Calvino writes, "and it labors not to reproduce but to distance the past." Art involves this self-annihilating, self-making labor, emerges only from this crucible of consciousness. I think memoir usually avoids it altogether.

But memoir, I can imagine someone objecting, aims less at being art than history, seeks not to distance the past but to reclaim it. It seems to me unsuccessful at this as well. On the personal level, it fails for the reasons I've mentioned above. It employs the tactics of art without accepting the consequences. It is true but not believable in the deepest sense, feels less like history than timid fiction. And on the cultural level, memoir seems to me less a reclaiming of history than a further fragmentation of it, one more admission that we share no stories, no binding myths, that the only antidote to alienation is selfhood, and the only means to selfhood is to dig around in one's own life.

The truth, finally, is that most memoirs aim neither at art nor at history but at some simulacrum of both, wherein the strictures of both fact and form can be evaded. That everyone seems inclined to write and buy memoirs these days seems to me less a triumph of memory than a symptom of failing cultural imagination.

▼ ▲ ▼

Walking out of the Stanley Spencer show at the Palace of the Legion of Honor, my friend and I had a disagreement that reveals much of our respective ambitions and temperaments. He thought the paintings were too idea-driven, too reliant on subject matter for their emotional effects. I loved the prodigality of the pictures, the rude humanity and juxtapositions, their conflictedness about security and desire (this especially). We moved into a discussion of poetry, one that we have had before. For my friend, subject matter is almost irrelevant; imagination is what counts, as it manifests itself in a singular style. This is Modernism, I guess (which is Romanticism), though it seems to me that the greatest poems of the Modernists all have clear, major subjects. More and more what I want is some complete saturation of the actual, to feel some part of the real world wanting me to make it into words, not merely my imagination trying to attach itself to reality or being amazed at how reality arranges itself around it. "Anecdote of the Jar" seems to me a meaningless poem. Or no, it's pure meaning, the mind untainted by any real involvement with the world. Useless to me.

▼ ▲ ▼

I don't want the graceful fluency of Wilbur or Merrill (though I admire both), but neither do I want poems that are disrupted and self-consciously ugly merely for the sake of being so. That's just one more rote piety. Things can't simply be "put there" as I've heard some critic say in praise of some poet. The craft, the shaping intelligence, the individualized but recognizably historical form (not "traditional," *historical,* animated by the living history of forms) – these are everything to the successful poem. Disruption as a principle is as stifling as Romantic notions of beauty. Chaos often inhabits a poet's most perfect words, but it does so as, for the most part, it inhabits our lives – constant but without any identifiable form by which we can recognize it, unobtrusive but always almost overwhelming. How to bring this feeling, this anxiety, into *form*? Willful disruptions of language or content or tone aren't true to the terror I feel, which is tiny and quiet and pervasive, woven into experience itself.

▼ ▲ ▼

The old-fashioned way of housebreaking a puppy is to rub its nose in its own waste. There's a good deal of twentieth-century literature that operates on the same principle. This is no doubt a necessary thing, in that we humans have fouled our own house in the past hundred years, and one function of art is to point out our foulness, to render our despair into apprehensible form. Another function of art, though, one

that has deep roots in all previous centuries, is to actually try and pro-
vide some means of healing and direction. It is to give hope.

> Try to remember this: what you project
> Is what you will perceive; what you perceive
> With any passion, be it love or terror,
> May take on whims and powers of its own.

These lines from Wilbur seem to me a very wise statement about
both art and life, and how much one's own will and imagination have
to do with shaping those things. They also seem to me a lens through
which to read much of American poetry since Modernism. Lowell
wrote a strange, sad letter late in his life in which he said that really
what he remembered about his life, what struck him most at the end,
was the happiness. This is strange and sad because there's no way you
would ever guess at this happiness from Lowell's work. There is
something stunted and partial about an art that apprehends only
trauma and anxiety. Though it lacks Lowell's intensities, Wilbur's
own work – with its largeness of spirit, its resolute focus on the
world outside the self, its capacity for convincing celebration – does
serve as a useful corrective and counterweight in this regard. It's
quite possible that he'll turn out to be the more durable poet.

▼ ▲ ▼

Being oblivious to one's own time is one kind of danger for a poet; it
results in the sort of "period poetry" that characterizes the Geor-
gians or all those triple-named, numbing versifiers that surrounded
Dickinson and Whitman. But being *too* aware of the abstract histor-
ical and cultural forces that are at work in one's own time, convincing
one's self that one actually sees them, is another. When Eliot dismissed
The Waste Land as merely "a bit of rhythmical grumbling," it was not
mere false modesty or defensiveness. An artist realizes the extent to
which his work records or enacts his culture only retrospectively.
Eliot's poem seems to us the very embodiment of Modernism, a
whole societal consciousness apprehended and formalized, but it

occurred first for him in the nerves: he lived it into form. You could compare it with *The Bridge,* which often seems like a dogged project, as if it were an artifact before one word of it were set down.

▼ ▲ ▼

Reading Timothy Dekin's posthumous book, *Another Day on Earth,* I think of Schoenberg saying of Webern's quartets that they were "absent of self-pity," contrasting them with Mahler's symphonies. Dekin's poems are not absent of self-pity, but neither are they corrupted by it. Indeed, one of the most moving things about poems such as "Imagine" or "Occasional Uncles" is the way a certain sentimentality is allowed into the poem but not, finally, into the poet. That is, sentimentality, which takes the form of an urge toward self-pity, is present in the poem, but not its comforts or obfuscations. The result is a truer density of experience; for which of us really experiences grief without some element of self-pity? Because one art succeeds by stoic exclusions – and Webern's does – doesn't preclude another art from succeeding by broad, sometimes very messy inclusiveness. (I mean emotional inclusiveness here, not necessarily breadth of subject matter or looseness of form.) In a way, what Schoenberg is reacting to is simply Romanticism, for what he says of Mahler's symphonies is equally true of Beethoven's, and you could lay the same judgment against Wordsworth, Coleridge, and even, though to a much lesser extent, Keats. (It's there in "When I have fears," for example, but utterly absent from "This living hand.") Dekin is nothing if not a Romantic, though a completely modern, which is to say a completely haunted, one:

> He loved her, but he used his love like a rope:
> Half hitch, slipknot, thief, figure eight, or noose.
> Meanwhile, she found a lover who made love
> Seem simple, trite, old-fashioned as a rose.
>
> Now see him smash the pictures that she left,
> Then glue them back together in his mind –

That cell where he is always in control
To solve, resist, inflict, and yet be kind;

Or torture himself with pictures of their touch,
Or with a frightening hatred, freeze them to
Statues on an imperishable bed
He must dishevel, strip, change, make anew,

As if those lovers never tired of lust,
Or held each other with a love
That he, too passionate for ordinary feeling,
Cannot imagine being jealous of.

("Imagine")

▼ ▲ ▼

Technique has everything to do with this. So much contemporary poetry has a self-enthralled quality to it. I don't necessarily mean that it's obsessed with the self, though almost always in mediocre art one smells, as Iris Murdoch said, "the fumes of personality." What I mean here, though, is that in much contemporary poetry you feel conspicuously one of two things: either the poet is very self-conscious about his means of expression and never lets you forget that, or there's a kind of implicit, self-congratulatory pleasure at not worrying much about the means of expression. In the first instance, you get work that's endlessly coiled into itself, too reflexive to say anything clear about the world. *I'm a poem!* it screams at you in every line. In the second, you get work that's too slack to say anything memorable about the world. You feel the poet wrote it while eating breakfast; you can almost hear him chewing.

▼ ▲ ▼

There is a type of artist whose genius inheres wholly in contested technique. He may indeed have virtuoso abilities, but he won't find his signature work until some coincidence – collision, more likely – of circumstance, psychological urgency, and perfected technique causes him to realize that everything he's learned so far suddenly *will not do.* At this point either the pressure of his frustration, despair, and even elation at this impasse warps his forms into a new way of saying things, or he relaxes into an enjoyable, forgettable virtuosity. Beethoven and Yeats are obvious examples of artists who made this change.

Post-Romantic ages have tended to prize artists who in some way resist their gift, or for whom there is some sort of expressive enmity between inherited technique and individual feeling. Indeed, our assumptions about the nature of "voice" and the ways in which an artist must either change or stagnate have become so entrenched that I sometimes think we overlook or deprecate a different relationship an artist might have with virtuosity, wherein a perfected technique is neither contested nor relaxed into, but transcended. Mozart is an example in music, Merrill in poetry.

I've drawn a line with Romanticism, and that is when the distinction becomes much clearer, but temperament more than time determines this distinction. If we could eliminate the implicit value judgment, we could draw the line between the active versus the passive. Beethoven and Yeats project themselves upon a body of technique. Mozart and Merrill inhabit technique so thoroughly (and are such geniuses – an important point to make) that even the most codified gestures within it become newly expressive. These gestures may not be *personally* expressive: Mozart is more anonymous than Beethoven, just as Merrill is more anonymous, in terms of style, than middle and late Yeats. But there is a transcendent purity and clarity of tone in Mozart and Merrill (or Bishop, Tennyson, Herbert) that you can't find in an art whose style, as with Beethoven and Yeats (or Lowell, Browning, Donne), bears so clearly the stamp of self. At times, it seems an ebullience beyond occasion, pure joy, at others something closer to a sadness for the mastery of sadness – that there could be such a thing.

▼ ▲ ▼

The tombstones in the old Confederate section of the cemetery in Lynchburg, Virginia, are so weathered that you have to put your face right next to them to see the names. And the pest house, where contagious people were kept until they died, has been made into an exhibit, with everything recreated inside as it might have been, and a florid recording of the miseries they must have suffered. And certainly it must have been hellish, I think, looking in at the straw pallets on the floor, the sawdust and single stark basin, dreaming the heat and delirium. You would have lain here and seen graves dug day after day, wondering which one was your own, enduring the drone of the flies, their bristly and horribly specific appendages, sometimes maybe a woman's laughter rivering in from the nearest houses, at once easing and intensifying the pain. It would take literature to get at this, I thought; somehow history, even at its worst, is too easily titillating. There is a kind of pleasure to be had from the details of extravagant, anonymous pain, which is certainly not the only reason why tourists flock to concentration camps in Germany, or why the first question we all want to ask when hearing of a suicide is how the act was done, but is sometimes one reason for both; or why I leave this cemetery feeling inadequate to it, soiled even, as if this kind of idle imagining of detail unattached to specific people, these events that happened to no one, were a deep violation. And to make these people specific, to have these events happen to someone, you'd need a life, not simply a name.

▼ ▲ ▼

We reveal more of ourselves by the way we represent our pasts than we do by what those pasts contain. In life as well as in art – or at least in those lives and works of art to which I am most attracted – there is a sense in which style *is* content. Martha Nussbaum has written of the erotic element in the stories we tell each other, the way love either starts or is stymied in those early, vulnerable moments when someone fashions for our benefit, and we for theirs, a self made of language. If it's true that this first infatuation, if it is to deepen into love, must send its roots into reality, that we must fall finally not for the character in another's stories but for the sensibility out of which that character emerged, it's also true that, for those whose imagination rivals their memory, love forever retains some sense of this initial unreality, its seed a dream we once had of another person, they of us. There is pain in this, and danger. People adept at self-invention never completely escape the suspicion that, as any relationship deepens, they are loved less for who they feel themselves truly to be than for the half-fictions with which they've half-revealed themselves to, half-plied another person.

Writing is a similar, safer kind of seduction. Even if there aren't many writers who would go as far as Faulkner, who once said he wanted to be obliterated as a person, wanted to be known only for his books, there are plenty for whom writing is a realm of alternative, preferable selves. This may have nothing to do with the creation of a character. The existence one acquires may be formal, some finish of feeling and thought the writer knows he or she lacks in life, some completion or consummation that experience never quite affords: "He lies with one to long for another," as Basil Bunting wrote of the poet. Whatever the result, the impulse is similar to the one that Satan, with sudden realization, expresses at the outskirts of Eden in *Paradise Lost*. "Which way I fly is Hell," he says, "myself am Hell." He wants to be where he is not. The place where that is possible isn't a place, though for a writer, for a moment, language seems like one.

▼ ▲ ▼

There is nothing for it, the self-doubt, the recriminations, the persistent sense of futility and failure. Acknowledgment no matter how small, a publication or prize, a word of praise from a friend – this is all a sort of alcohol (though widely varying in its quality) to which most writers turn or try to turn, attempting to numb the too-lucid sense of self that makes you sit listening with unadmitted vigilance for the click of the mailman's steps. Nothing comes, or something comes and it's nothing, and you rise from your mangled pages to wander streets the rest of the afternoon, edging uneasily into bookstores ("I just like the quiet now," is how an unbelieving friend of mine once explained her love for empty churches), sitting with an air of self-conscious solitude in a coffee shop or through a tedious matinee, one more hour filled and failed. There is nothing for it. The same street sounds and smudged light, evening intensifying the day's evasions, fog feeling its boneless way in off the ocean, nowhere to go but home. And nothing there but the same room, the same blank page to which you sit down, night and doubt around you like some denser medium that you'll either learn to breathe, or be buried by.

▼ ▲ ▼

Art and life, memory and imagination, process and product, ambition and survival: all the lovely, illusory dichotomies. I like Eliot's description of the poet as someone who is always taking disparate experiences and forming new wholes; like it, that is, except for the "always." Eliot, even more than most poets, knew the terror and value of long silences, when you don't feel like a poet at all, and eating breakfast and making love have nothing whatsoever to do with each other, and you sit down at your desk to create whatever you can – categories, perhaps, if only in the hope of escaping them.

I do believe in these distinctions. I do believe that art, even the most vital and various of it, arises out of some absence or rift in the life, that power of imagination is very often tied to pain of memory, and that the forms of art will never fill or heal the wounds of life. And then, in the midst of writing a poem, or even reading one, if only for a moment, I believe – well, in something beyond these distinctions. René Char: "The same blows that cast him to the ground projected him at once far ahead into his life, toward the future years when, wounded, he would no longer bleed from the iniquity of one being." This is memory *as* imagination, ambition *as* survival – the wound a sort of root-hold for the larger life and art that, in both senses of the phrase, grow out of it.

1993–2006

Notes on Poetry and Religion

Art is like Christianity in this way: at its greatest, it can give you access to the deepest suffering you imagine – not necessarily dramatic suffering, not necessarily physical suffering, but the suffering that is in your nature, the suffering of which you must be conscious to fulfill your nature – and at the same time provide a peace that is equal to that suffering. The peace is not in place of the sorrow; the sorrow does not go away. But there is a moment of counterbalance between them that is both absolute tension and absolute stillness. The tension is time. The stillness is eternity. With art, this peace is passing and always inadequate. But there are times when the very splendid insufficiency of art – its "sumptuous Destitution – / Without a Name," in Dickinson's phrase – can point a person toward the peace that passeth understanding: George Herbert, Marilynne Robinson, T.S. Eliot...

▼ ▲ ▼

Language can create faith but can't sustain it. This is true of all human instruments, which can only gesture toward divinity, never apprehend it. This is why reading the Bible is so often a frustrating, even spiritually estranging, experience. Though you can feel sometimes (particularly in the Gospels) the spark that started the fire of faith in the world – and in your heart – the bulk of the book is cold ash. Thus we are by our own best creations confounded, that Creation, in which our part is integral but infinitesimal, and which we enact by imagination but cannot hold in imagination's products, may live in us. God is not the things whereby we imagine Him.

▼ ▲ ▼

You cannot really know a religion from the outside. That is to say, you can know everything about a religion – its history, iconography, scripture, etc. – but all of that will remain inert, mere information, so long as it is, to you, myth. To have faith in a religion, any religion, is to accept at some primary level that its particular language of words and symbols says something true about reality. This doesn't mean that the words and symbols *are* reality (that's fundamentalism), nor that you will ever master those words and symbols well enough to regard reality as some fixed thing. What it does mean, though, is that you can "no more be religious in general than [you] can speak language in general" (George Lindbeck), and that the only way to deepen your knowledge and experience of ultimate divinity is to deepen your knowledge and experience of the all-too-temporal symbols and language of a particular religion. Lindbeck would go so far as to say your religion of origin has such a bone-deep hold on you that, as with a native language, it's your only hope for true religious fluency. I wouldn't go that far, but I would say that one has to submit to symbols and language that may be inadequate in order to have those inadequacies transcended. This is true of poetry, too: I don't think you can spend your whole life questioning whether language can represent reality. At some point, you have to believe that the inadequacies of the words you use will be transcended by the faith with which you use them. You have to believe that poetry has some reach into reality itself, or you have to go silent.

▼ ▲ ▼

I think it is a grave mistake for a writer to rely on the language of a religion in which he himself does not believe. You can sense the staleness and futility of an art that seeks energy in gestures and language that are, in the artist's life, inert. It feels like a failure of imagination, a shortcut to a transcendence that he either doesn't really buy, or has not earned in his work. Of course, exactly what constitutes "belief" for a person is a difficult question. One man's anguished atheism may get him closer to God than another man's mild piety. There is more genuine religious feeling in Philip Larkin's godless despair and terror than there is anywhere in late Wordsworth.

▼ ▲ ▼

I don't mean to suggest that Larkin was a Christian without knowing it. Milosz does something along these lines with Camus ("if he rejected God it was out of love for God because he was not able to justify Him"), and it seems awfully close to spiritual condescension. Similarly, I once heard someone respond to Larkin's "Aubade" by saying that, while undeniably beautiful and moving, the poem illustrated perfectly the condition of any person who did not accept Christ. This just won't do. It's not sufficient for Christianity to stand outside of the highest achievements of secular art and offer a kind of pitying, distancing admiration. If Christianity is to have any contemporary meaning at all, it must contain, be adequate to, and inextricable from modern consciousness, rather than simply retreating into antiquated beliefs and rituals. And modern consciousness is marked by nothing so much as consciousness of death. Can one believe in Christ and death in equal measure? Is this degree of negative capability possible? Paul Tillich pushes toward it in theology, as do, in very different ways, Jürgen Moltmann and Dietrich Bonhoeffer, but I can't think of any English-language poets after Eliot who have achieved this (or even tried).

▼ ▲ ▼

Poetry is not written out of despair, which in its pure form is absolutely mute. The poetry that *seems* to come out of despair – Larkin's "Aubade," for instance, late Plath – is actually a means of staving it off. A negative charge, simply by virtue of realizing itself, of coming into existence, becomes a positive charge. Whole lives happen this way, sustained by art in which, at some deep level, life is denied. There can be real courage in such lives and art, though it is very easy to move from engaging despair to treasuring it, to slip from necessity into addiction. This is when poetry's powers begin to fail.

▼ ▲ ▼

Art needs some ultimate concern, to use Tillich's phrase. As belief in God waned among late nineteenth- and early twentieth-century artists, death became their ultimate concern. Dickinson, Stevens, Beckett, Camus – these are the great devotional poets of death. Postmodernism sought to eliminate death in the frenzy of the instant, to deflect it with irony and hard-edged surfaces in which, because nothing was valued more than anything else, nothing was subject to ultimate confirmation or denial. This was a retreat from the cold eye cast on death by the Modernists, and the art of postmodernism is, as a direct consequence, less urgent. I suspect that the only possible development now is to begin finding a way to once more imagine ourselves into and out of death, though I also feel quite certain that the old religious palliatives, at least those related to the Christian idea of Heaven, are inadequate.

▼ ▲ ▼

"Death is the mother of beauty" is a phrase that could only have been written by a man for whom death was an abstraction, a vaguely pleasant abstraction at that. That's not really a critique of "Sunday Morning," one of the greatest poems of the twentieth century. Death is an abstraction for all of us, until it isn't. But for the person whose death is imminent and inescapable, nothing is more offensive, useless, or wrongheaded than phrases such as "Death is the mother of beauty."

Remove futurity from experience and you leach meaning from it just as surely as if you cut out a man's past. "Memory is the basis of individual personality," Miguel de Unamuno writes, "just as tradition is the basis of the collective personality of a people. We live in memory, and our spiritual life is at bottom simply the effort of our memory to persist, to transform itself into hope, the effort of our past to transform itself into our future." In other words, we need both the past and the future to make our actions and emotions and sensations mean anything in the present.

Strictly speaking, though, the past and the future do not exist. They are both, to a greater or lesser degree, creations of the imagination. Anyone who tells you that you can live only in time, then, is not quite speaking the truth, since if we do not live out of time imaginatively, we cannot live in it actually. And if we can live out of time in our daily lives – indeed, if apprehending and inhabiting our daily lives *demands* that we in some imaginative sense live out of time – then is it a stretch to imagine the fruition of existence as being altogether outside of time?

Death is the mother of beauty? No, better to say that beauty is the mother of death, for it is the splendor of existence that so fires the imagination forward and backward into our own unbeing. It is the beauty of the world that makes us more conscious of death, not the consciousness of death that makes the world more beautiful.

▼ ▲ ▼

I always find it a little strange to meet a poet for whom religion holds no instinctive resonance whatsoever. Most poets are sympathetic to the miraculous in all its forms, though they are also usually quite promiscuous with their sympathies. Still, there are exceptions. Thom Gunn used to say that there wasn't a religious bone in his body, and I can't recall a single instance from his work that uses religious language as a shortcut to the ineffable. (For an absolutely scrupulous use of religious language and imagery by an unbeliever, look at "In Santa Maria del Popolo.") On the other hand, Gunn's work is virtually devoid of mystery (look at "In Santa Maria del Popolo"). It does not contain (or aim for) moments of lyric transcendence; it offers no ontological surprises. This is not necessarily a specifically religious distinction. Larkin, though his work is absolutely rooted in reality, and though it seems quite clear he didn't believe there was anything beyond it, could never completely repress that part of himself that yearned for transcendence, and his work is full of moments in which clarity of vision and spiritual occlusion combine to mysterious lyric effect. In Gunn's work, by contrast, you sense there was no hunger that the world could not satisfy.

▼ ▲ ▼

One of the saddest things I know are the words Keats is reputed to have uttered just before he died: "I feel the horrible want of some faith – some hope – something to rest on now – there must be such a book." Part of the pathos here is simply the fear and hunger; it is terrible to watch someone die in a rage of unbelief, and there is every reason to think that, had he lived a normal life, Keats would have come to a different accommodation with death, either with or without religious faith. Another part of the pathos though is in the fact that even here, even on his deathbed, Keats can only imagine deliverance as a book, as literature. Keats was a large-souled, warmhearted, altogether companionable person, but the tragedy of his death was that he did not have a chance to outgrow his youthful devotion to "poetry" – to the idea of it, I mean. You cannot devote your life to an abstraction. Indeed, life shatters all abstractions in one way or another, including words such as *faith* or *belief.* If God is not in the very fabric of existence for you, if you do not find Him (or miss Him!) in the details of your daily life, then religion is just one more way to commit spiritual suicide.

▼ ▲ ▼

It is common for people to regret or even renounce their earlier lives. It is common for poets to use language such as "I had to forget everything I ever learned to make way for new work" or "You must learn all the rules so that you can break them." This is, paradoxically, clichéd thinking, a symptom of our fragmented existences rather than a useful ingenuousness or regenerative naïveté. Art – including our own, perhaps especially our own – should help us to integrate existence rather than mark it off. We should learn to see our lives as one time rather than a series of separate times. I find it difficult to believe in radical conversion stories – Saul on the road to Damascus and all that. I think you can test the truth of a man's present against his past; indeed, I think you have to. Our most transfiguring spiritual experiences are merely the experiences we were trying to have all our lives, which is to say that we are not so much transfigured as completed.

2006

IV

▼ ▲ ▼

The Druid Stone: Thomas Hardy*

H is philosophy, that crocheted fatalism, matters no more than any other poet's. The poems are less determined by it than a typical anthology selection indicates. "Hap," "The Convergence of the Twain," "Channel Firing," "Nature's Questioning," "The Subalterns" – these aren't *terrible* poems, I guess, but none of them is Hardy at his best, and all are "philosophical" in a paint-by-numbers way.

Edwin Muir, who began writing poetry in his midthirties, said that he came to it with a certain inevitable "deference to ideas." Hardy turned his primary attention to poetry near sixty, and he'd never had a mind too fine to be violated by an idea. ("Hap," with those subtle "purblind Doomsters," dates from his midtwenties.) Certain habits of mind were *set*. The wonder is the emotional clarity and flexibility he retained within those habits. Is there another post-Metaphysical poet besides Dickinson who so deftly handles thought like feeling, feeling like thought?

He's weakest at his extremes (in terms of content, I mean; his style has no extremes), either when he completely forgets his philosophy and writes virtuoso poems of pure description, or when he becomes a stage director for a production of Hardy's Gloom, and ghosts begin clunking around the poems like bad actors. He's at his best in that shadow world between object and idea, phenomena and numina, the living and the dead. Here is "The Shadow on the Stone":

> I went by the Druid stone
> That broods in the garden white and lone,
> And I stopped and looked at the shifting shadows
> That at some moments fall thereon

Selected Poems. Edited by Robert Mezey. Penguin, 1998.

From the tree hard by with a rhythmic swing,
    And they shaped in my imagining
To the shade that a well-known head and shoulders
    Threw there when she was gardening.

        I thought her behind my back,
        Yea, her I long had learned to lack,
And I said: "I am sure you are standing behind me,
    Though how do you get into this old track?"
    And there was no sound but the fall of a leaf
    As a sad response; and to keep down grief
I would not turn my head to discover
    That there was nothing in my belief.

        Yet I wanted to look and see
        That nobody stood at the back of me;
But I thought once more: "Nay, I'll not unvision
    A shape which, somehow, there may be."
    So I went on softly from the glade,
    And left her behind me throwing her shade,
As she were indeed an apparition –
    My head unturned lest my dream should fade.

This is probably my favorite Hardy poem. The first two lines of the
last stanza seem to me a bit repetitive (if there's a determinative ele-
ment in Hardy, it's form), but I love the touch of "Druid," suggesting
some ancient and altogether alien mysticism, the way the second
stanza concludes and ramifies with "belief," the simultaneous satis-
faction and desolation of the rhyme it makes with "grief." I love the
use of that word "unvision," which of course isn't a word, suggesting
the extent to which we *will* certain kinds of visionary experience out
of our lives. Some knowledge must be partial in order to be knowl-
edge, the poem tells us, and there are experiences we can have only if
we never quite have them.

2

He makes patterns, not forms. Certain ideas about composition and
the effects of poetry held by the Modernists – Eliot's auditory imagi-
nation, Frost's piece of ice riding on its own melting, Malraux's idea
of the poet haunted by a voice with which words must be harmonized

– simply don't make much sense when considered in relation to Hardy. Much of his work, even some of the best of it, seems banged together. He'll almost wreck a lovely poem like "The Voice" by rhyming "listlessness" with "wistlessness." Some find this charming.

It's true, as Larkin said, that each poem manages to make its own little tune, and it's true that this is an immense accomplishment. But the tunes usually feel like accompaniments to the message rather than expressions of it. (Just calling them "tunes" is telling.) You don't spend thirty years as a novelist without acquiring a strong sense of language as *means*. There is something decidedly functional about the patterns of Hardy's poems.

This isn't merely a Modernist distinction. Coleridge: "whatever lines can be translated into other words of the same language, without diminution of their significance, either in sense, or association, or in any worthy feeling, are so far vicious in their diction." Much of Hardy feels provisional, as if each poem were made out of whatever resources he had at hand at that very moment. I can imagine alternatives for "listlessness" and "wistlessness" without "diminution of their significance."

This *is* a qualitative distinction, then, at least in one sense. If your criterion for great poetry is the abstract, ultimately undefinable quality of "form," that sense of inevitability, of perfected utterance, then you will have to say that Hardy is not a great poet. Eliot said as much, if a bit indirectly: "at times his style touches sublimity without ever having passed through the stage of being good." Read in the context of Eliot's own ambition as a poet (can any poet's criticism ever be read out of this context?), this is brilliant, at once recognizing and clearly identifying something of Hardy's power, as well as subtly suggesting what it was in Hardy's poetry that made it inconsistent with Eliot's experience of the greatest poetry.

Another alternative, of course, would have been for him to revise his definition of what constitutes greatness in poetry.

3

Still, few great poets have written worse. I don't think Hardy is served very well by those who would turn his faults into virtues, who

see the lapses in taste as somehow warrants of authenticity or sincer-
ity. This argument takes one of two forms. John Crowe Ransom ex-
cused the bad writing because he felt that "the ignorance behind it is
the condition of the innocence and spontaneity we admire." Robert
Mezey, in his introduction to the welcome new *Selected Poems,* justi-
fies the bad writing because it's deliberate.

Neither of these explanations seems to me very convincing. Ran-
som's is patronizing: Hardy in a loincloth. He'd both written and read
too much to be taken for a noble savage. Mezey, following Hardy's
own prompt, perhaps, makes two false assumptions: that stylistic
roughness is somehow more "sincere" than writing with high finish,
and that sincerity is something one can simply apply to a poem.

Seamus Heaney has written of that moment when a poet whose
education and experience have outstripped his origins first pauses
before using some local word or expression. This is to be fallen,
Heaney says, and no amount of willful regression or assumed igno-
rance can recover the context in which that word or phrase was used
unconsciously. The task for a poet at such a crossroads is to find a way
of incorporating the word or expression without violating either it or
his own distanced consciousness.

You can think of this dilemma in terms of style as well. Once a
poet learns something of finish and balance and coherence, of *style,*
he can't simply violate his learning for the sake of making his art
more "rustic." You can't *affect* authenticity.

Not that this is what Hardy did. I think it more likely that, despite
his own ex post facto explanations about wanting to seem "a little
careless," the bad writing in Hardy is a result of his idea about the
function of poetry. It's telling that when he decided to turn his atten-
tion to verse, what most excited him was the prospect of countering
"the inert crystalized opinion" of contemporary society. He had
ideas he wanted to express, and if they wouldn't quite fit into the pat-
terns he had in mind for them, well, yes they would.

This is just one more contemporary assumption about poetry that
he frustrates. Auden, one of Hardy's most acute critics, was once
asked that endlessly fascinating question of whether writing poetry
could be taught. He drew a familiar distinction between the student
who loves simply to play with language and the one who has ideas,

saying that there was some hope for the former. It's tempting to imagine a very young Hardy – well, a very short Hardy, at any rate – being asked by drought-faced old Auden why he wants to learn to write poetry and replying soberly, "Because I have things to teach you, Sir."

4

He is clear. This can be troublesome, not because it leaves you with nothing to say (this can be a relief), but because your reaction to a given poem can feel more complicated than the poem itself seems to warrant. There is something, not obdurate, not obscure, not riddling, but *mysterious* about such simplicity.

Auden once defined poetry as "the clear expression of mixed feelings." This is an apt description of how a Hardy poem works, so long as one doesn't confuse his particular effect with ambiguity. If you think of a writer like Frost, whose clarity seems in some ways similar to Hardy's, the distinction becomes apparent. A typical Frost poem (a good one, I mean) – "The Road Not Taken," say, or "The Most of It" – contains different, sometimes diametrically opposed meanings depending upon your perspective. Frost is *faceted:* meaning glints off of different edges of the poem as you change your approach. There are multiple meanings and mixed feelings in a Hardy poem, too, but only one dimension. Consider "The Division":

> Rain on the windows, creaking doors,
>   With blasts that besom the green,
> And I am here, and you are there,
>   And a hundred miles between!
>
> O were it but the weather, Dear,
>   O were it but the miles
> That summed up all our severance,
>   There might be room for smiles.
>
> But that thwart thing betwixt us twain,
>   Which nothing cleaves or clears,
> Is more than distance, Dear, or rain,
>   And longer than the years!

This is a poem of emotional estrangement. It's also very much a love poem. Only after the first stanza do we get any indication that it's not *purely* a love poem, and that initial sense of longing, of a remediable loneliness, of *love,* haunts the rest of the poem. Even without the conflictedness, the "Dear" in the penultimate line would be technically brilliant. As it is, that pause for the endearment, and the subtle change from its first usage six lines earlier, is wrenching.

There are poems that make you think about life, and there are poems (not many) that make you immediately feel your own. The former, like the Frost poems, lead you deeper into the particular experiences they are: you contemplate *them.* The latter seem to cast you back into experience itself, and what you're left contemplating is not so much the poem, which seems transparent, but some part of your own life it has recalled, which is anything but. This, I think, is why the complexity of one's reaction in such cases can seem incommensurable with the simplicity of the poem that has caused it. The particular poems of Hardy that accomplish this effect will vary from reader to reader, of course, but it's hard for me to imagine that one could read all the way through him without it ever happening.

5

He is wise. That sounds like a swooning platitude (Hardy causes his enthusiasts to embarrass themselves just as often as he does his detractors), until you consider how rarely one wants to apply that word to poets, even great poets. Eliot was encompassing, magisterial, ferociously intelligent, but *wise?* The word won't stick. Nor does it seem appropriate for the glacial aestheticism of Stevens, for all those inscrutable moons and masques of Yeats. Some poets aim at wisdom, or at Wisdom, and invariably end up in some version of self-parody: Frost with his yuk-yuk rusticism, Wordsworth grown pompous and "moral."

What makes poetry wise is similar to what makes a person wise, though wisdom in one in no way guarantees its presence in the other. It has to do with a broad, humane moral intelligence of which one is relentlessly suspicious, with an ability to perceive the world outside of the self and yet to *have* a coherent self. It has to do with an awareness of the dangers of sophistication as well as of an ignorant naïveté. Confucius: "When nature exceeds culture, we have the rustic. When culture exceeds nature, we have the pedant. Only when nature and culture are balanced, do we have the *chun-tzu*." John Clare is the rustic, Ezra Pound the pedant. Hardy, though he would no doubt have sniggered at the word (and perhaps because of that), is the *chun-tzu*.

Balance. Anyone who goes into poetry in a major way becomes aware of how strong the pull toward the inhuman can be. I don't mean toward the fantastic or surreal, but toward a certain kind of perfected experience, some dream of permanence, of a form into which all of this too various and fallible life can perish. "Oh that I once past changing were," George Herbert writes. A good deal of great poetry, from Keats to Eliot to Hart Crane to Dylan Thomas, has arisen out of the tension between submitting to and resisting this impulse. This is the point at which poets begin talking about escaping from personality, about being the least poetical things in existence, about some "line you must not cross." A good deal of bad poetry, or at least half-realized poetry, has been written by poets who submitted too thoroughly to that impulse, who, like Swinburne, like Crane and like Thomas, strayed beyond the farthest margins of consciousness, only to have their experiences break apart upon their reentry into language.

Then there are a few poets in whose work one never feels this impulse, whose poems tease us not out of thought but into it, not toward eternity but time. Bishop and Williams are two such writers. Hardy, who in one poem describes himself as a "time-torn man," is another. They may not be content with this world, but they are reconciled to it. Their work is more concerned with, to borrow a distinction from Iris Murdoch, the "busy contingent" rather than the "still icon." It may be about suffering, but the poems themselves never become emblems of it, never quite harden into objects of contemplation. And if such poets are given some glimpse of experience beyond the physical, it is likely to be in something like shadowed leaves on a stone, which, the very plainness of the language seems to imply, are probably just shadowed leaves on a stone.

Is Hardy, then, great? Pound thought so, for reasons along the lines I have noted, that he caused one's own life to become vividly present in one's consciousness. "Have you a better test of true poetry?" Pound asked. The question seems to me less invulnerably rhetorical than he intended. Much of the greatest art does not recall your own life to you. You don't "relate" to Lear. Indeed, I think there is often something impersonal and austere, some cold and uncompanionable remoteness, to the greatest art. Though Mezey describes Hardy's poems as "an eye without an I," my own feeling is that the self in the poems, the I, is never really, to use Joyce's phrase, "refined out of existence." I have a profound sense of the time-torn man behind these poems, of a single life lived (unlike, say, Eliot, whose work is one long passionate lament for a life not quite lived). Hardy's poems are still mired in life, you might say, still warm with it. They are probably as good as poetry gets while remaining fully human.

2000

A New Mode of Damnation?: Hart Crane

"I am only interested in adding what seems to me something really new to what has been written," Hart Crane, trying to explain his meager production, wrote in a letter in 1921. He was twenty-two years old. Already behind him were three of his anthology pieces – "My Grandmother's Love Letters," "Black Tambourine," and "Chaplinesque" – the last two of which exhibit the formal finish and distinctive idiom characteristic of his mature style. Already stirring and warring within him were the contradictions that his poetry was one long attempt to, if not reconcile, at least contain: formal order versus undiscriminated experience; affirmation and enthusiasm versus skepticism and despair; high-styled devotional intensity versus earthbound affections and ordinary life. If the age demanded an image of its accelerated grimace, it got one in Hart Crane, though in too over-specialized a form for the age to recognize, as he well knew. "I admit to a slight leaning toward the esoteric," Crane continued in that same letter, "and am perhaps not to be taken seriously."

Crane was taken seriously, though, both by himself and by the enclosed community that was the literary culture in general. He was born into a time of truly great criticism. That his work attracted the attention of some of the greatest of those critics – Allen Tate, Waldo Frank, R.P. Blackmur, and Yvor Winters, notably – meant that it enjoyed the sort of serious readership that work of such forbidding difficulties usually precludes. Crane's confidence was certainly bolstered by this attention. On the other hand, that those critics were so ruthlessly and publicly honest with each other (the situation is simply impossible to imagine today) meant that those difficulties, and the fundamental weaknesses in Crane's poetry they revealed, were pointed out with unsparing proficiency.

I take my title from Winters's book *Primitivism and Decadence,* which pounds the pulpit of reason to make its case against the sort of late-Romantic excess that Winters thought Crane exemplified. The two men met only once, but they carried on an extensive correspondence during the period of Crane's most intense creativity. Though he was primarily a poet then, from the beginning of the relationship Winters was a sort of self-appointed Apollonian antidote to Crane's Dionysian disorder. Winters was the budding young poet-critic, awesomely learned, respectably married, disciplined, already leaning toward, if not quite stiffened into, the iconoclastic critical opinions for which he is now best known. Crane was uneducated (in a formal sense) but literary to the bone, openly homosexual, itinerant, frequently jobless, broke, drunk. Each man, I think, recognized something of himself, or some possible version of himself, in the other. Crane's poetry is as clenched as his life was chaotic. Winters's prose has the slightly crazed feel of any carefully crafted sanity. Poetry was where the two men met, the overwhelming focus of the relationship, and their responses to each other constitute some of their clearest and most emphatic declarations about the art.

The relationship ended abruptly and acrimoniously a couple of years before Crane's suicide in 1932, when Winters wrote an unfavorable review of *The Bridge* in *Poetry.* Although Crane thought he'd been sandbagged and responded with calm ferocity in a final, brilliant letter refuting Winters's arguments and denouncing his methods ("the cog-walk gestures of a beetle in a sandpit"), it seems probable that Winters, in a rather spectacularly heavy-handed way, meant to do Crane some good. Winters thought *The Bridge* was not simply a failure but a potentially lethal one, its shortcomings symptomatic of a poetry – and, by extension, a mind – that was submitting to experience rather than mastering it. He would eventually come to believe that such poetry required a kind of "possession" of the artist by experience and feeling, which he likened to demonic possession. As he believed that to respond to such poetry required a similar submission from the reader, a dangerous relaxation of rational intelligence, he felt that Crane, though a truly great talent, could only be useful to subsequent poets and readers as a negative example. There was greatness and

nobility about Crane, but he was in the end a "saint of the wrong re-
ligion." One went to him, Winters said, to learn to recognize and
avoid "a new mode of damnation."

One doesn't need to make the theological leap to understand
something of what Winters was talking about. There is a quality of
formal immediacy or expressiveness to Crane's poems. When I first
read him, though I understood the poems only intermittently, I knew
that I had come upon something I needed, and it's still this initial,
half-baffling formal energy that compels my deepest response to
Crane. By "immediacy" I don't mean to suggest immediacy of mean-
ing so much as immediacy of feeling. There is a fierce defensiveness
to most of Crane's poetry; the formal finish, which is always durable
and occasionally impenetrable, exists more as a means of withstand-
ing experience than enacting or understanding it. Often the better
part of what you feel in a Crane poem is what you don't feel, the
chaotic life and experience that haven't come within its control. Life
and experience aren't excluded from the poems, but they often exist
at the edges or in the interstices of a poem, so that the feeling is in-
tense but unspecific, or it is specific in a way that is to some extent
personal, having its origins as much in a reader's state of mind as in
the literal meaning of the words.

In speaking of Crane's poems in this way, I open myself up to a
charge that Thomas Parkinson makes in his good book *Hart Crane
and Yvor Winters: Their Literary Correspondence.* Parkinson points
out that a common tendency among critics has been to think of
Crane's poems not as denotative arrangements of language subject to
specific interpretations but as abstract formal spaces within which
feeling – usually the critics' own feeling – occurs. The most obvious
analogy is with music, though Crane's poems are not "musical" in
quite the same way as are the poems of, say, Eliot. In Eliot's most lyri-
cal passages – the last section of *Ash-Wednesday,* for example, or in
parts of "Little Gidding" – the movement is outward: you feel the lan-
guage straining to get beyond language, seeking to express some-
thing beyond itself. Crane's poems, by contrast, seem screwed into
themselves; there is a locked, intractable quality to them. What
movement there is – and I don't feel much – occurs internally. Walter

Pater's definition of architecture as "frozen music," which Crane himself refers to once in his letters, comes to mind. With Crane one feels less the releasing element of sound than the focusing pressure of shape, less the dynamic movement of meaning away from the words of the poem than the concentration of meaning into some compressed and static, and therefore bearable, form.

Crane certainly intended this response to his poems, this sort of indefinite intensity, at least to some degree. In a note he wrote to accompany "For the Marriage of Faustus and Helen" he speaks of his ambition to distill the entire experience of a poem into something like a "single, new word, never before spoken and impossible to actually enunciate, but self-evident as an active principle in the reader's consciousness henceforward." In a letter to Harriet Monroe defending his poem "At Melville's Tomb," he writes of a "logic of metaphor" contained within the poem ("Your poem reeks with brains," is her succinct – and not *wholly* unwarranted – response), and in another to Sherwood Anderson he holds up John Donne's "The Expiration" as an exemplary example of "interior form," which he defines as "a form that is so thorough and intense as to dye the words themselves with a peculiarity of meaning, slightly different maybe from the ordinary definition of them separate from the poem." All of the explanations contain some idea of enclosure or compression, of the poem as a self-sufficient, self-justifying space. There is some way in which a reader must get inside of Crane's poems, which often present what seem to be deliberate strategies of resistance.

It is a poetry at once recognizably Modernist and oddly unplaceable. The inferior work, and especially the early work, of many poets often feels like period pieces. Much of Crane feels like period pieces from a period that never existed. You can't trace his influence into recent poetry in the direct way that you can see Ashbery emerging out of Stevens, Duncan out of Pound, or any number of poets out of Williams. Crane pushed two of the chief characteristics of Modernism – the use of, or perhaps just the acceptance of, indeterminate context and the emphasis upon establishing an absolutely individuated idiom – about as far as they could go. It isn't simply that entire poems or passages are self-contained and obscure, but often within individual poems a single line will have a sudden shining autonomy to it, a classical feel and clarity, but one that, because it occurs without definite context or tone, is disorienting. The effect is of an utterance that is at once summative and strangely vacant, as in the last line of "Praise for an Urn":

> Scatter these well-meant idioms
> Into the smoky spring that fills
> The suburbs, where they will be lost.
> They are no trophies of the sun.

His idiom, too, has an extravagant, willful singularity about it. A familiar – and useful – cliché of poetry is that it turns the personal feeling or experience of the poet into a form that is not merely personal, a form that can be experienced by a stranger. Keats's statement that poetry ought to strike a reader like a "fine remembrance" is a more sophisticated version of this cliché, because contained within Keats's statement is the suggestion of something like a collective unconscious: poetry becomes a means of both forging and remembering the links between us, of discovering and securing our common humanity. Keats's emphasis, though, is on subject matter, on *what* is being said or perceived. This changes somewhat with some of the Modernists, and particularly with Crane, who at least partially or occasionally transferred that historical emphasis upon subject matter to idiom. It is as if the ambition became to create a *voice* that was absolutely individuated and yet accessible, representative. Crane was elated at the first positive responses to his poems because it meant to him that his "own natural idiom," which he then defined as "the very blood and bone" of himself, was not the prison he sometimes feared it to be. For if André Malraux was right when he said that "a poet is haunted by a voice with which words must be harmonized," it sometimes seems as if Crane was haunted by a voice with which *no* words could ever quite be harmonized. Words are what the poems are made of, of course, but the completed poems retain something of that original impulse, that quality of hauntedness and insufficiency.

I'm not suggesting that Crane's poetry is an exercise in something called "pure form," or that its meaning is expressed wholly or even primarily by means of abstract patterns of sound and structure. Poetry is neither art nor music, finally. Its capacity for conveying meaning abstractly is limited, and a poetry that has simply given up trying to convey meaning, though it may offer certain diversions, is no way to spend a life, either as a reader or a writer. Content matters, as Crane well knew. There are passages clearly intelligible in the most literal sense, and even the most difficult of the poems will usually disclose themselves if a reader finds his or her way into that interior logic.

What is notable, though, is that often when the poems do become clear, it is to express a desire for some sort of stillness or permanence. This is one of the most conspicuous examples of the way in which Crane's poems embody severe contradictions. He *seems* to be a kind of twentieth-century Whitman, celebrating change, expansiveness, inclusiveness; but often what you feel in the poems is either the locked quality I have noted, that severe form and finish, or this longing for an idealized, frequently lifeless stasis. Thus in "The River," which is perhaps the single best section of *The Bridge,* the opening lines replicating the passing of images from a seat on a train (which are wonderful, and almost anomalous in Crane) give way to the much more rigidly controlled iambic pentameter quatrains with which he was more comfortable. And though the poem apparently exalts (and romanticizes) the life of hoboes, their constantly changing experience and the sensory freshness that comes with that, its most powerful lines either contain an image of and longing for permanence:

> Each seemed a child, like me, on a loose perch,
> Holding to childhood like some termless play

– or situate the speaker at some fixed point longing for places into which he can never quite move, for emotional experiences which he can never quite have:

> Trains sounding the long blizzards out – I heard
> Wail into distances I knew were hers.

For all of his enthusiasm and appetitive energy, Crane never really stopped thinking of poetry as a place of refuge. The letters written during the last year or so of his life, when he had for the most part

given up poetry for the role of professional *poète maudit,* become no-
tably less interesting, but there is a poignancy in the very fact of their
decline. Perhaps there is a point in every poet's life when one is faced
with either radically enlarging the range of life that is made available
to the work, and thus relinquishing to some extent the hold one has
on one's work, the hold one has on one's life, or withdrawing into
technical virtuosity or silence. In the relatively late poem "Island
Quarry" one can see Crane at this point, frozen by the stark parting
of the roads in front of him, yet answering to the dilemma with clar-
ity and honesty:

> – It is at times as though the eyes burned hard and glad
> And did not take the goat path quivering to the right,
> Wide of the mountain – thence to tears and sleep –
> But went on into marble that does not weep.

Whether one believes that in the end poetry failed Crane or he
failed poetry depends, I suppose, upon one's perspective. Winters
felt that it was very definitely the latter, or that poetry failed Crane
only because Crane had misunderstood the nature of the relationship
between poetry and life. It is essential, Winters felt, that readers of
Crane understand this primary failure: "Crane... possessed... the gift
of style without the gift of thought... [he offers] us limited regions in
which [he] may actually aid us to grow, to come to life." Implicit
within this statement is a definition of great poetry – that which
helps us "come to life" – as well as of a great poet, which for Winters
entailed the complete mastery of talent and experience. The extent
to which one accepts these definitions will determine where one lo-
cates Crane among the century's major poets.

As for myself, I think that Winters was at least partially right. He
underestimated the extent to which Crane's poems might help one
"come to life," because to respond intensely but indefinitely to the
world is still to respond. It's quite possible to be jolted in the general
direction of life by an art that doesn't itself know the precise way. As
Pound wrote, "a work of art, any serious work, vivifies a man's total
perception of relations." I think my original response to Crane was
just such a positive charge, a vivification if not yet a clarification.

At the same time, Winters identified the danger of making one's poetry into merely a kind of conductor for a strong current called experience. If he went too far in the other direction, insisting upon the poem as a hard-wired network of technique wherein experience was governed, his conservatism was nevertheless that of a man who knew exactly what was at stake. It won't do to romanticize what happened to Crane, to use his suicide to somehow authenticate the intensity of the poems, but one must also recognize, as Winters did, that the neurosis and accelerating anxiety that led Crane to kill himself have something to do with the very particular charge that runs through his art.

Winters's assumption, though, is that all poets have a choice in the matter, that Crane could have willed his way into a steadier sort of writing and life and still written great poetry, and was not, as it sometimes seems, defenseless against his own gift. Coleridge once made a very perceptive comment about Shelley which is equally applicable to Crane: "Shelley was a man of great power as a poet, and could he only have had some notion of order, could you only have given him some place whereon to stand, and look down upon his mind, he would have succeeded." Both poets did succeed, of course, though perhaps not in the greater terms that Coleridge is implying. Age is the most obvious limitation for Shelley, though I don't think it's an adequate one for Crane. Crane's letters reveal an artistic maturity that few poets of any age attain. If he sometimes seems to have seen the work ahead of him with a paralyzing clarity – his letters detailing his plans for both "Faustus and Helen" and *The Bridge* are simultaneously impressive and deadening – and if he did to some extent confuse meaningful experience with mere turbulence, as if one weren't truly in one's life unless one were being overwhelmed by it, he nevertheless had the kind of scope, prehensile ambition, and highly developed sense of form and structure that characterize great poets.

But there is some point at which, if one is to both write great poetry as well as survive it, this hard distinction between form and experience, or between poetry and the world, must be eased or reconciled. As unlike as Winters and Crane seem as poets, they are similar in that each used poetry to either control or withstand the world and experience. In Winters's poems – the later ones, I mean, after he had seen the dangers and made his choice – there is a mismatch between the formal control and the experience allowed into the poem. Over and over you feel Poetry pinning Experience to the mat while God counts to three. Crane is the better poet because you sense in his poems the enormous pressure of what's been left out, but there is still a sharp discrepancy – and even antagonism – between form and experience. Sometimes form gets the upper hand in the way I've pointed out: the poem doesn't express feeling; it's haunted by it. In other poems experience overwhelms the form, which becomes distorted, inadequate, fragmented, though you can feel as a sort of elegiac overtone the wholeness it had in mind. *The Bridge* has something of this quality, though the quintessential example of this sort of poetry is *The Waste Land,* which, not at all coincidentally, was written by the one contemporary poet whom Crane considered a serious rival.

There is, I think, another, greater sort of poetry. It occurs when the forms of one's mind somehow become, during the moment of the poem, coextensive with the forms of the world, when the words with which Malraux's haunting interior voice is harmonized are so adequate and inevitable that the voice is both appeased and harnessed, utterly contained and yet cast beyond itself, as if it had its origins in currents of life greater than the poet's own. One of the best expressions of this that I know of comes in Book 1 of *The Prelude,* when Wordsworth has just recounted his experience of stealing a boat one night and being reproached by all of nature:

> but after I had seen
> That spectacle, for many days, my brain
> Worked with a dim and undetermined sense
> Of unknown modes of being; o'er my thoughts
> There hung a darkness, call it solitude
> Or blank desertion. No familiar shapes
> Remained, no pleasant images of trees,
> Of sea or sky, no colours of green fields;
> But huge and mighty forms, that do not live
> Like living men, moved slowly through the mind
> By day, and were a trouble to my dreams.

The greatest poetry has something of these huge and mighty forms in it. In *The Prelude* the measured motion of the verse, the steady currents opening into moments of suspended attentiveness, have about them something of these forms that this passage describes. The form of the poem isn't imitative but participatory. Such art requires the sort of absolute attention to technique that you find in Crane, but, because it depends upon some reconciliation between one's interior voice and the world, some fine remembrance and invention of a time when those two things didn't seem so separate, it also involves elements of balance, order, clarity, closure, unity of design. Will has something to do with achieving these things, though only insofar as it enables a poet to wait, to resist either forcibly imposing order on experience, or allowing one's forms to warp under the pressure. The characteristics I have listed are not ones we normally associate with high Modernism, though I do think that Eliot, in both *Ash-Wednesday* and *Four Quartets,* achieved this greatest, most sustaining sort of poetry.

Crane was less successful than Eliot, in his life as well as in his art. His leap into the sea in 1932 is almost too conveniently and conclusively symbolic. The poet who in *The Bridge* had written of water as the place where the "word" was tested seems to have tried to put his poetry to some ultimate test. The poet who in "Voyages" had equated the immensity of the sea with the immensity of his own love, seen clearly the self-annihilating appeal and danger of each, seems to have tried to pay the cost of some ultimate consummation. *Damnation* is not quite the right word, and yet it's not quite the wrong one, either. If living gods embarrass us, we nonetheless retain some idea of fatedness, in the sense that character is fate; and even the most earthbound poets I know cling to some ghost of the notion that poetry is a means to other orders of existence. For those poets who cling to this notion more fiercely, whose gods are gone but not the gravitational force they exerted, the elation of perception is inevitably accompanied by the pain of separation. Crane was such a poet, his gift to some extent an affliction. Thus the word *damnation* has a certain secular accuracy.

Certainly Crane knew his shortcomings as well as anyone. Though one of his earliest letters mentioning *The Bridge* speaks of it hopefully as "a mystical synthesis of America," in one of his last, most forceful letters to Winters he admits that "those richer syntheses of

consciousness which we both agree as classing as supreme" are be-
yond him. To a limited extent I agree with Winters regarding Crane's
limitations, but I still very much admire and want to affirm the sort of
poetry that he did write. I believe there is always a place in poetry for
the stylistic extravagance of a Crane, for the doomed ambition that
seeks "to lend a myth to God." His failures – the spectacular over-
writing, the weak-kneed rhapsodies and sentimental mysticism – are
too intimately bound up with what is great in his work to distinguish
neatly between them. But his unremitting intensity, his fusion of
forms of the past with the life of his own time, and his refusal to evade
his severe conflictedness about issues of form and style, life and art:
these seem to me exemplary. "There is constantly an inward struggle,"
as Crane wrote in a late letter, which was not to Winters but seems to
anticipate his petrified rightness, "but the time to worry is when there
is no inward debate, and consequently there is smooth sliding to
the devil."

1997

Pure Honey, Pure Gall:
Edna St. Vincent Millay*

I

She was born in 1892 in Rockland, Maine, to an affable, hapless man and a virago who soon scuttled him. Childhood was a full library and an empty larder; from the former she learned to think of her life as a legend, from the latter the will to make it so. At five she read the word *paramour* and fell into a swoon. At twelve she walked calmly out of school when her principal, driven finally mad by this wisp of a girl who insisted on being called "Vincent," hurled a book at her and shouted that she'd run the school long enough. She was named for a hospital, not a saint.

"Renascence" made her famous, a long poem written when she was nineteen. It was a different time, when not only individual books of poetry were reviewed in daily papers but sometimes individual poems; when some of the best critical minds of the country could become not simply involved but apoplectic over the announcement of a national poetry contest. She didn't win the contest in question, as it happened, but the clamor that ensued brought her more attention than if she had. The age had found a voice for its immediate, sensual energies, and Millay, after a flurry of letters and a few judiciously included photographs, was launched.

In some fundamental sense she never looked back. When her fame

The Selected Poetry of Edna St. Vincent Millay. Edited by Nancy Milford. Modern Library, 2002.

Savage Beauty, by Nancy Milford. Random House, 2001.

What Lips My Lips Have Kissed: The Loves and Love Poems of Edna St. Vincent Millay, by Daniel Mark Epstein. Henry Holt, 2001.

threatened to estrange her from her mother and sisters, she simply
lifted them out of their existence into hers. When any infatuation
threatened to define her, she slipped free, always with her love for the
idea of experience intact. *Pure, virginal, childlike* – these are the
words her contemporaries used over and over for her, even as she cut
a wide and very public swath through libertine Greenwich Village.
She learned what her country was learning, to wield an innocence
without compromising it, to remain as elusive to herself as she was to
the people who fell for her.

And fall for her they did. Poets and publishers, barkeeps and
diplomats, men and women and amalgamations thereof all fell under
Millay's spell, often at the same time. There is a decade and a half
during which any biographer who tries to keep track of Millay's af-
fairs begins to sound like the announcer at a horse race. Never,
though, is there any question about who was holding the reins:

> I, being born a woman and distressed
> By all the needs and notions of my kind,
> Am urged by your propinquity to find
> Your person fair, and feel a certain zest
> To bear your body's weight upon my breast:
> So subtly is the fume of life designed,
> To clarify the pulse and cloud the mind,
> And leave me once again undone, possessed.
> Think not for this, however, the poor treason
> Of my stout blood against my staggering brain,
> I shall remember you with love, or season
> My scorn with pity, – let me make it plain:
> I find this frenzy insufficient reason
> For conversation when we meet again.

Everyone loved it. Edmund Wilson, who would become the most
powerful critic of the time, and whose brief affair with Millay would
be the high point of his own hearty erotic life, believed Millay to be
great in the old-fashioned, heroic sense of that word. Thomas Hardy
thought America's two significant contributions to world culture
were recessional buildings (by which he meant skyscrapers, good old
Hardy) and the poetry of Edna St. Vincent Millay. Even the lovers

whose lives she mined for material remained mostly devoted to her, or at least in a sort of lobotomized awe.

Most of all, though, the public loved Millay. Her books sold thousands of copies within the first few weeks of printing. At the height of the Depression she was bringing in the contemporary equivalent of three hundred thousand dollars a year *from her poetry.* There were weekly national radio broadcasts. There were reading tours in which she didn't so much appear as emanate, all voice and velvet gown, at once ethereal and sensual, imperious and vulnerable. Partly her audience loved this presence, and partly they loved the poems. Mostly, though, they loved the way one revealed the other, each poem a pane through which to look at a life. Millay ignored the Modernists, who returned the favor, but in one way she leapt beyond them. She was confessional before there was such a thing.

In its essence, it wasn't a pose. The casual sexual rapacity, the constant travel and activity, the alcohol in volumes that would have bleared a bull elephant – this was costing her, physically as well as mentally, more than she admitted, either to others or to herself. But however lightly all those thousands of readers quoted her most famous epigram about the candle burning at both ends, Millay truly meant it. She lived in a kind of continuous present, and there is something both admirable and terrible in the extent to which she wedded her art to immediate experience; admirable because she sustained it, terrible because to do so required being blind to the wreckage.

In her thirties Millay married Eugen Jan Boissevain, partly, one suspects, out of pure fatigue. Not that Boissevain wasn't an interesting man. Dutch, monied, Hollywood handsome, he was a bon vivant with a taste for difficulty, the sort of man who would dive into the Seine in evening clothes to save a stranger from suicide, who deliberately addicted himself to morphine for the sole purpose of giving his love an example of quitting. Lacking in himself the singular passion that defines a life, Boissevain had the wherewithal to attach himself to people who did (his first wife was Inez Milholland, a leader of the women's suffrage movement), as well as the strength and complexity of character to remain utterly himself in their shadows. His devotion to Millay was absolute, and for the rest of his life he took care of all her needs to the extent that any one man could.

There's little left to tell – little, that is, that will make this person any more apparent. There was a Pulitzer Prize, which she was the first woman to win. There was George Dillon, the twenty-one-year-old golden boy of poetry with whom Millay absconded to Paris for a time. There was morphine, Millay's last great passion, which she went at with the same ravening intensity with which she'd gone at all the rest. These and a thousand other facts she will not inhabit now. Millay tumbled down the stairs one night in 1950, legendary to the last. "I have been ecstatic," she left behind in her journal, "but I have not been happy."

2

Millay's reputation as a poet was in decline by the time of her death. Her books have stayed in print, but it wouldn't be inaccurate to say that her poetry has had no discernable influence on twentieth-century poets. (Confessionalism would have happened without her.) The reasons for this are fairly obvious, and they have little to do with resentment of her fame, or her conservative sense of form, or even the morally admirable, aesthetically awful political poems she wrote at the end of her career. If Millay ascended in part for extraliterary reasons – her beauty, the way she seemed to embody a zeitgeist, her professional cunning – she sank for purely literary ones.

In everyday life the evolution of language is an incremental (or decremental), hardly definable sort of thing. In literature there are definite rifts. Any poetry that gets caught on the wrong side of a seismic shift is likely going to sink, at least for a while. The literary language Millay was born into may not have been completely rotten, but it was very ripe. Except for a couple of instances, she seems never to have investigated or needed a more flexible idiom. As late as 1930 she could begin a poem, "Gone in good sooth you are." She had a splendid ear for preexisting poetic cadence (Shakespeare's and Tennyson's, primarily), and almost none for the language in the air around her. It is as if a master chef locked herself in a house filled from floor to ceiling with half-blackened bananas. Nothing to do but make pudding – lots and lots of pudding.

It's taken a while, then, to discover what is worth saving in Millay, to hear the poetry amid all the pretty writing. She had a talent for astringent, memorable epigrams. At a time when most epigrams tended toward the gnomic or the coy – "April is the cruellest month," "Rationalists would wear sombreros," that sort of thing – Millay wrote many old-fashioned detachable maxims, if not exactly the sort you'd want to stitch on a sampler:

> Who builds her a house with love for timber
>   Builds her a house of foam.
> And I'd liefer be bride to a lad gone down
>   Than widow to one safe home.

("Keen")

> That which has quelled me, lives with me,
> Accomplice in catastrophe.

("Theme and Variations")

Indeed, Millay's entire imagination was in a sense epigrammatic, in that she was constantly reducing, in both the positive and negative senses of that word, complicated experience into beautiful truths. It's strange that a mind so devoted to the intensity of experience could be so confident of formulating it, that a person so devoted to the body could, as a poet, be so consistently abstract. This tension is the most salient feature of her style.

Millay is all ear, no eye. "I am waylaid by Beauty," she writes in one poem, and she invariably was. There is not a single instance in Millay of the sort of head-clearing metaphorical originality that R.P. Blackmur once said "added to the stock of available reality," and that marks certain periods more than others. (The Modernists and the Renaissance poets have it, for instance; the Victorians and the Augustans mostly don't.) Millay's method, like Tennyson's, is to employ a limited set of images in emblematic, usually anthropomorphic ways. She doesn't see the world, she sings it:

> Thus in the winter stands the lonely tree,
> Nor knows what birds have vanished one by one,
> Yet knows its boughs more silent than before:

> I cannot say what loves have come and gone,
> I only know that summer sang in me
> A little while, that in me sings no more.

It's worth noting how "recollected in tranquility" this is. For all the emphasis on impulse and immediacy in Millay, for all the poems in praise of Dionysus (she once enclosed twenty-seven new sonnets with a love letter), Millay's best poems, finally, occur not in the grasp of passion but in its wake. In love she is usually pure honey, in lust pure gall. Neither is quite real. The latter is better, though usually, as in the sonnet I quoted in the first part of this essay, it seems a somewhat glib inversion of sentimentality. Somewhere in between the two, though, when the ecstasy of an occasion subsides to the rigor of a form, or when the abstract language of her passion resolves into something that is not quite nostalgia, not quite indifference, and not quite love, Millay comes alive. She is even, at times, specific:

> She had forgotten how the August night
> Was level as a lake beneath the moon,
> In which she swam a little, losing sight
> Of shore; and how the boy, who was at noon
> Simple enough, not different from the rest,
> Wore now a pleasant mystery as he went,
> Which seemed to her an honest enough test
> Whether she loved him, and she was content.
> So loud, so loud the million crickets' choir...
> So sweet the night, so long-drawn-out and late...
> And if the man were not her spirit's mate,
> Why was her body sluggish with desire?
> Stark on the open field the moonlight fell,
> But the oak tree's shadow was deep and black and
>   secret as a well.

This is from "Sonnets from an Ungrafted Tree," a series of poems written from the voice of a woman who finds herself taking care of a dying man she's never truly loved, though it seems she's spent most of her life with him. There's more complexity of experience in these poems than anywhere else in Millay. Gone is the tendency to stamp an epigram, gone the obvious biographical context (one that I can find, at any rate: neither of her most recent biographers even mentions this sequence). The language is still merely gestural in places ("mystery," "sweet," "secret") and there's that familiar trope of losing sight of shore, but this, again, is simply how a Millay poem works. She takes the bluntest materials and occasionally makes some cut sharper than you could have expected, uses stock poetic images and ideas and somehow renders some truth of feeling as stark and unplumbable as this poem's closing image.

Randall Jarrell once famously defined a good poet as someone who, in a lifetime of standing out in thunderstorms, managed to get struck by lightning five or six times; double that and you were great (though, presumably, charred). The truth is, though, that Millay wrote some twenty poems well worth remembering but no single poem with sufficient complexity, or singularity of voice, or reach, or *something,* to be great. She loved her limitations too much to ever transcend them, but loved them with enough discipline to make them durable. She was overrated by her own time but is underrated now. Her work warrants a revival, though she could have used an editor with less of a sweet tooth. This new Modern Library edition ought to come with a shot of insulin.

3

Any poet lives two lives. There's the life of dates and places, ambitions and degeneracies, money and love and the lack thereof–the life, in short, that everyone leads. Inside of this or raveled up with this is the life of artistic consciousness, which, no matter how directly it may seem to derive from events and actions, bides its own time, and bears its own pains, and either acquires and sustains some existence independent of that biological life to which it's tied, or dies with it.

Biographers and critics rarely get at the latter. Walter Jackson Bate does it for Keats, Peter Makin for Bunting, Richard Poirier for Frost. What I am talking about is something more than merely focusing on the work in equal proportion to the life or scrupulously setting one in relation to the other. It involves some understanding that the engagement between a poet and the books she reads is something more intimate than "influence," the link between life and language not reducible to "subject matter." Most lasting art is made by people who believe with everything in them that art is for the sake of life, but who live otherwise; when a life is particularly furious or frivolous, though, when its dimensions seem greater than the work that emerges out of it, this can be a hard thing to keep in mind.

Nancy Milford doesn't even try. *Savage Beauty* is less about a poet than a phenomenon, less a work of criticism than enthusiasm, less a book than a magazine profile run amok. Maybe, just maybe, given the very particular way that Millay linked her poetry with her sexuality, there's some case to be made for including intimate physical descriptions. But to have her bounding into a room having just discovered her clitoris, to breathlessly imagine her lovers ("His lips were so soft, it was like kissing the flesh of a girl's nipple"), to give us even the color and sparseness of her pubic hair – this, finally, is not to take either your subject or your readers very seriously. To be sure, Milford loves Millay, has been completely consumed by her for the past thirty years. This, to put it gently, is the problem: "By now I had an inkling of the furies that drove the Millays, and I was wary of their enchantment. I didn't know then the strength of that pull on women, or that one cannot be wary enough."

Daniel Mark Epstein's book, *What Lips My Lips Have Kissed: The Loves and Love Poems of Edna St. Vincent Millay,* is more focused, more intelligent, and a bit more discreet, though there are certainly enough passages to suggest that the "pull" Milford felt isn't as gender-specific as she thought. (Here is Millay just before she charges George Dillon: "She gazed at the youth, her eyelids lowering slightly, her nostrils flared.") Epstein is interested exclusively in Millay the love poet, the poems written at the quick of the senses, and he's good at distinguishing her heat-of-the-moment style from poets whose primary force is loss, as well as describing the course she negotiated between physical inspiration and what he calls "emotional entropy." I wish this book were more informed and pressured by Epstein's own engagement with poetry, that he didn't slide so easily off the work into the life. But that, perhaps, is to ask for a more interior, less determinedly commercial book than he ever intended to write.

In any event, neither of these writers comes close to giving a sense of the consciousness that created Millay's poems. I can't think of many poets as difficult to get at in this regard. Millay confesses everything and reveals nothing. She wrote no critical prose that might cast the poems in a different light, and the poems themselves, like her persona, don't articulate an inner life so much as fend it off. It wouldn't be accurate to say that she developed a pose along the lines of late Frost, for Millay *was* this welter of impulse and instinct and averted consciousness from first to last. "To change your language you must change your life," Derek Walcott has written. Millay never changed either. Whatever stillness there is inside all this surface turbulence, whatever life inside the legend, she won't disclose them easily.

She *is* in there, though, somewhere. The fact is, it takes a good deal of intelligence to write a real poem, however deliberately obscured or erratically applied that intelligence may be in a life. It also requires some latent, coherent sense of self (even if a poem is, as Eliot thought, a means of escaping this), though that self as it is revealed outside the work may be too fragmented and too fugitive to find by way of conventional biography. Reading through these recent books on Millay, I had to return continually to the poems to remind myself of these things. There is a silence at the center of Millay, both the woman and the poet, one which at rare moments she seems to have been aware of, and which she's still waiting for someone to hear: "Nobody speaks to me. People fall in love with me, and annoy me and distress me and flatter me and excite me and – and all that sort of thing. But no one speaks to me. I sometimes think that no one can."

2001

Eight Takes

A.R. AMMONS *

It's beginning to seem as if A.R. Ammons can write books faster than you can read them. He has always been the sort of poet who seems to need to spin his wheels for a while before getting any traction. In his recent work the ruts have been getting notably deeper, but there are still moments when his writing rises out of habit into real poetry, reminding you again of how good this poet can be:

> if you can
> send no word silently healing, I
>
> mean if it is not proper or realistic
> to send word, actual lips saying
>
> these broken sounds, why, may we be
> allowed to suppose that we can work
>
> this stuff out the best we can and
> having felt out our sins to their
>
> deepest definitions, may we walk with
> you as along a line of trees, every
>
> now and then your clarity and warmth
> shattering across our shadowed way

However. This new poem, *Glare,* is three hundred pages long. Much of it, particularly after the first fifty pages or so, is simply a kind of disposable poetry, not without its casual pleasures – the cleverness, the nimble wordplay and associative progression of each section – but

---

* *Glare.* W.W. Norton, 1998.

neither requiring nor rewarding much sustained attention. It often reads like a first draft, which is astonishing in one sense, because few people could ever write this well at one go; depressing in another, because Ammons was once so much better than this. The poet who once wrote poems of such severe impersonality that they seemed stripped of human presence, yet charged with a very particular human consciousness, now finds no detail of his own life too dull to leave out. (Or too embarrassing: some of the more priapic passages in this book are beyond parody.) The poet who once actually wrote the *poems* that could never be mistaken for anyone else's is in *Glare* simply proclaiming his own iconoclasm:

> I reject European clutterment because
> we fought to put that ocean between
>
> us. I identify with no sort or kind

Besides being wrong as a description of his own poetry and mind (without the "clutterment" of British Romanticism, and in particular Wordsworth, Ammons's poetry wouldn't exist in the form that it does), this is affectation, the raised-by-the-wolves routine, Ammons making himself into an American caricature just as Frost eventually did. The results for the poetry – leaden language, disingenuous self-deflations, formal complacency, faux wisdom – are the same.

But Ammons insulates himself against most of these criticisms. *Glare* is so constantly self-deprecating, undercutting its own ideas and embracing its own first-thought-best-thought spontaneity, that it manages to mock in advance any critic conventional enough to question the quality of the *writing*. *Glare* is a sort of poetry in real time. At one point, after three pages of poetry, Ammons tells us that he's been writing for fifteen minutes. It's hard to know just how to take this, whether Ammons is being serious or coy, but it's not hard to determine that what you've been reading is superficial, more interesting as an idea of poetry than as an actual poem. He speaks of "finding the form of the process," by which he seems to mean something more than the way in which certain poets – Hopkins, say – manage to retain some sense of the process of composition within their finished forms. Ammons's ambition in *Glare* seems to be to make the finished form of the poem *indistinguishable* from the process of composition. But form, if it is to have any meaning at all, must involve some degree of culmination, both of the process of composition and of life. The achievement of form is painful precisely because of how unlike life it is, because of all the life that gets burned off as the poem comes into being. The achievement of form is restorative because of the life that gets focused and saved. I don't see any way around this, even for the most inclusive or "expansive" poems. *Glare* is meant to contain a kind of immediacy of experience and thought, but because the formal decisions are fixed at the outset there is a mechanical, prefabricated feel to much of it. It isn't the process of experience that one gets from the poem but processed experience, couplets clipped off by the adding-machine tape, plopping out like sausages.

WILLIAM MEREDITH [*]

There is an anecdote about William Meredith attending an opera with his friend Robert Lowell. Looking around at the packed opera house, Lowell is said to have remarked sorrowfully that there probably wasn't a person in the place who knew who the two poets were, to which Meredith replied, "That's as it should be, Cal." Apocryphal or not, that's not a bad place to begin with Meredith's poems, which avoid both Lowell's elephantine egotism and his mercurial energy, his neurosis and his greatness. Meredith aligns himself with those "who persist in being at home in the world," and the poems that issue out of such a right relation are unfailingly equable, unadorned, well-crafted, clear. The equanimous moral awareness of the poems is completely devoid of self-righteousness or sententiousness, but it depends for its existence upon a climate of thought and feeling that is relentlessly mild. And mildness, as Meredith himself points out, "can enervate as well as heat."

Meredith is well aware of his own limitations. Too aware, perhaps. An outright declaration of modesty is not always a guarantee of

Effort at Speech: New and Selected Poems. TriQuarterly Books, 1997.

eradicated ego. When Stephen Spender says, "I think continually of those who were truly great," he gives himself away with that "truly." I don't think Meredith's disclaimers contain this sort of duplicity, but there is, for me at least, a tediousness in being reminded so often of how cheerfully resigned he is to his own "minor" status. You wish there were a little disruptive anger in it, or an "Andrea del Sarto"-like ambivalence at not having been touched by the gods more intensely. Perhaps it's just a personal predilection (as opposed to everything else in this review, of course, which I'm channeling straight from the mind of God), but I'm put off by poetry that attempts to "ingratiate," as Meredith states quite explicitly is his goal.

It is for this reason that I prefer the poems in which Meredith isn't talking about poetry, or at least is going about it with a good deal of humor, as in *Hazard, the Painter.* At his best, Meredith is a poet of suburban decency (it's a crowded neighborhood, I know, but few have Meredith's technical skill): emotionally ingenuous, cautiously sage, intelligent, diffident, clever. The isolation and anxiety that fueled so much of the poetry of Lowell's generation are mostly foreign to Meredith, though his work doesn't seem an evasion of these feelings so much as a lucky anomaly. He is very much a poet of relationships, which are usually unsentimentally celebrated, as in the lovely "Accidents of Birth":

> but you, up from the clay yourself,
> as luck would have it, and inching
> over the same little segment of earth-
> ball, in the same little eon, to
> meet in a room, alive in our skins,
> and the whole galaxy gaping there
> and the centuries whining like gnats –
> you, to teach me to see it, to see
> it with you, and to offer somebody
> uncomprehending, impudent thanks.

This *Selected Poems* is full of such steady, sturdy work, the sort of poetry that presumes that someone other than poets and academics will be reading it. (A foolish presumption at the moment, perhaps, but maybe that's what we need more of.) If, as Joyce thought, great art is a process of refining one's self out of existence, perhaps there is a lesser but still valuable art that is a process of refining one's self *into* existence. When you finish this book by Meredith, you have a strong sense of the man who wrote it, of a life well lived. But if it's the quality of the life and character in the poems which accounts for a large part of their strength, it's the consistent craftsmanship which keeps them from being merely a diary of that life. In a time when so much of our poetry is either companionable but craftless, or highly wrought but affectless, Meredith's poetry charts a viable, pleasurable middle course.

JOHN PECK*

Read John Peck for an extended length of time and you can palpably feel the furrows on your face deepening. There is no ease in this poet. Knotted, crabbed, bookish, Peck's poems are always difficult, frequently incomprehensible. He is like a sculptor whose clay keeps hardening faster than he can finish what he has in mind for it. Some pieces he leaves in various states of incompletion; some he touches up with a jackhammer. The result is a lot of strange, misshapen things that seem the fruit of some peculiar solitude, a mind that is often too screwed into itself to make itself known. This sort of obscurity is not a virtue. It never is. So anyone coming to Peck for the first time – and he's still not at all well known – needs to know that persistence pays off with this poet, frequently in the form of splendid passages embedded in the wreckage of otherwise unreachable poems, and occasionally in the form of entire poems that are beautiful and clear (well, there is *some* ease in this poet).

Great poetry is first of all sound. If a poet has no sense of cadence and form as expressions of feeling, then the limits of his or her accomplishment are quite small. Such poets are limited to their perceptions, to *what* they have to say. (Rarely does a poet have such perceptual genius that it transcends a rudimentary formal sense: Marianne Moore.) The gift for making language itself into feeling rather than merely

* *M and Other Poems.* TriQuarterly Books, 1996.

feeling's vehicle is just that, a gift. Peck has it:

> *That was the first day. Now that it has passed, I see*
> *further into the weave and two wheatfields spreading,*
> *one packed in moonlight where a hunched sweating mower*
> *labors in silver, laying his ghost swathes down alone,*
> *faithful to something hidden, disturbingly faithful, for*
> *he fails to see the village gather in a long file and go*
> *into the church, and does not hear their faint chanting.*
> *Gazing along his acre I feel the grain in fingers*
> *rise and the long cells arch and lock, and feel the dead*
> *uneasy in the wakeful earth.*

This is from "M," the mysteriously titled long poem that constitutes slightly less than half of this book.* I understand slightly less than half of the poem, though the parts that I do understand, and the others that I don't quite understand but nevertheless feel ("yet I saw little / in a seeing way"), seem to me truly excellent. I think the poem is about the possibilities of commitment – to a god:

> Humankind
> seeks bond with the shattering hand within and above and
>   anteriorly beyond,
> trying to see, to save.

To another person:

> at the midpoint, the between, in the two of them
> extracted to the one they make elsewhere abundantly.

And to a polity, as in these lines about Gandhi:

> As if a hillside of humanity were turned over
> and all that spirit were poured through one point.

Underlying all of these, though, is the poem's constant questioning of perception itself, and what it is really *about* in the end is a deep commitment to, and faith in, language:

---

*Mr. Peck has written me since this review was published. "M" is simply the Roman numeral for one thousand, which is the number of lines in the poem. Not so mysterious after all.

The way
through primal tone leads to strange seeing.

Peck, like Eliot, understands the way in which the best poetry is first of all a physical thing, its sounds and rhythms experienced bodily. "M" is everywhere charged with this "strange seeing."

Peck is heavily indebted to the Modernists, particularly Eliot and Pound. From them he derives that physical formal sense (which is a gift, but it's seeing it elsewhere that teaches one to trust it), as well as his capacity to modulate between the lyrical and the discursive, the imagistic and the philosophical. But Peck is also open to Basil Bunting's charge against the Modernists that their poetry derived too much from books and not enough from life. (Bunting was including himself.) There is an incongruity to the fact that Peck argues in his work for an immediacy of life and experience ("a knowledge not from books, theory from bone / and darkness") and yet often employs a style that is essentially sealed off from the understanding of others, from the life and experience that aren't his own. I think Eliot was simply wrong when he asserted that the poetry of his own time had to be "difficult," and I think poets of our own time often make the same mistake. The real difficulty is in being clear. Some of the writers who figure prominently in Peck's poetry – Virgil, Dante, Frost, Tolstoy – illustrate the possibility of attaining a surface clarity without sacrificing depth or complexity. I wish Peck were more often clear; his obscurity is a serious weakness. But it's so rare to come across a poet of this quality, a poet who can really *write,* that the difficulties are worth working through. And by the time one gets to the end of "M," it does seem that something, in life as well as in poetry, has been "notched forward":

When I had gotten to the summit, I stood there long into
deepening haze, looking. There was less and less to see,
that part was over, but the whole of it I felt
piercing through, as a hawk whistled near my head, unbending,
    to sail down.

GJERTRUD SCHNACKENBERG *

Gjertrud Schnackenberg's best book is her first, *Portraits and Ele-gies,* though her best single poem is probably the much-anthologized "Supernatural Love," from her second book, *A Lamplit Answer,* which also contains the lovely poem "Snow Melting." If the implicit judgment here is harsh – the latter work doesn't measure up to the earlier – I would immediately temper it by saying that some of the earlier work seems to me a substantial and rare accomplishment. I think people will be reading some of these poems for a long time.

Schnackenberg's particular gift is for a kind of clear density, for making many different strands of experience part of a single, deceptively simple weave. Difficulty dissolves into the fluent lines and surprising rhymes of the finished poem. It's an Elizabeth Bishop sort of gift (and Schnackenberg at times writes every bit as well as Bishop), though much of the later work, with its literary and historical freight that feels like borrowed authority, is closer to Robert Lowell. Someone may one day explore Schnackenberg's ideas of and relation to authority – the way her father in "Supernatural Love" becomes a kind of god, or the extent to which so many poems are pinioned to famous (almost exclusively male) people or works of art. For now, I just want to say that my favorite poem of hers is "Darwin in 1881" (favorite and best aren't necessarily the same thing), a splendid character study of the naturalist in the last moments of his life:

> Now done with beetle jaws and beaks of gulls
> And bivalve hinges, now, utterly done,
> One miracle remains, and only one.
> An ocean swell of sickness rushes, pulls,
> He leans against the fence
> And lights a cigarette and deeply draws,
> Done with fixed laws,
> Done with experiments
> Within his greenhouse heaven where
> His offspring, Frank, for half the afternoon
> Played, like an awkward angel, his bassoon
> Into the humid air

Supernatural Love: Poems 1976–1992. Farrar, Straus and Giroux, 2000.
The Throne of Labdacus. Farrar, Straus and Giroux, 2000.

So he could tell
If sound would make a Venus's-flytrap close.
And, done for good with scientific prose,
That raging hell
Of tortured grammars writhing on their stakes...

In a way Schnackenberg's work enacts one of the chief difficulties of poets in our time: what will I write *about*? When a poet spoke for a community, that was more obvious, and even when those ties had been largely severed, there was still a subject in the loss. You feel Schnackenberg at this point in her first book, one section of which concerns itself with imagined (I guess they are imagined) inhabitants of a house she has come to live in, and you feel her drifting beyond this point in subsequent books, which are almost exclusively about other works of art or dead artists. The poems are consistently impressive, but there is something increasingly pinched and narrowed about them. There are certain words you can't imagine her using, certain experiences you can't imagine her treating. Raw colloquialisms, the rough textures of contemporary experience, the body's whole rude chaos of decay and need – these seem to have no place in her poems. By the time you get to her most recent book, *The Throne of Labdacus,* a numb book-length poem focused on the nameless slave who saved Oedipus (I don't know if I would have even figured this out without the book jacket information), you feel very strongly the force of these refusals, and not as warped formal energies in the way you feel this dynamic in, say, Hart Crane, but simply as refusals.

Each poet's deepest test is different, and what we call risk in one may be the mildest sort of security in another. A poet who finds it too easy to bleed onto her pages may need a sort of verse tourniquet; a poet who finds it too difficult may need a knife. There are poets who ought to be locked in libraries for years without pen or paper, and some need nothing so much as a decade at Disneyland. I have in the past inveighed so heavily against the cozily anecdotal, the broken-prose confessions, the whole contemporary mush of *me, me, me,* that I find it strange to come across a poet whose work I truly admire but which seems to me not personal enough, evasive in the very impeccability of its style. And yet I think it's no accident that "Supernatural Love" returns to the subject matter that enlivened Schnackenberg's first book, that "Snow Melting" seems to be about the very painful end of a relationship:

> Tonight this small room seems too huge to cross.
> And my life is that looming kind of place.

Both poems are like islands of genuine feeling in a sea of mere technique.

In the end, of course, it's the islands that will be remembered, and not the waters by which a poet made her way between them (or, in this case, from them). We forget how rarely a poet of substantial early achievement "develops," as well as how common it is to have simply a decade or so of real originality over the course of one's life. That we can't know this about ourselves is, I suppose, a kind of grace.

MAY SWENSON [*]

May Swenson isn't nearly the potpourri poet that the throbbing title, flowery cover, and cloying section headings ("Selves," "Visions," "Heavens," etc.) of this posthumous collection might make you think. Preciosity *is* a weakness of hers, it's true, a sort of daft-aunt verse in which at one point she's splashing about in "the tinkling streams / of innocence," at another generously offering her dildo to Emily Dickinson. (A dildo being, you degenerates, a flower.) Turn the page, though, and you can find a weirdly erotic dream of being devoured by snakes; or a poem about the problems of excretion in wild places:

> Little I knew
> a gale this night would wash, and then
> wind-wipe my rump over the rail.

("The Beauty of the Head")

Or a most unauntlike kind of piety:

> Oh Heavenly Father leave us the illusion
> of the flies who cluster the lake of urine

[*] *Nature.* Mariner, 2000.

gushed by the horse in the fetid prison
of his stall
and the bliss and energy that spins them
as they bathe and dip their sugar there

("Yes, the Mystery")

Susan Mitchell in her introduction compares Swenson to Hopkins,
and in terms of the textures of the poems – the impasted abundance,
the beautifully abraded language – as well as the focus on the physical
world, the comparison seems apt. Both are ceaselessly praised for the
quality of their eyes, though both are primarily aural rather than
visual poets. (Change a word here or there, and "The Windhover"
could be about a helicopter.) A poet of the eye – Bishop, Williams,
early Snyder – says, "This is the world." Such a poet is effaced in some
sense for the sake of the thing seen. (Sometimes *too* effaced: Bishop,
Williams, early Snyder.) By contrast, though she may be nowhere in
the poem, a poet whose predominant sense is sound says with every
line, "This is my vision of the world." You don't write a real poem
without imposing some sort of vision, but some visions are more
peremptory than others. "I showed who's god around here," Swen-
son writes at the end of one poem, revealing that "Heavenly Father"
I quoted above to be a piece of pure rhetoric. Almost always in a
Swenson poem you feel the presence of the *makar:*

Angular eels of light
scribble among the buttes and crinoline
escarpments. Thunder's organ tumbles
into the stairwell of the gorge.
When rain and mist divide their veil,
westering sun, a palette knife, shoves into the cut
colors thick and bright, enclabbering
every serrate slant and vertical;
hard edged, they jut forward,
behind, beside them purple groins and pits
in shadow. Shadow within shadow beneath a shawl
of shadow darkens, and we dare not blink
till light tweaks out.

("The North Rim")

It pleases me to read this, to feel a poet taking such patient plea-
sure in the textures of the language, but in truth I don't *see* very much
of this scene. Eels "scribble"? Rain and mist "divide their veil"? The
colors are merely "thick and bright"? At the end, though, in the mi-
nor music "blink" and "tweaks" make of the day's vanishing and the
need to see it, I feel that familiar pang of sense enlivened by sound.
I'm not so sure I've ever actually seen this moment either, but the
rightness of the words makes me feel that I must have, or now could.

A lot of people are going to find a lot of Swenson merely decora-
tive, and there's a truth to the accusation that I can't fully refute. It's
disconcertingly easy to drift in and out of much of her poetry because
there seems to be so little at stake, or because the real stakes of her ro-
mantic merging with nature are elided:

> Here, in an Eden of the mind,
> I would remain among my kind,
>   to lake and hill, to tree and beast married.

> ("A Lake Scene")

This is the sort of sentimental nature poetry that makes you want to
hug a logger. It would be overstating things to say that Swenson is ac-
tually at her best when she's not writing about nature, because there
is such an abundance of splendid, memorable physical description in
this book. I would say, though, that she's strongest when her descrip-
tive powers are put at the service of, and even at times flattened out
by, some ordinary, overt human emotion. This happens in poems
such as "View to the North" and "Staring at the Sea on the Day of the
Death of Another," in both of which an image opens or even thins
away (instead of accreting, her usual method) into a clear and empty
awareness of the poet's own death, and it happens in the moving
"Pigeon Woman," one of the rare poems to take another person as a
subject. You can't "love" nature, finally, though the end of "Pigeon
Woman," without swooning music or cluttered ornament, hints at
the massive loneliness that might drive someone to believe she can:

> Ruddy-footed
> on the lime-stained paving,

purling to meet her when she comes,
they are a lake of love. Retreating
from her hands as soon as empty,
they are the flints of love.

DEREK WALCOTT[*]

Reading Derek Walcott can be like listening to some grand cathedral
music that's all tangled up in its own echoes: it's lovely, most defi-
nitely, but it can sometimes be tough to tell one note from the next. I
know several people who find him too "gorgeous," who sense a hol-
lowness in the high rhetoric. To my mind, the criticism reveals less
about Walcott's work than it does about typical American taste in
contemporary poetry. At this particular cultural moment, we seem to
save our highest praises either for a poetry written in the personable,
conversational tones of our predominant style, or for a highly in-
flected "experimentalism" that cries out for critics to explain it. Billy
Collins or Jorie Graham. There's little feeling for any poetry that
seems at all "grand," whose style, with its internalized sense of for-
mal and historical tradition, calls conspicuous attention to itself as an
extension of that tradition, thereby seeming to speak with a voice
that is greater than the poet's own. It's too male, too pretentious, too
self-aggrandizing, just too damn much. This accounts for the recent
elevation of Bishop's poetry over Lowell's (how else to explain it?), as
well as for most people's preference for the later, lazier Lowell rather
than the Miltonic lines of *Lord Weary's Castle,* in which he was a
great poet. The comparison with Lowell is apt not only because Wal-
cott has been quite obviously influenced by Lowell (and, occasionally,
overwhelmed by him) but also because, at his best, Walcott writes at
that level. And though it surprises me to say it, because so few poets
sustain their creative capacities into old age, *The Bounty* is among
Walcott's best work.

There is little in the book that won't be familiar to readers of Wal-
cott's earlier poetry. There are the same island landscapes; the same
literary allusiveness; the same tidal lines that seem always almost too
much for the iambic measure that periodically reclaims them; the

The Bounty. Farrar, Straus and Giroux, 1997.

same density of texture that is occasionally decorative and occluding, but mostly wonderful:

> The sound rushing past the car windows, not the sea but cane,
> the night wind in your eyes like a woman's hair, the fresh
> fragrances, then the lights on the hills over Port of Spain,
> the nocturnal intimacies that stroke the flesh.
> Again, the night grows its velvet, the frogs croak
> behind fences, the dogs bark at ghosts, and certainties
> settle in the sky, the stars that are no longer questions.

This is, I guess, "Keatsian" in its sensuousness, but *The Bounty* isn't the book of a man with his nose pressed to the sweetshop window. Poets revive their work in various ways, but one of the most ruthlessly consistent truths about poetry is the part death so frequently plays in that revival. As teeming and "bountiful" as this book is, there is a persistent feeling of bareness and even destitution to it, a sense that all of the inventiveness and linguistic fertility, all of this grand sound, is being offered up in the face of voids more immense than any poem can fill. It is, quite literally, a book of endings, elegiac not only in its subject matter, but also, in a way, in its forms. You can feel these poems moving ineluctably toward their final lines, toward "closure," and it's notable how often the endings of the poems are the points at which the writing is best, as if those echoes were trailing off, everything coming clear. What prevents these endings from seeming forcibly imposed upon the poems, merely artful evasions of the actual death that is the poems' subject, is the sense they retain of their own inadequacy and limits, that utter absence underlying their crafted permanence. The effect is like that of a bell whose vibrations continue to trouble the air when the sound is gone, life at once completed and ramifying:

> Therefore, I foresee myself as blessedly invisible,
> anonymous and transparent as the wind, a leaf-light traveller
> between branches and stones, the clear, the unsayable
> voice that moves over the uncut grass and the yellow
> bell of an allamanda by the wall. All of this will soon
> be true, but without sorrow, the way stones allow
> everything to happen, the way the sea shines in the sun,
> silver and bountiful in the slow afternoon.

That's all that I have space to quote. There are passages that are equal to these, and a couple that are better than these, on most of the pages in this book. Yes, the descriptions sometimes sag under a heavy adjectival weight; yes, there is occasionally a note of self-importance in Walcott's frequent references to his own "gift"; and yes, it sometimes seems that every line has been burnished to the same unseeable sheen. But in its imaginative abundance; in the immediacy and intensity of its passions and its achievement of a voice that is so much more than merely personal; in the evidence it gives of a craft that is wholly mastered and yet still vulnerable to living experience; and in its music – above all in its abiding music – *The Bounty* seems to me a great book.

ELEANOR WILNER[*]

It often seems that some of the notions we've inherited from the Modernists – Eliot's auditory imagination, Williams's "No ideas but in things" – have in contemporary workshop culture devolved into the belief that poets ought not think when they write, that poetry is a place where you check your intelligence at the door. There have been various reactions against this tendency – Yvor Winters, J.V. Cunningham, much of Neo-Formalism – but they've usually been weakened by having simply ignored Modernism.

Eleanor Wilner's work is a more formidable alternative and advance. Thought occurs in her poems, and her poems have definite subjects, not infrequently the sort of big-game themes that wreck lesser writers: war, environmental degradation, justice, sexism. As with most poets, her chief strength, which is her ability to treat ideas in her poems without lapsing into propaganda or tendentiousness, is raveled up with her chief weakness. Many of her poems suffer from wordiness, the sense you get that too much of the poetry has been sacrificed to the initiating idea. Her *New and Selected* is at least a hundred pages too long, and you come away from many poems more impressed with the moral earnestness than the formal accomplishment, the quality

---

[*] *Reversing the Spell: New and Selected Poems.* Copper Canyon Press, 1998.

of the mind rather than the quality of the writing. But there are many poems in this book in which Wilner manages to negotiate her way between statement and music, in which *what* is being said registers on a consciousness that has been first awakened by the play of the language. The opening lines of "High Noon at Los Alamos" are as good an example as any:

> To turn a stone
> with its white squirming
> underneath, to pry the disc
> from the sun's eclipse – white heat
> coiling in the blinded eye: to these malign
> necessities we come
> from the dim time of dinosaurs
> who crawled like breathing lava
> from the earth's cracked crust, and swung
> their tiny heads above the lumbering tons
> of flesh, brains no bigger than a fist
> clenched to resist the white flash
> in the sky the day the sun-flares
> pared them down...

A poet who has a certain kind of mythical or allegorical impulse, whose imagination is most enlivened by the representative or transcendent image or experience, is in a difficult, occasionally quite painful position when she inhabits a time when there are no living myths, no definite truths to allegorize. Much of Wilner's work arises out of this tension. She seems to be best known as a poet of revisionist myth, and many of her poems are reworkings of familiar mythological stories. These are inventive enough, but like so many of the contemporary poems of this sort (and it does seem a trend), it often seems that the purpose of the poem is not to recover or reanimate some of the myth's mystery and meaning, but merely to expose some underlying assumption contained therein. The poems have a doggedness to them, which comes over in the prosaic writing. Much more compelling are those poems which, though they have an odd allegorical or parable-like feel to them, have no definite mythological reference (or their references are ones of which I'm ignorant, always a distinct possibility), or when some recognizable event is made strange and given an otherworldly aura because the exact source of the perception is withheld. Among these poems are "Landing," "The Messenger," "Being as I Was, How Could I Help..." (this one comes from an existing myth, but I get the same sense from it), "The Pillar," "Abstraction," "The Round Fish," and what is perhaps the single best poem in the book, "Bat Cave."

Wilner's work is somewhat difficult to quote from. She is not a poet of line-by-line astonishments (like, say, Plath), nor does she often have pieces that are notably better than the whole poems in which they occur (Walcott). With Wilner it's usually all or nothing. I have focused on these poems of unmoored mythical feeling because they seem to me her most original, though there are poems on a wide variety of subjects in this book, many of which are excellent in more conventional ways. What you will not find, however, is much change of style. Though there is an added depth and complexity to the thought of the more recent poems, tonally and formally they are not substantially different from the poems in Wilner's first book. She is a poet of somewhat limited stylistic range, though she can exercise considerable force within it. So much of contemporary poetry (and poets' prose, for that matter) seems to want too desperately to be liked, or to be a kind of public relations campaign for the poet's personality. Wilner's work avoids these charges absolutely. It is impersonal but passionate, its imaginative energy directed outward rather than inward, toward the world rather than the self. As troubling as some of the poems are (and these aren't poems that aim to ingratiate), it's a relief to come across work in which a moral intelligence is matched by aesthetic refinement, in which the craft of the poems is equal to their concerns. She deserves serious readers.

JAY WRIGHT*

I have little feeling for the whole of poets. Slogging all the way through Frost or Stevens can leave me grumpy and blunted toward both, and I'd rather eat a copy of *The Cantos* than read it again. And these are poets I love. Jay Wright is not a poet I love, though for years

* *Transfigurations.* Louisiana State University Press, 2000.

I've carried early lines of his in my head as a kind of totem against abstraction and interiority:

> An aching prodigal,
> who would make miracles
> to understand the simple given.

("Beginning Again")

I took on this review because of those lines (he's changed the first one, if I remember correctly); I wanted to come to terms with the kind of poet who could write them. After six hundred and nineteen pages of closely packed poetry, though, after ten dogged and increasingly despairing days of reading (I'm making about a penny an hour at this point), those lines and the rare others like them have begun to seem like the tiniest of lights in the densest of fogs:

> I order your allegiance, now:
> >to the signs' immaculate
> >appearance, a sortie
> >into divinity's turbulence;
> >to the irruption of desire's cocoon,
> >and its emerging;
> >to the spirit's turning and return
> >to the master's voice;
> >to the token of divine serenity;
> >to love's conception, birth
> >and revelation.
> I would have you grow in the signs' unfolding.
> I would discover you in the resurrection of sacred things.

("The Abstract of Knowledge / the First Test")

The absolute lack of specifics, the clichéd language, the vatic tone, the descent into palpable absurdity (*irruption of desire's cocoon?*) – I don't know what to say about this except that it's by no means the worst passage I could have chosen, and that it's fairly representative of the bulk of this book. It's an icemaker for the frozen sea inside of you.

Harold Bloom and others have praised Wright for his fusion of myths and sources. The ambition is more laudable than the accomplishment. Wright is at his best when he's most grounded, both to sound and to reality. In terms of intensity, if not consistency, he can be as beautiful as he can be bad:

> I will lay you a limbo
> of soft afternoons,
> with peacocked drinks
> and street dances...

> ("Beginning Again")

> I know this country by the myth of the rose,
> those linden tenors, lilting swords, unruly loves,
> larcenous runts who rise from the mist at the peak
> of an insurmountable passion.

> ("Twenty-Two Tremblings of the Postulant")

> one has to learn to live with winter,
> a wood cat with a devouring patience
> and a tempered ear for the softest harmonics of resignation.

> ("Nuestra Señora de la Paz")

I'm willing to work pretty hard at a poet who can write like this. Wright can be particularly difficult to get at, though, because he has written a considerable amount, and some of his best writing is buried in among his worst. Before you can enjoy the sweet relief of that middle quotation above, for example, which seems to me immediately compelling as a piece of rhythm and sound even if there's some delay of sense, you get this anvil of abstractions dropped on you:

> Flight's image defines
>   the conjunction of your besieged foot
> with the zodiac of a timeless god's
>   weightless grief.

How much better Wright would have been served by a judicious selection, one which carved away or at least pruned back some of the mystical bluster for the sake of the stranger, earthier music that, if it can shuck this book, will survive it. For my money, which alas is no money, such a selection would certainly include "Beginning Again,"

"Night Ride," "Tensions and Resolutions," "The Body," "Twenty-Two Tremblings of the Postulant," parts 2 and 4 of "Boleros," "Nuestra Señora de la Paz," and "The Healing Improvisation of Hair."

I can imagine someone objecting that the Wright I'm selecting is narrowed and more conventional, that I've made little effort to come to terms with the elaborate system of names, signs, and symbols that constitute his vision. They would be right. I did read every page of this book, but sometimes – when a poem would begin with, say, "Beauty is splendor veritatis, a radiance of truth" – the mule of my mind would balk, and I might have plowed a few furrows without it. Admittedly, I have little patience for poetry that is self-consciously vatic. (Shelley, though I have read him hard, occupies almost no space in my consciousness, and I love Robert Duncan in his minor moments, not his major ones.) This resistance may make me less than an ideal reader for Wright, at least in terms of his major projects. In his moments of fidelity to the simple given, though, when reality is the means rather than the price of transcendence, he does seem to me to justify the claims he makes in some of his last, best lines:

> I carried my life, like a stone,
> in a ragged pocket, but I
> had a true weaving song, a sly
> way with rhythm, a healing tone.

> ("The Healing Improvisation of Hair")

1997–2001

So Fierce and Sweet the Song:
George Mackay Brown

For contemporary American poets a poetry of place almost always means a poetry of missing places. Whether because of itinerancy or the pace of change, American poets don't inhabit the same places they inhabited as children, much less the places where their parents and grandparents were children. Some tend in memory a kind of ambered past which no longer has anything to do with an actual place (think of Philip Levine's Detroit); others actively seek out sites on which to feed their feelings of dislocation and dispossession (Richard Hugo's drive-by elegies are an example). And if the proliferation of poems written about distant familial history may be partly explained by current literary fashion, it's also a genuine expression of personal and cultural need, an attempt to inhabit some more permanent past, as if by rooting themselves in a place of their own making, American poets might grow more knowingly out of it.

The poetry of George Mackay Brown, who died in 1996 after having lived his entire life in the Orkney Islands off the coast of Scotland, illustrates some of the possibilities that are open to a poetry that is free of this anxiety. Vivid and direct, densely physical, crafted in the way of things built for use and not for show, his poems are saturated with actual life, though it sometimes happens to be the life of centuries ago. History was not a nightmare from which Brown was trying to awaken. It was a world so much like his own that to pay attention to the world around him was to pay attention to the past, to endure its ordeals was to receive its myths:

> Some December midnight
> Christ, lord, lie warm in our byre.
> Here are stars, an ox, poverty enough.

> ("A Child's Calendar")

Brown's poems are not anachronisms. Poets may take their sub-
jects from other centuries (and the localized historical continuity of
Brown's world made this especially fruitful), but their styles must, in
one way or another, come from their own. The poets that Brown read
and absorbed are implicit in every line he wrote. There are echoes of
Dylan Thomas ("my seapink innocence") and Hopkins ("I plucked
the loan of a curl of raw kale"); a lovely, early trace of Yeats:

> On every kind of merriment they frown.
> But I have known a gray-eyed sober boy
> Sail to the lobsters in a storm, and drown.
> Over his body dripping on the stones
> Those same old hags would weave into their moans
> An undersong of terrible holy joy.

> ("The Old Women")

Somewhere between this half-chanted tide of sound and an overly
self-conscious manipulation of it, somewhere in the realm of Basil
Bunting's "Baltic plainsong speech," Brown's best poems lie.

There is something hard and unbudgeable about these few poems
for which he will be remembered. They are craggy and impersonal,
sharply focused, unfussy, efficient. Even the poems that deal with vi-
olence or disorder have a reflective feel about them, feel *told*. But
there is often in their chiseled finish a volatility, a sense that instinct
and appetite, life outside the mind, have been momentarily charmed
into form. This is from "The Laird's Falcon":

> Steadfast himself, a lord of space,
>   He saw the red hulk of the sun
>   Strand in the west, and white stars run
> Their ordered cold chaotic race;

> Till from lucidities of ice
>   He settled on a storied fist,
>   A stone enchantment, and was lost
> In a dark hood and a sweet voice.

Within this material density, though, holding it together and
making it strong, are images of atomic precision, "sun pieces /

Between forge and wincing anvil." This clarity, along with Brown's tactic of employing a slightly archaic-sounding language of archetypal phrases and kennings, gives some of the poems a runic mysteriousness and power. Indeed, the best moments in Brown's poetry occur when the densities of syntax and action open into passages of head-clearing calm, a calm made all the more moving for the pain – linguistic and otherwise – that it took to get there:

> They are glad, all women, at a man's stillness –
> In the cradle lying, quiet as apples,
> In the trance after love,
> Even carried in from boarfang or whalequake:
> In wombfold again laid, her utter man.

Although these lines from *Fishermen with Ploughs* don't sound anything like Edwin Muir, the older Orkney poet who was responsible for getting Brown's first book published, the aim underlying them is not unlike that which informs much of Muir's poetry. *Fishermen with Ploughs* follows the life of "a tribe of fisher people" from the ninth century through the twentieth. Though some of the latter poems become a bit reactive and dogmatic (progress, for Brown, is a "Dragon"), it's in this book that Brown's project of enacting living experience within a larger pattern of history and myth is most evident and successful. It's a project he shared with, and probably to some extent learned from, Edwin Muir.

Muir's poems, though, with their classical antecedents, can sometimes be oddly inert, embalmed instead of enacted in mythic pattern. Brown's poetry never seems such a dogged project, never feels so *literary*. His characters – his tinkers and lairds, fishermen and old women – are at the edge of legend, either coming or going. Myths are quickened with a current of living experience, and the living characters are enlarged with myths they've not quite died into. Anyone who would sing something true of such people, Brown implies in "Old Fisherman with Guitar," must have participated intimately in the ordeals and delights of their life:

> So fierce and sweet the song on the plucked string,
> Know now for truth
> Those hands have cut from the net

> The strong
> Crab-eaten corpse of Jock washed from a boat
> One old winter, and gathered the mouth of Thora to his mouth.

One can't will oneself into this sort of authenticity, of course. When American poets, trying to create a past to inhabit, either refuse or forget their own separateness, do not weave into the solidest realities of that imagined world their knowledge of its loss, the result is soft nostalgia. In an odd way, though he is a different species of poet from Brown, it's a poet like James Schuyler, with his gossipy sponginess, his meandering anxieties and sudden precisions, who comes closest to writing an American poetry of living place. But Schuyler's urban world was not contained enough, either in terms of its apprehensible experience or its history, to enable the sort of historically coherent and culturally summative poetry of Brown. (Perhaps such a poetry simply can't be written of twentieth-century cities, which are not continuous, discrete places. *The Waste Land* is an expression of modern urban consciousness; its history is international, its physical details only incidentally of London.)

To be sure, such containment has its limitations. The tonal range of Brown's poetry is quite small. Not only is it inadequate for the longer, later poems, which are pretty consistently dull, there are whole realms of experience – humor, changefulness, sudden passion and personal vulnerability – that seem unavailable to Brown's poetry, to which it seems positively resistant. This doesn't matter, finally, in the face of the achievement, is probably a necessary component *of* the achievement. Robert Frost once said that all a poet could hope for was to write a couple of poems that future readers might find it difficult to get rid of. The surest way to do this is with sound, forms of such clear musical feeling that they are hard to forget. George Mackay Brown was crafting his own sturdy, plainsong version of such poems right up until the end of his life:

> We are folded all
> In a green fable
> And we fare
> From early

Plough-and-daffodil sun
Through a revel
Of wind-tossed oats and barley
Past sickle and flail
To harvest home,
The circles of bread and ale
At the long table.
It is told, the story –
We and earth and sun and corn are one.

1996

The Created and the Made:
Janet Lewis and the Uses of Convention*

W hat is good about Janet Lewis's poetry is not singular, what is
moving not personal, what will be lasting not much. Like her
husband, Yvor Winters, she wrote out of a Renaissance sensibility,
and there is something both admirable and merely contrived about
the aesthetic stances of both. The styles and beliefs of the Renais-
sance poets were fashioned out of and expressive of their own time,
whereas the forms and style of Lewis and Winters, right down to the
choices of subject matter, the archaisms, the ease with abstractions
and inversions, always have an air of entrenchment and implicit re-
nunciation about them. At their best, such poems remind one of what
does not age in art – clarity, music, definitive theme – as well as the
kind of force that a mind that is either somewhat mild (Lewis) or
somewhat crazed (Winters) can acquire in the armor of old forms. At
their worst, they can seem merely quaint.

Lewis is at her best when both content and form have sharp con-
tours to them, in poems that neither use the words *soft* or *sweet,* nor
feel that way. Notwithstanding the inversions, and excepting
"Country Burial" and "Snail Garden," she is at her best when she
rhymes, and can occasionally make a music that has the lightness and
grace of a Campion, as in her lovely "A Lullaby":

> Lullee, lullay,
> I could not love thee more
> If thou wast Christ the King.
> Now tell me, how did Mary know
> That in her womb should sleep and grow
> The Lord of everything?

* *Selected Poems of Janet Lewis.* Edited by R.L. Barth. Swallow Press, 2000.

Lullee, lullay,
An angel stood with her
Who said, "That which doth stir
Like summer in thy side
Shall save the world from sin.
Then stable, hall and inn
Shall cherish Christmas-tide."

Lullee, lullay,
And so it was that Day.
And did she love Him more
Because an angel came
To prophesy His name?
Ah no, not so,
She could not love Him more,
But loved Him just the same.
Lullee, lullee, lullay.

At other times she writes with something closer to the straightforward, expository precision of earlier, "Nativist" Renaissance writers – Turberville, perhaps, or a much calmer Ralegh. Here is "Days":

Swift and subtle
The flying shuttle
Crosses the web
And fills the loom,
Leaving for range
Of choice or change
No room, no room.

Neither poem leaves much room for criticism. It's worth pointing out the way the rhymes vary in their positions from stanza to stanza in "A Lullaby" (and the unconventional Christianity, in which this world is loved as much as the next, a human as much as a god) or the way one word is left without a rhyme in "Days," art enacting life, wherein there is always some mistake or failure that no amount of imagination or regret can change. That the word is *web* sharpens the effect, because it suggests that such a mistake or failure isn't isolated but woven into the whole of one's work, one's self. Swift and subtle.

And familiar. Perhaps there is a distinction, a technical or formal distinction the origins of which are psychological, to be drawn in poetry between the created and the made. "Only someone mistaken about himself," E.M. Cioran writes, "someone ignorant of the secret motives behind his actions, creates." This is an idea of art as a means of self-exploration, of form finding itself as a process coextensive with the mind's extending and exploring its own dimensions. (Go in fear of psychiatrists, is the vulgar corollary.) "Mind in its purest play is like some bat," Richard Wilbur writes,

> That beats about in caverns all alone,
> Contriving by a kind of senseless wit
> Not to conclude against a wall of stone.
> . . . .
> And has this simile a like perfection?
> The mind is like a bat. Precisely. Save
> That in the very happiest intellection
> A graceful error may correct the cave.

("Mind")

The made, by contrast, results when mind and form are fixed at the outset, and the conventions of art are used as a means of articulating content. The mind is like a bat, period. The created is a higher thing, beyond question, but it would require an impoverished sort of austerity to exclude the made from one's definition and experience of art. In the work of the best poets – Richard Wilbur, for example – there is always an admixture of the created and the made. And in the work of the best periods – the Renaissance, for example – there are always a large number of poets working quite comfortably, even anonymously, within viable conventions.

Viable conventions. Accepting the conventions is not the issue here. No art exists without conventions. The issue, for individual poets as well as for a literary culture, is to what extent those conventions are effective in defining the dimensions of contemporary experience. Are they too worn out for, or do they merely ignore, the farthest darknesses, as is the case with poets who use traditional forms in no discernably different way than they were used three hundred years ago? Are the conventions too ill-defined and individualized to be built upon, as is the case with late-twentieth-century free verse? In the case of the former, the dimensions of the cave, or one corner of it, are known too well. In the latter, there's some sharpness of perception and navigation that's lost. In either case, the guano piles up.

The created depends upon the made, and vice versa. Eliot once divided literary history into two distinct, alternating phases of experimentalism and consolidation. Without the former, an art atrophies; without the latter, its projects become more and more merely singular. In retrospect, one of the more surprising aspects of Modernism, a movement of great innovation and experimentation, is not simply how culturally and personally conservative were many of the poets engineering it, but the technical conservatism of some of its greatest poems. Eliot is anchored to iambics. "Sunday Morning" is masterfully executed blank verse. And what of the best poets of the time, Frost and Yeats? "But they weren't quite Modernists," I can hear someone objecting. Precisely.

The point here is not that poets need to write in traditional forms. It's hard for me to see how a serious poet would simply reject them out of hand (how brittle and dated some of those arguments seem from the seventies and eighties), but some of my favorite poets of the second half of the twentieth century – Schuyler, Ammons, Niedecker – seem to have found little need for them. The point I want to make is that the greatest innovations occur in direct proximity to the stage at which conventions become merely conventional, and *therefore,* in order for an art to advance, it is imperative that its conventions be clearly definable, that its gains, whatever they are, be consolidated. I would argue that, with free verse, ours have not.

We're a nation of creators. It isn't simply in art that experimentation, the idea of it, has been made into a sort of self-consuming tradition, or that individualism has been not simply valued above any sort of collective identity but somehow made into a collective identity. Change *is* our tradition, you might say, the individual our highest authority. Our chief strengths are our enormous energy, individual initiative, and flexibility, which we have developed at the expense of depth and durability. It's a formula that has proven to be wonderfully effective for an economy, less so for a culture.

Our poetry, however far it might seem to be from the general culture, has mirrored this tendency, especially since Modernism. One can see not simply in the writers whom we most exalt – think of John

Ashbery or Jorie Graham – but in the language that we use to talk about them, that we value the contingent over the fixed, process over product. It has become an almost automatic truism that a poem must "enact" experience, although the better part of any art has always been that which simply records or describes experience. With free verse, we've made instinct into a technique, rather than the quality that extends technique. We have exalted the created at the expense of the made, and in the process have created a climate that is inhospitable to minor poetry, which generally requires hard edges, sharp focus, and some degree of inherited technique. And in such a climate the projects of our would-be great poets – from *The Bridge* to *The Cantos,* on through Ashbery and Graham – have become full of airless, unconnected interiors, endless little culs-de-sac of consciousness into which fewer and fewer readers are willing to crawl.

Which brings me back to Janet Lewis, finally. Her work is less an antidote to or advancement of contemporary tendencies (because she simply ignores them) than a respite and reminder of the uses of given convention, the focusing power of anonymous craft. She is one of those poets – they were everywhere in the Renaissance – for whom poetry is less a means of understanding and apprehending life than a means of marking and commemorating it. It's not a feeling of what it means to be conscious that you'll get from these poems, but a description of what consciousness is, not a mind testing and extending the boundaries of reality and itself, but one comfortable with the given dimensions of both. For Lewis, the world is as real as the language that names it, Heaven a bankable radiance just beyond, and art a measured means of apprehending both:

> This is the many-mansioned, built in air,
> The timelessly returning, built of time;
> The only halls to which she may repair
> Who long since passed beyond the reach of time.
>
> Since she so loved this, ever I find her here
> When men have laid their personal strife aside
> That this impersonal grace may hold the air,
> Whereby my loss is, for a time, denied.

> ("Music at a Concert")

Temperament as much as talent determines the nature of ambition. There are sparks of an altogether different, more consuming fire in Larkin's lovely but narrow range, whereas even Lowell's fourteen-liners have a Promethean reach to them (but a pygmy's grasp). Poetry was not Janet Lewis's life. There's no obsessiveness, no neurosis, no formal fire into which you can feel a life being steadily fed. She *knew* herself. But out of that knowledge, through seven decades of writing until her death in 1998, she made five or six poems that, to this reader, seem durable enough to begin making their way now without her.

2001

Free of Our Humbug: Basil Bunting*

All through my twenties I read Basil Bunting with a kind of avid awe. The sounds and forms of his poems seemed to me at once remote and exemplary, too singular to learn from in any direct way, perhaps, and yet guiding examples nonetheless. I loved the aural imperative of the verse, which you hear before you understand, or which, in a sense, to hear *is* to understand. I loved the dense textures, the sculpted syllables, the way the lines seem almost to bristle with contempt for anything extraneous or merely ornamental. Most of all, I loved the way you can feel the form of this poetry over large stretches of verse, the way it accretes without losing precision, is in some major way as abstract as music yet never loses specificity. You cannot exhaust a poetry like this:

> A mason times his mallet
> to a lark's twitter,
> listening while the marble rests,
> lays his rule
> at a letter's edge,
> fingertips checking,
> till the stone spells a name
> naming none,
> a man abolished.
> Painful lark, labouring to rise!
> The solemn mallet says:
> In the grave's slot
> he lies. We rot.

> *(Briggflatts)*

What I'm wondering, then, is why, at the age of thirty-seven, and not having read Bunting carefully for some years, should I have

* *Complete Poems.* Edited by Richard Caddel. New Directions, 2003.
Basil Bunting on Poetry. Edited by Peter Makin. Johns Hopkins, 1999.

found making my way through his *Complete Poems* in the past few weeks *so damned hard?*

▼ ▲ ▼

Bunting was born in Northumbria – Wordsworth country, a poet he revered – but it took a long time for his life and work to find their way back there. (The best book on Bunting – indeed, one of the very best books on a single poet that I know of – is Peter Makin's *Bunting: The Shaping of His Verse.*) He had a Modernist's life, in a sense – Paris and Rapallo, Pound and Eliot and Yeats, the range of languages and learning, the romp through cultures and times. He was in the mix.

And yet, in a way, he wasn't. Bunting's first substantial book didn't come out until he was fifty, so he was always a very marginal figure. Even more than that, though, Bunting was *in* life in a way that Eliot, with his fastidious repressions and deflections, and Pound, with his dogged intellectualization of everything, and even Yeats at times, with his masques and mysticism, weren't. Bunting had no time for theories, programs, or dogma of any sort and could be searing in his contempt of them. He lived and wrote very close to the ground.

Close, but not rooted, at least not until late in life. Restive, self-educated, fiercely independent, Bunting lived with great range and at great risk. He worked as an editor, a sailor, a music critic, was a foreign correspondent for the *Times* in his forties, a lowly proofreader for a provincial newspaper in his fifties. He lived at sea – alone – for a year. He went from serving rough prison time as a conscientious objector during World War I to being head of all British intelligence in Persia in World War II. It says something about his character that neither of these roles was out of character. *Briggflatts*, his masterpiece, and certainly one of the best poems of the twentieth century, is governed both by a contemplative quietism that Bunting associated with Quakerism and the violence that he saw both forging and deforming culture through the centuries. Can a meditation be both focused and raucous? That's what *Briggflatts* feels like.

To read Bunting is mostly to read that poem. He didn't write much. Even a casual glance at the dates of composition reveals long years of silence between poems. Pound's influence is everywhere in the early work, and there is very little that doesn't seem either merely precocious or massively pretentious. The series of "sonatas" that Bunting wrote from his midthirties on can be striking in random moments, and some of the brief odes are fully intact and truly beautiful. It's strange, though, how consistently provisional – or perhaps peripheral – it all feels, how there seems to be no coherent center from which the poems issue, until *Briggflatts* – which, by the way, was begun when Bunting was well past sixty. If he hadn't written that poem, I'm not sure we'd read him now.

▼ ▲ ▼

Briggflatts, then. If I tell you that the poem is about lost love – or, more accurately, renounced love – I will have told you everything and nothing. The opening section – which is just a knockout, the best thing Bunting ever wrote – tells the story of a boy and girl in their teens accompanying her father, who is a stonemason, to a graveyard to erect a tombstone, then going back to the girl's house, where the boy and girl make love. That's it, really. The rest of the poem is about poetry, history, devotion, delight, despair. There is a good deal of description of landscape, all splendid. Only near the end does the poem become unexpectedly direct again, when we learn the full force of that early experience, and the pain and regret that, it seems, the poet has both preserved and suffered his entire life:

> Fifty years a letter unanswered;
> a visit postponed for fifty years.
>
> She has been with me fifty years.
>
> Starlight quivers. I had day enough.
> For love uninterrupted night.

Bunting called the poem an "autobiography." He also claimed that his poems were for "unabashed boys and girls" to enjoy. Bunting could be a bit coy. If *Briggflatts* is autobiographical, it's autobiographical in the way *The Waste Land* is: tracking down every reference in the poem to an event in the life is a fool's errand. And if you've got an unabashed boy or girl lolling around your house reading Bunting right now – friend, you've got a problem.

The poem is difficult, and it's ridiculous to pretend otherwise. It does work at a primary aural level that is available, I think, to any reasonably intelligent person who is willing to read slowly and aloud (Bunting: "Reading in silence is the source of half the misconceptions that have caused the public to distrust poetry"); and I don't think that a genuine experience of the poem necessitates recognizing every allusion and tying together the many, many lacunae. Still, your experience will be considerably enhanced if you know something about St. Cuthbert, Eric Bloodaxe, Aneurin and Taliesin, the Lindisfarne Gospels, Dante, the sonata form, Domenico Scarlatti, and the navigational techniques of Nordic Vikings. Bunting himself is little help. "Notes are a confession of failure," he said, "not a palliation of it."

▼ ▲ ▼

Here's what I did. I read through the poems – not successfully. I reread that Makin book. I read all of Bunting's prose I could find, including the recently published lectures he delivered to students late in his life in Vancouver. (Mercilessly dull! – I think he wanted to turn them all into bankers.) It made no sense to write a negative review of the poems, because I knew (I could *hear*), even in the midst of my resistance to them, that they were great. The only solution was to bring that resistance into my reading, and thus into my review.

I am *tired* of the techniques of Modernism, tired of the allusiveness, the fragments, the difficulty, tired of the emphasis *on* technique. As deeply as I believe in the power of language to express meaning abstractly, and as much as I love poets like Hart Crane and T.S. Eliot, whose ambitions were like Bunting's in this regard, more and more I want an art that is tied to life more directly. This is a complicated matter with Bunting, though. Bunting's great fear was words uttered in excess of knowledge, and by knowledge he meant lived experience. In terms of precision of observation, concision of language, and veracity of detail, the line between life and art is very tight indeed in his work. In another way, though, the life of the poems is constantly being subsumed by the style.

Bunting had a son he never saw. His American wife, pregnant at the time, left him and went with their two daughters back to Indiana. I don't know the moral dynamics of the situation. What I do know is that Bunting wrote a lovely poem many years later when he got word of his son's death. Here is the first stanza of "A Song for Rustam":

> Tears are for what can be mended,
> not for a voyage ended
> the day the schooner put out.
> Short fear and sudden quiet
> too deep for a diving thief.
> Tears are for easy grief.

Two things are interesting about this poem. First, it has a specific occasion, which makes it nearly anomalous among Bunting's work (and rare among the work of the high Modernists in general). Like the adolescent love scene from *Briggflatts,* "A Song for Rustam" is more direct, clearer, and more immediate than anything else Bunting wrote. The other interesting thing about the poem, though, is simply what it's saying: *Tears are for easy grief.* The line implies both a psychology and an aesthetic. Any feeling that is too immediate is too easy, and it is not to be trusted until it has been turned into something else. "Take no notice of tears," the poet exhorts himself – or Bloodaxe rather, the figure into whom he's suddenly dissolved at the end of section I of *Briggflatts* – "lest / insufferable happiness impede / flight to Stainmore," which is to make loss the fuel of all accomplishment, and all experience the ghost of some lost ideal ("He lies with one to long for another"). And what is accomplishment? For Bunting, more than anything else, it was poetry. And what is the lost ideal? "All arts," he wrote, "are concerned only with form in the end."

Well, I don't buy it – though I have long bought it, have even peddled these notions myself. As lovely and direct as "A Song for Rustam" is, there remains something weirdly occluded about it, something brusque, something – I hesitate to say this – simulated. The same is true of the grief in *Briggflatts*. I just don't *believe* the feeling expressed in some of the lines I've quoted about this singular lost intensity, this fifty-year-old grief. It seems to me very "literary." You're not a man at sixteen, you're a gland. To locate your life's ideal in that instant is, finally, deeply sentimental, and there is a direct connection between this psychological occlusion or willed immaturity and the idolatry of form, or technique, or style – whatever you want to call it.

Art is about more than form in the end. It is also about life, about truth – and not simply the kind of musical truth that Bunting claimed for the autobiographical element of *Briggflatts,* but something much more basic and accessible. Don't misunderstand me: when I argue for a more direct connection between life and art, I don't necessarily mean the *poet's* life. Lord knows that tendency has run amok. I do believe, though, that poetry must attend as scrupulously, cling as fiercely, to the breadth and mess of experience as it does to the forms that are its essence. Bunting tilted the scales too heavily toward the latter, as did Crane and Eliot, whose general statements about life or efforts at wisdom are similarly compromised.

Of course, as Eliot himself said, it isn't the job of a poet to convince us of *what* he believes, but *that* he believes. Crane and Eliot were better at this than Bunting, if only because they were both more given over to their respective delusions. And that's the real rub: I don't think *Bunting* believed in his own grief, at least not in these instances I've noted. *Briggflatts* was prompted by a visit from a young poet and Bunting's subsequent desire "to write something for these younger chaps to read." As always you have to take into account Bunting's tendency to be coy and dismissive in his comments on his own work, but the subject matter does feel a bit trumped-up, feels very much *like* subject matter. And here is how "A Song for Rustam" ends:

> Truth that shone is dim,
> lies cripple every limb.
> Where you were, you are not.
> Silent, heavy air
> stifles the heart's leap.
> Truth is asleep.

▼ ▲ ▼

When I told a friend, a good poet and professor, that I was going to write something about Bunting, she said that she'd never really read him, and then expressed dismay at how some poets simply vanished. This surprised me, both the fact that she hadn't read Bunting and the perception that he was overlooked. Subsequent conversations, though, both with poets and nonpoets, have convinced me that my friend's experience is not at all anomalous. Bunting is still somewhat off the radar.

He shouldn't be. There are English poets of the past half-century whom I would recommend to general readers above Bunting – Hughes and Larkin, notably. And I do think that Bunting might have been a better poet if he hadn't come of age during Modernism, or at least had been more resistant to its most reader-resistant characteristics. But there are effects and intensities in Bunting that few poets of any time can touch. I don't know of anyone who could more utterly fuse sight and sound:

> Wind shakes a blotch of sun,
> flatter and tattle willow and oak alike
> sly as a trout's shadow on gravel.

("Uncollected Odes: II")

Or carve language so closely to what Bunting called "the structure of event" that to read the lines aloud is to feel the physical fact of what they describe:

> Crew grunt and gasp. Nothing he sees
> they see, but hate and serve. Unscarred ocean,
> day's swerve, swell's poise, pursuit,
> he blends, balances, drawing leagues under the keel
> to raise cold cliffs where tides
> knot fringes of weed.

(*Briggflatts*)

Or make a music that so steadfastly refuses to rise above physical facts, refuses to be separate from *things:*

Under sacks on the stone
two children lie,
hear the horse stale,
the mason whistle,
harness mutter to shaft,
felloe to axle squeak,
rut thud the rim,
crushed grit.

(*Briggflatts*)

Or so often simply take your breath away with the beauty of individual passages:

Furthest, fairest things, stars, free of our humbug,
each his own, the longer known the more alone,
wrapt in emphatic fire roaring out to a black flue.

(*Briggflatts*)

Articulating my own objections to Bunting's work mostly dissolved them. You can't read poetry with some ideal conception of it in mind any more than you can live that way. I am not moved by the ostensible subjects of Bunting's poetry and find myself frustrated if I attend too closely to the poems at basic levels of narrative and psychology. The way to read Bunting, I think, is to trust him utterly at the level of music, and little at the level of subject matter.

Read this way, the poems can be quite moving, in part simply for the fact of their deflections. I think what Bunting meant in "A Song for Rustam," finally, though he may very well not have known it, is not that tears are for easy grief, but that tears are for specific grief. And what that poem laments is less the specific loss than the inability to fully feel it – the inability to *ever* have fully felt it. *Briggflatts* is no different, a vast soundscape in which the real grief can never quite be found, either because the poet couldn't see it himself, or wouldn't let himself see it, or simply because the grief is so much deeper than any detail of his own life – *lacrimae rerum.* Bunting seems implicitly to acknowledge this last possibility by attaching a coda to the poem, which, like most everything he wrote, is at once close and remote, strangely incomplete and utterly finished:

A strong song tows
us, long earsick.
Blind, we follow
rain slant, spray flick
to fields we do not know.

Night, float us.
Offshore wind, shout,
ask the sea
what's lost, what's left,
what horn sunk,
what crown adrift.

Where we are who knows
of kings who sup
while day fails? Who,
swinging his axe
to fell kings, guesses
where we go?

2004

V

Love Bade Me Welcome

Though I was raised in a very religious household, until about a year ago I hadn't been to church in any serious way for over twenty years. It would be inaccurate to say that I have been indifferent to God in all that time. Even a casual glance through the essays in this book reveals not only how thoroughly the forms and language of Christianity have shaped my imagination, but also a persistent existential anxiety. I don't know whether this is all attributable to the century into which I was born, some genetic glitch, or a late reverberation of the fall of Man. What I do know is that I have not been at ease in this world.

Poetry, for me, has always been bound up with this unease, fueled by contingency toward forms that will transcend it, as involved with silence as it is with sound. I don't have much sympathy for the Arnoldian notion of poetry replacing religion. It seems not simply quaint but dangerous to make that assumption, even implicitly, perhaps *especially* implicitly. I do think, though, that poetry is how religious feeling has survived in me. Partly this is because I have at times experienced in the writing of a poem some access to a power that feels greater than I am, and it seems reductive, even somehow a deep betrayal, to attribute that power merely to the unconscious or to the dynamism of language itself. But also, if I look back on the poems I've written in the past two decades, it almost seems as if the one constant is God. Or, rather, His absence.

There is a passage in the writings of Simone Weil that has long been important to me.* In the passage Weil describes two prisoners who are in solitary confinement next to each other. Between them is

---

* See "An Idea of Order," in this volume.

a stone wall. Over a period of time – and I think we have to imagine it as a very long time – they find a way to communicate using taps and scratches. The wall is what separates them, but it is also the only means they have of communicating. "It is the same with us and God," she says. "Every separation is a link."

It's probably obvious why this metaphor would appeal to me. If you never quite feel at home in your life, if being conscious means primarily being conscious of your own separation from the world and divinity (and perhaps any sentient person after Modernism *has* to feel these things), then an idea or image that can translate that depletion into energy, those absences into presences, is going to be powerful. And then there are those taps and scratches: what are they but language, and if language is the way we communicate with the divine, well, what kind of language is more refined and transcendent than poetry? You could almost embrace this vision of life – if, that is, there were any actual life to embrace: Weil's image for the human condition is a person in solitary confinement. There is real hope in the image, but still, in human terms, it is a bare and lonely hope.

It has taken three events, each shattering in its way, for me to recognize both the full beauty, and the final insufficiency, of Weil's image. The events are radically different, but so closely linked in time, and so inextricable from one another in their consequences, that there is an uncanny feeling of unity to them. There is definitely some wisdom in learning to see our moments of necessity and glory and tragedy not as disparate experiences but as facets of the single experience that is a life. The pity, at least for some of us, is that we cannot truly have this knowledge of life, can only feel it as some sort of abstract "wisdom," until we come very close to death.

First, necessity: four years ago, after making poetry the central purpose of my life for almost two decades, I stopped writing. Partly this was a conscious decision. I told myself that I had exhausted one way of writing, and I do think there was truth in that. The deeper truth, though, is that I myself was exhausted. To believe that being conscious means primarily being conscious of loss, to find life authentic only in the apprehension of death, is to pitch your tent at the edge of an abyss, "and when you gaze long into the abyss," Nietzsche says, "the abyss also gazes into you." I blinked.

On another level, though, the decision to stop writing wasn't mine. Whatever connection I had long experienced between word and world, whatever charge in the former I had relied on to let me feel the latter, went dead. Did I give up poetry, or was it taken from me? I'm not sure, and in any event the effect was the same: I stumbled through the months, even thrived in some ways. Indeed – and there is something almost diabolical about this common phenomenon – it sometimes seemed as if my career in poetry began to flourish just as poetry died in me. I finally found a reliable publisher for my work (the work I'd written earlier, I mean), moved into a good teaching job, and then quickly left that for the editorship of *Poetry*. But there wasn't a scrap of excitement in any of this for me. It felt like I was watching a movie of my life rather than living it, an old silent movie, no color, no sound, no one in the audience but me.

Then I fell in love. I say it suddenly, and there was certainly an element of radical intrusion and transformation to it, but the sense I have is of color slowly aching into things, the world coming brilliantly, abradingly alive. I remember tiny Albert's Cafe on Elm Street in Chicago where we first met, a pastry case like a Pollock in the corner of my eye, sunlight suddenly more itself on an empty plate, a piece of silver. I think of walking together along Lake Michigan a couple of months later talking about a particular poem of Dickinson's ("A loss of something ever felt I"), clouds finding and failing to keep one form after another, the lake booming its blue into everything; of lying in bed in my high-rise apartment downtown watching the little blazes in the distance that were the planes at Midway, so numerous and endless that all those safe departures and homecomings seemed a kind of secular miracle. We usually think of falling in love as being possessed by another person, and like anyone else I was completely consumed and did some daffy things. But it also felt, for the first time in my life, like I was being fully possessed by being itself. "Joy is the overflowing consciousness of reality," Weil writes, and that's what I had, a joy that was at once so overflowing that it enlarged existence, and yet so rooted in actual things that, again for the first time, that's what I began to feel: rootedness.

I don't mean to suggest that all my old anxieties were gone. There were still no poems, and this ate at me constantly. There was still no God, and the closer I came to reality, the more I longed for divinity – or, more accurately perhaps, the more divinity seemed so obviously a *part* of reality. I wasn't alone in this: we began to say a kind of prayer before our evening meals – jokingly at first, awkwardly, but then with intensifying seriousness and deliberation, trying to name each thing that we were thankful for, and in so doing praise the thing we could not name. On most Sundays we would even briefly entertain – again, half jokingly – the idea of going to church. The very morning after we got engaged, in fact, we paused for a long time outside a church on Michigan Avenue. The service was just about to start, organ music pouring out of the wide open doors into the late May sun, and we stood there holding each other and debating whether or not to walk inside. In the end it was I who resisted.

I wish I could slow things down at this point, could linger a bit in those months after our marriage. I wish I could feel again that blissful sense of immediacy and expansiveness at once, when every moment implied another, and the future suddenly seemed to offer some counterbalance to the solitary fever I had lived in for so long. I think most writers live at some strange adjacency to experience, that they feel life most intensely in their recreation of it. For once, for me, this wasn't the case. I could not possibly have been paying closer attention to those days. Which is why I was caught so off-guard.

I got the news that I was sick on the afternoon of my thirty-ninth birthday. It took a bit of time, travel, and a series of wretched tests to get the specific diagnosis, but by then the main blow had been delivered, and that main blow is what matters. I have an incurable cancer in my blood. The disease is as rare as it is mysterious, killing some people quickly and sparing others for decades, afflicting some with all manner of miseries and disabilities and leaving others relatively healthy until the end. Of all the doctors I have seen, not one has been willing to venture even a vague prognosis.

Conventional wisdom says that tragedy will cause either extreme closeness or estrangement between a couple. We'd been married less than a year when we got the news of the cancer. It stands to reason we should have been especially vulnerable to such a blow, and in some ways love did make things much worse. If I had gotten the diagnosis some years earlier – and it seems weirdly providential that I didn't, since I had symptoms and went to several doctors about them – I'm not sure I would have reacted very strongly. It would have seemed a fatalistic confirmation of everything I had always thought about existence, and my response, I think, would have been equally fatalistic. It would have been the bearable oblivion of despair, not the unbearable, and therefore galvanizing, pain of particular grief. In those early days after the diagnosis, when we mostly just sat on the couch and cried, I alone was dying, but we were mourning very much together. And what we were mourning was not my death, exactly, but the death of the life we had imagined with each other.

Then one morning we found ourselves going to church. *Found ourselves.* That's exactly what it felt like, in both senses of the phrase, as if some impulse in each of us had been finally catalyzed into action, so that we were casting aside the Sunday paper and moving toward the door with barely a word between us; and as if, once inside the church, we were discovering exactly where and who we were meant to be. That first service was excruciating, in that it seemed to tear all wounds wide open, and it was profoundly comforting, in that it seemed to offer the only possible balm. What I remember of that Sunday though, and of the Sundays that immediately followed, is less the services themselves than the walks we took afterward, and less the specifics of the conversations we had about God, always about God, than the moments of silent, and what felt like sacred, attentiveness those conversations led to: an iron sky and the lake so calm it seemed thickened; the El blasting past with its rain of sparks and brief, lost faces; the broad leaves and white blooms of a catalpa on our street, Grace Street, and under the tree a seethe of something that was just barely still a bird, quick with life beyond its own.

I was brought up with the poisonous notion that you had to renounce love of the earth in order to receive the love of God. My experience has been just the opposite: a love of the earth and existence so overflowing that it implied, or included, or even absolutely demanded, God. Love did not deliver me from the earth, but into it. And by some miracle I do not find that this experience is crushed or even lessened by the knowledge that, in all likelihood, I will be leaving the earth sooner than I had thought. Quite the contrary, I find life thriving in me, and not in an aestheticizing Death-is-the-mother-of-beauty sort of way either, for what extreme grief has given me is the very thing it seemed at first to obliterate: a sense of life beyond the moment, a sense of hope. This is not simply hope for my own life, though I do have that. It is not a hope for Heaven or any sort of explainable afterlife, unless by those things one means simply the ghost of wholeness that our inborn sense of brokenness creates and sustains, some ultimate love that our truest temporal ones goad us toward. This I do believe in, and by this I live, in what the apostle Paul called "hope toward God."

"It is necessary to have had a revelation of reality through joy," Weil writes, "in order to find reality through suffering." This is certainly true to my own experience. I was not wrong all those years to believe that suffering is at the very center of our existence, and that there can be no untranquilized life that does not fully confront this fact. The mistake lay in thinking grief the means of confrontation, rather than love. To come to this realization is not to be suddenly "at ease in the world." I don't really think it's possible for humans to be at the same time conscious and comfortable. Though we may be moved by nature to thoughts of grace, though art can tease our minds toward eternity and love's abundance make us dream a love that does not end, these intuitions come only through the earth, and the earth we know only in passing, and only by passing. I would qualify Weil's statement somewhat, then, by saying that reality, be it of this world or another, is not something one finds and then retains for good. It must be newly discovered daily, and newly lost.

So now I bow my head and try to pray in the mornings, not because I don't doubt the reality of what I have experienced, but because I do, and with an intensity that, because to once feel the presence of God is to feel His absence all the more acutely, is actually more anguishing and difficult than any "existential anxiety" I have ever known. I go to church on Sundays, not to dispel this doubt but to expend its energy, because faith is not a state of mind but an action in the world, a movement toward the world. How charged this one hour of the week is for me, and how I cherish it, though not one whit more

than the hours I have with my wife, with friends, or in solitude, trying
to learn how to inhabit time so completely that there might be no dis-
tinction between life and belief, attention and devotion. And out of all
these efforts at faith and love, out of my own inevitable failures at
both, I have begun to write poems again. But the language I have now
to call on God is not only language, and the wall on which I make my
taps and scratches is no longer a cell but this whole prodigal and all
too perishable world in which I find myself, very much alive, and not
at all alone. As I approach the first anniversary of my diagnosis, as I
approach whatever pain is ahead of me, I am trying to get as close to
this wall as possible. And I am listening with all I am.

2006

Notes

Aside from the references in footnotes, the following books were under review.

A PIECE OF PROSE

A Way of Happening, by Fred Chappell. Picador, 1998.

Shooting the Works, by W.S. Di Piero. TriQuarterly Books, 1996.

The Enemy's Country, by Geoffrey Hill. Stanford University Press, 1995.

The Work of Poetry, by John Hollander. Columbia University Press, 1997.

The Cure of Poetry in an Age of Prose, by Mary Kinzie. University of Chicago Press, 1993.

The Judge Is Fury, by Mary Kinzie. University of Michigan Press, 1995.

A Poet's Guide to Poetry, by Mary Kinzie. University of Chicago Press, 1999.

Oblivion, by Donald Justice. Story Line Press, 1998.

All the Rage, by William Logan. University of Michigan Press, 1998.

Modern Poetry After Modernism, by James Longenbach. Oxford University Press, 1997.

Twenty Questions, by J.D. McClatchy. Columbia University Press, 1998.

Jackdaw Jiving, by Christopher Middleton. Carcanet, 1998.

Road-side Dog, by Czeslaw Milosz. Farrar, Straus and Giroux, 1998.

Bardic Deadlines, by Geoffrey O'Brien. University of Michigan Press, 1999.

The Sounds of Poetry, by Robert Pinsky. Farrar, Straus and Giroux, 1998.

Between the Iceberg and the Ship, by Anne Stevenson. University of Michigan Press, 1998.

What the Twilight Says, by Derek Walcott. Farrar, Straus and Giroux, 1999.

Poetry and Consciousness, by C.K. Williams. University of Michigan Press, 1998.

FUGITIVE PIECES (II)

Blake, by Peter Ackroyd. Knopf, 1996.

Another Day on Earth, by Timothy Dekin. TriQuarterly Books, 2002.

A NEW MODE OF DAMNATION?: HART CRANE

O My Land, My Friends: The Selected Letters of Hart Crane. Edited by Langdon
    Hammer and Brom Weber. Four Walls Eight Windows, 1997.

Hart Crane and Yvor Winters: Their Literary Correspondence, by Thomas
    Parkinson. University of California Press, 1978.

SO FIERCE AND SWEET THE SONG: GEORGE MACKAY BROWN

Fishermen with Ploughs, by George Mackay Brown. Hogarth Press, 1979.

Following a Lark, by George Mackay Brown. John Murray Publishers Ltd., 1996.

Selected Poems, 1954–1992, by George Mackay Brown. University of Iowa Press,
    1996.

"Finishes: On Ambition and Survival" is dedicated to Dabney Stuart.
"An Idea of Order" is dedicated to Denise Levertov.

The dates following each essay are the dates of composition, not nec-
essarily of publication.

About the Author

Christian Wiman is the author of two books of poetry, *The Long Home* (1998), which won the Nicholas Roerich Prize, and *Hard Night* (2005). His poems and his critical and personal essays appear widely, in such magazines as *The Atlantic Monthly, Harper's, The New York Times Book Review,* and *The New Yorker.* He is the editor of *Poetry* magazine.

Copper Canyon Press gratefully acknowledges
Lannan Foundation for supporting the publication and
distribution of exceptional literary works.

LANNAN LITERARY SELECTIONS 2007

Maram al-Massri, *A Red Cherry on a White-tiled Floor: Selected Poems*

Norman Dubie, *The Insomniac Liar of Topo*

Rebecca Seiferle, *Wild Tongue*

Christian Wiman, *Ambition and Survival: Becoming a Poet*

C.D. Wright, *One Big Self: An Investigation*

LANNAN LITERARY SELECTIONS 2000–2006

Marvin Bell, *Rampant*

Hayden Carruth, *Doctor Jazz*

Cyrus Cassells, *More Than Peace and Cypresses*

Madeline DeFrees, *Spectral Waves*

Norman Dubie, *The Mercy Seat: Collected & New Poems, 1967–2001*

Sascha Feinstein, *Misterioso*

James Galvin, *X: Poems*

Jim Harrison, *The Shape of the Journey: New and Collected Poems*

Hồ Xuân Hương, *Spring Essence: The Poetry of Hồ Xuân Hương,*
translated by John Balaban

June Jordan, *Directed by Desire: The Collected Poems of June Jordan*

Maxine Kumin, *Always Beginning: Essays on a Life in Poetry*

Ben Lerner, *The Lichtenberg Figures*

Antonio Machado, *Border of a Dream: Selected Poems,*
translated by Willis Barnstone

W.S. Merwin
The First Four Books of Poems
Migration: New & Selected Poems
Present Company

The Chinese character for poetry is made up of two parts: "word" and "temple." It also serves as pressmark for Copper Canyon Press.

Since 1972, Copper Canyon Press has fostered the work of emerging, established, and world-renowned poets for an expanding audience. The Press thrives with the generous patronage of readers, writers, booksellers, librarians, teachers, students, and funders—everyone who shares the belief that poetry is vital to language and living.

Major funding has been provided by:

Anonymous (2)

Cynthia Lovelace Sears and Frank Buxton

The Paul G. Allen Family Foundation

Lannan Foundation

National Endowment for the Arts

Washington State Arts Commission

THE **PAUL G. ALLEN**
FAMILY *foundation*

NATIONAL
ENDOWMENT
FOR THE ARTS

WASHINGTON
STATE ARTS
COMMISSION

Copper Canyon Press gratefully acknowledges Mimi Gardner Gates for her generous Annual Fund support.

For information and catalogs:

COPPER CANYON PRESS
Post Office Box 271
Port Townsend, Washington 98368
360-385-4925
www.coppercanyonpress.org

▼ ▲ ▼

Ambition and Survial is set in ITC Bodoni Twelve Book with display titles set in Interstate. Book design by Valerie Brewster, Scribe Typography. Printed on archival-quality Glatfelter Author's Text at McNaughton & Gunn, Inc.